U.S. Trade Policy
Balancing Economic Dreams and Political Realities

JOHN M. ROTHGEB JR.
Miami University

CQ PRESS

A Division of Congressional Quarterly Inc.
Washington, D.C.

CQ Press
A Division of Congressional Quarterly Inc.
1414 22nd Street, N.W.
Washington, D.C. 20037

(202) 822-1475; (800) 638-1710

www.cqpress.com

☉ The paper used in this publication meets the minimum requirements of the American National Standard for Information Sciences—Permanence of Paper for Printed
Library Materials, ANSI Z39.48-1992.

Printed and bound in the United States of America

05 04 03 02 01   5 4 3 2 1

Cover design by Naylor Design

Library of Congress Cataloging-in-Publication Data

Rothgeb, John M.
    U.S. Trade Policy : balancing economic dreams and political
realities / John M. Rothgeb, Jr.
        p.   cm.
    Includes bibliographical references and index.
    ISBN: 1-56802-522-X (alk. paper)
    1. United States—Commercial policy—History.   2. Foreign trade
regulation—United States—History.   3. Free trade—United States—History.
4. Protectionism—United States—History.   I. Title:
    U.S. trade policy.   II. Title: United States trade policy.   III. Title.
HF1455 .R618 2001
    382'.3'0973--dc21   2001000764

Paul Rejai
Eminent scholar and friend

Contents

PREFACE

As the United States enters the twenty-first century, its trade with other countries plays a more important role than at any other time in its history. Trade is at the heart of American participation in a rapidly growing global economy. It has become a key element in the construction and maintenance of a prosperous economy that generates jobs, provides access to more goods than ever before, holds inflation in check, and allows Americans to sustain a standard of living that is the envy of people around the world. Beyond this, trade is increasingly used to sanction countries that engage in behavior the United States regards as unacceptable and to induce others to abide by values such as respect for human rights and the peaceful resolution of international disputes. In short, international trade is of fundamental and growing importance to the health of the American economy, to the American way of life, and to American foreign and national security policy.

American leadership in promoting international trade is also widely regarded as a key to the growing interdependence that ties many members of the global community to one another and that has led to an unprecedented era of peace and prosperity among many countries around the world. Beginning with the Bretton Woods System, which was set up in the waning days of the Second World War, and continuing through the Kennedy, Tokyo, and Uruguay Rounds of the GATT, the United States has taken the lead in creating the institutions and rules that currently govern international trade. Indeed, many of these institutions and rules can be properly understood only when they are placed in the context of the debate in the United States that led to their creation.

And yet, despite the undoubted value of trade to foreign policy and its undisputed role in the contemporary international system, it is often a neglected subject in academic discussions and in books designed to teach students about international politics and American foreign and security policy. This book is designed to fill that void by describing the evolution of American trade policy over the past several decades. It begins by discussing the constitutional grants of power and protectionist and isolationist traditions that guided trade policy in the years before the Great Depression. The book continues by considering the major issues that have shaped American policy as the United States has become ever more committed to eliminating trade barriers and building institutions to promote international commerce. It concludes with an analysis of the issues crowding the current American trade policy agenda.

To facilitate the understanding of the linkages between trade and foreign and security policy, this book places its subject matter in the broader strategic and political context that shapes the American response to the international issues it confronts. Among all the problems U.S. foreign policy decision makers face, trade is perhaps the most political. Trade decisions involve high stakes: any move toward promoting or restricting imports and exports affects billions of dollars in goods and services and has serious implications for the fate of millions of workers at home and abroad. In addition, decision makers often have strongly held ideological beliefs about the value of trade and its effect on local culture. Beyond this, trade frequently is regarded as a valuable tool in the arsenal of weapons available to policy makers as they work to resolve international disputes. Trade policy is therefore intricately bound to the political and military questions that confront U.S. policy makers.

In addition to linking trade to strategic and political issues, this book shows how deeply trade policy is affected by the interest groups that dot the American political landscape and how it is enmeshed in the larger institutional struggle between the president and Congress for control of American foreign policy. The examination of American trade policy provides students with an opportunity to see how international and domestic political forces interact to affect policy. Studying trade policy also provides an instructive lesson in just how much the traditional lines separating foreign and domestic policy have been obscured in the global political system of the new millennium.

ACKNOWLEDGMENTS

Several people played important roles as I prepared this book. I received editorial assistance from my wife, Sue; my mother, Carrie Lee; and my son, John, who read early versions of several chapters and offered helpful comments. Two graduate students at Miami University also provided valuable assistance. Chris Kelley helped me to set up and maintain the several computers I used when working on the project, and Benjamas Chinapandhu collected most of the information that I used when writing Chapter 9. Both have bright futures as scholars. In addition, the editorial team at CQ Press, including Charisse Kiino, Amy Briggs, and Belinda Josey, has been a model of professionalism, and Sabra Bissette Ledent provided valuable editorial support. Finally, I thank those who reviewed the manuscript and helped me to improve it: Kerry Chase at Tufts University, John Conybeare at the University of Iowa, Rick Doner at Emory University, Maurice A. East at George Washington University, Alan E. Kessler at the University of Texas at Austin, Stephen J. Silvia at American University, and David Skidmore at Drake University.

1 Introduction

On the morning of November 30, 1999, thousands of chanting demonstrators gathered around the Seattle meeting site. Many linked arms to form human chains; others sat down or stretched out on sidewalks or in the streets to block the many officials seeking to attend the conference. As limousines pulled up, they were surrounded by swarms of protestors attempting to prevent passengers from getting out. The badly outnumbered local security forces found they could do little to assist those people trying to make their way into the meeting place. Indeed, the more the police tried to gain control of the situation, the more raucous some of the protesters became.

By noon, the demonstrations had taken a more violent turn as small groups of protestors threw rocks, bottles, and other objects at police. Barricades were set up to block streets, piles of refuse were set ablaze, and the window-smashing spree that began left much of downtown Seattle in near ruins. Conference participants who had not yet left their hotels cancelled their plans to attend the meeting, while those who had tried to reach the conference beat a hasty retreat in the face of the melee.

Eventually, the National Guard was called in to restore order and to patrol the Seattle streets to guard against acts of misconduct. Most of those who had gathered to participate in the conference gave up hope of doing so and began leaving for home. The protestors also departed, but not without declaring a significant victory over the forces that the conference represented. Most swore to continue their fight at any future conferences designed to address the agenda prepared for the Seattle meeting.

As shocking as these events were, one of the biggest surprises for many was that the "battle in Seattle" was over a **World Trade Organization (WTO)** meeting. In other words, the issue that precipitated the largest and most tumultuous political demonstrations the United States had seen since the antiwar protests of the Vietnam era was not a bloody military campaign but trade. Tens of thousands of peo-

1

ple had flocked to Seattle to let the world know that they were fed up with trade and with the leading international organization dealing with trade-related issues, the WTO. For protestors, trade posed a threat to their lifestyles, to the environment, to workers in developing countries, and to the very independence of the United States. They believed that if something was not done, and done quickly, the ever-growing volume of international trade would destroy jobs at home and abroad, defile the air people breathe and the water they drink, and lead to the creation of a powerful international agency that would rob the United States of its sovereignty.

As described in the chapters that follow, these conceptions of international trade reflect a decades-old debate over whether American interests are best served by commercial contacts with other countries. Early opponents of such contacts, often called protectionists, saw trade as a tie that would bind the United States to countries that might exploit its resources for their own purposes and involve America in problems, including wars, in which it should have no interest. For the believers in **protectionism,** self-sufficiency was the ideal that should guide the United States, and the nation should draw on its own natural resources and on the skills of its people to produce the goods and services Americans needed. Beyond this, protectionists believed that international trade could stunt the growth of American nationalism by fostering linkages that could lead Americans to identify more with foreigners than with one another. Limiting trade not only would avoid this outcome, but also would encourage a sense of community as Americans interacted to their mutual commercial advantage to build a prosperous nation.

These protectionist views were opposed by another American tradition, **internationalism,** that regarded trade as the surest way to promote peace and prosperity for the United States. Internationalists believed trade could pull differing peoples together into mutually advantageous relationships that would promote understanding and eliminate the causes of violence and warfare. Internationalists also pointed to the economic benefits of trade such as larger markets and more efficient production, both of which could bring higher standards of living to everyone involved.

It was an internationalist proposal that led to the trade conference in Seattle in November 1999. The conference was called to initiate negotiations that would expand the commercial opportunities available to American businesses around the world. As internationalists saw it, Seattle was the ideal location for such a conference because of its linkages to the global system of trade, which had made it one of the fastest-growing and most prosperous cities in the United States. In many ways, Seattle was a symbol to internationalists of the extensive benefits of trade.

CONTROLLING U.S. TRADE POLICY

The riots that accompanied the Seattle WTO conference represented more than clashes between demonstrators and police; they were the latest manifestation of the contest between protectionists and internationalists for control of American trade policy. **Trade policy** may be defined as the rules and procedures that a government uses to regulate commerce between its own country and other countries. Because trade involves buying and selling goods and services on world markets, and because all governments attempt to regulate this buying and selling to the advantage of their own citizens, trade policy can be very complex, reflecting the impacts of a variety of social, political, and economic factors, both international and domestic.

Among the many forces that affect the development and implementation of U.S. trade policy, four stand out: (1) the strategic and competitive environment the United States confronts in the international arena; (2) the ideas policy makers and influential private citizens have about the role trade plays in handling American problems; (3) the beliefs special-interest groups have about how they are affected by the rules and procedures set up to regulate trade; and (4) the institutional rivalries that exist among elements of the U.S. government. Each of these forces plays a role in creating the political reality within which the alternatives of promoting trade or encouraging self-sufficiency have struggled to gain the upper hand over American trade policy.

The strategic and competitive environment confronting the United States sets the global context for trade policy. The strategic part of the international environment relates to the threats that other countries pose to American national security; the competitive environment pertains to the degree to which members of other societies market products in the United States and elsewhere, possibly undermining the ability of Americans to do business at home and abroad. Trade policy helps to solve strategic problems by giving the United States the carrot of more open American markets to encourage foreign cooperation and the stick of restricted access to American markets to punish foreign intransigence. As for competition, trade policy may be used both to shield American producers from foreign rivals and to open foreign markets to American goods, thereby providing Americans with better business opportunities abroad.

The ideas people have about the value of trade are related to the historical conceptions described earlier. Generally speaking, internationalists believe trade contributes to the solution of many of the problems confronting the United States; protectionists tend to believe that the best way to deal with difficulties is to isolate the American economy from international commerce. These differences were evident in debates about American trade policy throughout the twentieth century. For example, in the years between the two world wars internationalists regarded trade as the best way to limit conflict, end economic depressions, and help democracies as they struggled against totalitarian societies. For their part, protectionists felt that restricting trade could ensure American neutrality, prevent war, and insulate the United States from commercial trends that spread economic downturns from one society to another. During the Cold War, these differences appeared in disputes over the degree to which American markets should be opened to promote Western solidarity against communism and whether increasing east-west trade helped or harmed American security interests. In more recent years, disputes have centered on the effects of free trade agreements, the best approach to use in preventing Asian economic problems from affecting the American economy, and whether trade with China promotes or hurts both human rights movements in China and the national security of the United States. In each case, the validity of the arguments presented is in the eyes of the beholder, depending on whether one is more internationalist or protectionist.

The perceptions of special-interest groups about how they are affected by trade plays a big role in the arguments they make. Those groups that feel trade hurts their cause tend to see it in a very different light from those that believe they benefit. As will be seen throughout this book, trade has varying effects on different segments of society. Consumers benefit from trade because it provides them with a greater variety of goods and services at lower prices. Those who export or manufacture goods in several locations around the globe also benefit from trade because it allows them to do business in larger markets, which translates into higher sales and more profits. Those who produce for the local scene, however, often find trade problematic, for it opens the doors of the domestic market to foreign competitors who frequently sell goods that are equal to or better than those made locally. As a result, producers for the local market have a vested interest in impeding trade and often engage in political activity to pressure the government to restrict imports. They even may wage public opinion campaigns to convince the populace at large that trade is harming the greater public interest. Of course, those who benefit from trade also resort to political pressures and public rhetoric to swing people around to their point of view. No matter which side of the question a group favors, it has strong reasons to try to convince others that its position is the only reasonable approach to take. As a result, trade policy is extremely political, and political necessity plays a major role in molding economic arguments.

Institutional rivalries, the fourth factor affecting trade policy, are found both between the executive branch and Congress and within the executive branch itself. As described in later chapters, executive-congressional disputes arise in part because of the constitutional separation of powers that puts regulation of foreign commerce in the hands of Congress but negotiation of international agreements in the hands of the executive branch. Beyond this, the structure of Congress and of the American economy act to pressure members of Congress to pay attention to those who want protection from foreign competition. Thus the executive branch sometimes finds itself negotiating foreign trade deals that many in Congress find unacceptable because local producers are harmed. The controversy produced by such an arrangement is magnified by Congress's tendency to intervene in ongoing negotiations and to remind the executive branch that the final authority over trade resides in Congress.

Rivalries also exist within the executive branch, for virtually all cabinet departments have an interest in international trade. Most executive branch agencies try to carve out a role in the trade policy-making process so that they can influence policy to help the special-interest groups they serve. But because many of these special interests have differing views of how trade should be conducted, conflict is an inevitable part of policy making. Interestingly, these intra-executive branch disputes often are exacerbated by interactions with Congress because it is not unusual for members of Congress to feel that the interests of their constituents are best served by promoting the views of one executive branch department or agency over those of another. As a result, the policy-making process, with its pulling and tugging between the executive branch and Congress and within the executive branch, serves to dampen the ideals players may bring to the political game.

OBJECTIVES OF THIS BOOK

This book is designed to examine in detail how the forces just described affect American trade policy. Moreover, what ideals have inspired the political and other leaders who have formulated this policy? How have these ideals been molded by international strategic realities and by the rough and tumble of domestic politics as private special interests have conducted their own slugfest in a political process shaped by institutional rivalries? The policy-making process has changed over time. In the years before World War II, Congress dominated the process, and the values associated with self-sufficiency and protection from foreign competition held the upper hand over the ideals calling for expanding commerce. But with the onset of a succession of events, beginning with the Great Depression and followed by World War II and the Cold War, the proponents of increased trade found it possible to initiate a process that led to a slow but steady series of changes that transformed American trade policy and almost completely shifted the nature of the trade debate in the United States.

But the nature of the trade debate is not the only thing that has changed; both the relationships between private interests and Congress and the type of protection provided by the U.S. government have changed as well. Whereas it was once commonplace for producers who feared foreign competition to maintain such a cozy relationship with key members of Congress that they could almost dictate the shape of protectionist legislation, it is now nearly impossible for anyone to exert such influence on the legislative process. Likewise, the basic nature of protection has shifted from the high tariff walls of the first part of the century to the carefully crafted administrative procedures of today. In addition, the current policy-making process is circumscribed by international agreements that were unimaginable in the years before the Second World War. Indeed, even the terms of the discussion of trade have changed, for the debates about the value of protection and **isolationism** that previously dominated discourse have been replaced by discussions about both international commercial institutions and how they may better serve American interests and the best means for placing new items on the international negotiating agenda.

In short, American trade policy has changed substantially over the past seven decades. This book examines the evolutionary process that brought the United States from a society where most people viewed trade with suspicion to a society that today embraces foreign products and has assumed the role of an international leader in developing new rules and institutions to promote and regulate trade. In addition, this book investigates the issues that currently dominate the debate over American trade policy and considers the primary goals the United States is pursuing as the world enters the twenty-first century.

2 Protection, Free Trade, and Congress

A s the nineteenth century gave way to the twentieth, many Americans viewed foreign trade with suspicion. As they saw it, imports were stealing American jobs and depressing wages, hurting American businesses, retarding the growth of the U.S. economy, and providing foreigners with undue influence over American society and national security. In other words, foreign commercial activity was something patriotic Americans needed to watch carefully. Picking up on this cue—and long before there were televisions to broadcast commercials in which celebrities encourage their fellow citizens to "Buy American"— politicians, especially those from the Republican Party, depicted imports as a scourge. As one Republican campaign message of the time stated, "We are uncompromisingly in favor of the American system of protection [from foreign trade]. The President [Democrat Grover Cleveland] and his party . . . serve the interests of Europe; we will support the interests of America."[1]

NATIONALISTS AND THE AMERICAN SYSTEM

For Republicans, supporting American interests meant taking a nationalist approach to trade by creating formidable barriers to imports. The main such barrier was the **tariff,** a tax collected on goods entering the United States from other countries. For nationalists, tariffs served at least two purposes. First, they produced revenue for the federal Treasury. Indeed, until passage of the Sixteenth Amendment to the Constitution in 1913 (it allowed the government to collect income taxes), tariffs were the primary source of funds for the federal government. Second, tariffs protected American businesses. The **protective tariff** favored by Republicans was designed to force the prices of foreign-made goods to such high levels that American consumers would find comparable goods made in the United States more attractive cost-wise.[2] Goods made at home would then be guaranteed the lion's share of the home market; after all, Americans should buy and sell from one another before doing business with foreigners.

The Republican thinking about trade, the tariff, and protection built on ideas inherited from Alexander Hamilton, the nation's first Treasury secretary, and Henry Clay, an influential member of Congress in the first half of the nineteenth century. It also reflected the notions of anticolonialism and isolationism that were widespread in the United States in the early twentieth century.

Hamilton's trade program, presented in his *Report on Manufactures* (1791), was part of an overall plan for the economic development of the agrarian United States of the late eighteenth century. It was premised on the idea that American national security and prosperity depended on the United States reaching its full economic potential—that is, veering away from a predominantly agricultural economy toward support for industries such as shipbuilding and ironworking which were essential to maintaining a proper armed forces and which would lead to higher-paying jobs for American workers. Hamilton also recognized that by developing new industries, the United States would no longer have to depend on imports of foreign manufactured goods. At that time, and for many years afterward, most of these goods were provided by the United Kingdom, allowing it to continue to dominate its former colonies. This dependence on Britain not only hurt American national pride, but also introduced the possibility that Britain would use trade relations to exert unacceptable pressure on the United States, thereby forcing the new country to follow policies, both foreign and domestic, that suited the British Crown.

Hamilton proposed solving these problems by regulating trade. He calculated that if the prices of foreign manufactured goods were high enough, American entrepreneurs would set up businesses to produce similar goods. In such an **import substitution** approach to economic development, trade barriers are used to encourage the local production of goods formerly bought from foreigners. Higher prices for imports are a key factor in the establishment of new enterprises, because new firms almost always confront substantial start-up costs that they pass along to consumers in the form of higher prices. At the same time, new companies often have quality control problems that sometimes result in the manufacture of a less-reliable product than might be purchased abroad. During their early years of operation, then, new companies generally are forced to charge more for goods that might be lower in quality than imports. In Hamilton's day, unless a trading system forced the prices for foreign goods upward, America's infant industries would have little prospect of reaching adulthood.

A protective tariff was well suited for Hamilton's purposes. By taxing imports that were in direct competition with American-made goods, the United States could push prices to levels that would induce consumers to buy from American companies trying to compete with their better-established European rivals. Moreover, such a plan would encourage new ventures that might help to safeguard U.S. national security, such as iron and steel manufacturing and the development of a machine tool industry.

In addition to these advantages, tariffs were regarded as nearly ideal protective devices because they could be fine-tuned over time—that is, they could be levied on a product-by-product basis, allowing manipulation of the prices of specific items while leaving other goods unaffected. Thus foreign products such as bananas, coffee, or tea not grown in the United States could be taxed at a low rate or not at all so consumers would not be burdened unnecessarily by high prices. The level of tariffs also could be adjusted up or down as the ability of American enterprises to compete with foreign corporations changed. Indeed, early nationalists maintained that protection was temporary and that as American firms became stronger and better established, protective tariffs would be phased out entirely. And last but not least, the tariffs collected would enrich the federal Treasury and help the U.S. government cover its operating costs.

Another line of argument favoring protection was built on the need to provide ready markets for American production to guarantee employment and prosperity and to avoid having the United States become the dumping ground for cheap European goods made by exploited, underpaid workers. Reflecting these concerns, Henry Clay of Kentucky, who served in Congress for many years and as secretary of state from 1825 to 1829, was among the first to argue in favor of restricting imports to preserve the U.S. market for American producers. Clay and others worried that opening of the American market would not be reciprocated by foreign markets, leaving the United States to play the role of patsy in the game of international commerce. Under such circumstances, American businesses would be whipsawed, on the one hand, by the invasion of their home markets by foreigners and, on the other hand, by their inability to sell in the closed markets of other countries. The end result would be rising tides of bankruptcy and unemployment in the United States, while those in other countries enjoyed prosperity. As Clay and other nationalists from the mid-nineteenth century onward saw it, the U.S. government was duty-bound to guard against such a situation.

To avert foreign threats to American prosperity, nationalists advocated setting up an "American system" in which the nation's various economic interests and producers would be tied together in a complementary and mutually beneficial set of arrangements. For example, southerners would grow cotton, tobacco, and sugar for use as raw materials in mid-Atlantic and New England factories producing clothing, textiles, cigars, candy, soft drinks, and other goods for sale throughout the country. Midwestern farmers would grow the corn and wheat and raise the hogs and cattle needed to feed people in other parts of the country, especially in the rapidly growing cities spawned by industrial activity. Miners in Appalachia and elsewhere would supply coal and other raw materials for the growing iron and steel industry, and financiers in New York and other large cities would provide the credit American corporations needed to conduct business.

In short, the United States could, by combining its diverse natural, manufacturing, and agricultural resources with a policy of protection, create and maintain a self-sufficient (or autarkic) economy that would provide benefits to all without having to face the risks to prosperity that trade represented. Moreover, by concentrating on the creation and maintenance of domestic commercial networks, Americans could cement their ties of loyalty to one another, forge a great nation from what might at first seem an excessively disparate collection of peoples, regions, and modes of production, and become a thriving democracy that might serve as a symbol of hope for the rest of the world.

Finally, such a system would go hand in hand with the desire of many Americans for isolation from much of the rest of the world, especially Europe. Through the early 1900s, Americans generally regarded themselves as part of an endeavor to create a new and different society founded on democratic principles that would allow the common citizen to earn a decent living and have a voice in the conduct of public affairs. They believed their political and economic systems were distinctly different from those found elsewhere, and most especially Europe, where discrimination based on class, religion, and political affiliations was normal and where constant quarrels between countries meant frequent warfare. The conventional wisdom was that too close an association with Europeans would spell trouble for Americans. Antidemocratic European values might pollute and undermine the American system of democracy, and Europeans might seek to entice the United States to involve itself in European conflicts in the belief that American resources might prove decisive in swinging the outcome in their favor. Thus the self-interested commercial advantages that many expected from an American system of protection were reinforced by political arguments that warned of the dangers stemming from too close an association with Europe. And trade often was described as the type of relationship that could lead to trouble.

Overall, then, from its formation in the mid-1800s and for nearly a century thereafter the Republican Party firmly positioned itself in favor of a nationalist system of protection that it believed would promote prosperity, economic development, higher wages for American workers, and better prices for American farmers; guarantee markets for American production; safeguard the American system of democratic government; and maintain American national security. One of the linchpins in this system would be regulation of foreign trade by way of a protective tariff designed to limit the ability of foreigners to penetrate the U.S. economy and to play a key role in vital areas of American society. Indeed, according to the

Republicans of this period, their protectionist system was largely responsible for advancing the United States from its relatively feeble economic position before the Civil War to its international economic dominance of the early twentieth century. Moreover, Republicans proudly proclaimed that all of this was accomplished while preserving, and even enhancing, the American way of life and steering the United States clear of entanglements in European conflicts.

THE FREE TRADE ALTERNATIVE

Although many nineteenth- and early twentieth-century leaders believed that enormous advantages were associated with the nationalist approach to foreign trade, such beliefs faced significant economic and political challenges from the beginning. The centerpiece of the economic arguments against nationalism was the doctrine of **free trade.**

The Basic Economic Argument

Writing in 1776, the same year the United States proclaimed its independence from Great Britain, Scottish economist Adam Smith introduced the world to free trade and **capitalism** in his book *The Wealth of Nations.* In the years since Smith's book, and particularly since the end of World War II, free trade, which is at the heart of the so-called liberal approach to international commerce, has become an ideal against which American trade policy is often judged.

In *The Wealth of Nations* Smith was seeking to undercut the mercantilist view of trade that was popular in the eighteenth century. **Mercantilism** treated commercial activity as subordinate to the government's need to accumulate power and to strengthen the society it ruled. One vital ingredient in accumulating power was the acquisition of ever-larger stocks of bullion (gold and silver), which, in a time before paper currency was widely accepted, could be used both to finance government policy and to enlarge the military resources the government needed to expand its authority at home and abroad.[3] Two of the more widely pursued methods for increasing a government's stockpile of bullion centered on acquiring gold and silver mines, which led some governments to seek colonial outposts, and on manipulating one's **balance of trade** with other societies.

Establishing and maintaining a **favorable balance of trade** were viewed as the key to amassing more bullion. A favorable balance of trade was achieved when the value of a country's exports exceeded the value of its imports. In those days when bullion financed the acquisition of goods in international commerce, if a society could export a lot and import very little, then its overall balance of exports as opposed to imports would lead to an inflow of bullion. Using that reasoning, rulers adhering to mercantilist views promoted exports while often limiting imports.[4] Indeed, such leaders regarded self-sufficiency as an ideal state of affairs; after all, a self-sufficient society, by requiring few if any imports, could minimize its outflows of bullion and maximize its inflows of bullion through its own exports. Another advantage of self-sufficiency was that foreigners could not use an interruption in trade to exert political pressure.

Smith regarded the mercantilist treatment of trade as wrong-headed. For one thing, he questioned the mercantilist views of both wealth and the role of trade in the creation of a better society. Instead of defining bullion as wealth and viewing trade as a means of increasing one's hoard of bullion, Smith viewed bullion as a medium of exchange that facilitated trade. He also maintained that wealth was better understood as the availability of the goods and services needed by a society, and he argued that trade should be conceptualized as a process by which a society acquires from other societies the goods and services it wants but cannot produce for itself.

Indeed, capitalists like Smith tended to emphasize a society's ability to import, because imports provided the amount and variety of things people needed to raise their standard of living; exports simply provided the income to finance imports. Therefore, unlike mercantilists who concentrated on one part of the trade picture (favoring exports and attempting to reduce imports), capitalists had a more complete picture of the process. They understood that a society could not import unless it exported, and that, likewise, a society could not export unless it imported so that other societies could earn the money needed to buy its exports.

Capitalists also recognized that international trade allowed each country to take advantage of its own unique natural resources, climate, and workers' skills to produce a relatively limited range of goods. Moreover, a *free* flow of international trade allowed all countries to obtain from others the products they either could not make for themselves or could make only at great expense. Trade, then, would allow the creation of an international division of labor, with each society specializing in the goods that its resources and other endowments would permit it to produce more efficiently than other societies. In effect, the international system would replicate on a grand scale the relationships that existed in the domestic arena where members of society worked at single occupations, each making far more than they could consume personally. Individuals could then sell their surplus production to others for the income they needed to buy the remaining goods and services that allowed them to maintain a standard of living higher than they could possibly attain if each household attempted to produce for itself everything it required. Such a system not only would allow everyone to gain access to more goods and services than they otherwise could, but also would provide the best-made products at the lowest prices because specialization would ensure that the goods would be made by those best suited for the task.

The system of international commerce that free traders envisioned and the efficiency and quality of production that they expected required one more ingredient, however: a hands-off approach by governments toward commerce. Free traders argued that within any one country natural competition among producers and buyers and consumers' tendency to shop for the best product at the best price would be a far more effective mechanism for regulating the economy than anything a government could devise. They advocated, then, a minimum degree of government intervention in the economic marketplace. The marketplace was defined as the process through which producers and consumers struck deals leading to the exchange of goods and services. Self-interest and competition were vital parts of this process. Self-interest was the desire of each actor to accumulate as many resources as possible and to have the highest standard of living attainable. In pursuing this goal, everyone in the marketplace would seek to buy the highest-quality goods at the lowest possible price, and producers would strive to make better goods than others and to sell at a low price lest they lose out to others making a similar good at a better price. According to the capitalists, government intervention in this process could result in favoritism toward one producer or buyer over others, exempting it from the natural competition of the marketplace.

A freely functioning market was needed at the international level as well. Any tariffs and other government measures intended to restrict the flow of commerce between countries and to encourage domestic businesses over foreign firms would undermine creation of the international division of labor and the proper functioning of the competitive processes needed to maintain an international marketplace.[5] This arm's-length relationship between the government and the marketplace was the source of the term **free trade.** As free traders saw it, the ideal commercial interactions take place in an environment largely void of government interference—that is, commerce is "free" of politics, including political restrictions (such as tariffs) on foreign trade, and protectionist policies are unacceptable.

Protectionism was the bane of capitalist trade because it distorted economies and tended to leave all but a selected few worse off than they might have been otherwise. One aspect of protection that capitalists found particularly pernicious was its practitioners' tendency to depict protection as an attempt to fight off an onslaught of imports. As capitalists saw it, protectionists were merely employing nationalist xenophobia to justify an economic practice that actually inflicted harm on consumers by guaranteeing a lower standard of living.

In general, calls for protection ring out from those industries that feel unable to compete effectively—that is, those businesses that believe that unrestrained international trade will bring with it a flow of imports that will rob them of sales in their home markets.⁶ Because a producer's inability to compete usually can be traced either to its higher prices or to its inferior goods, the protection granted to the noncompetitive producers in effect denies local consumers access to better-made or lower-cost foreign goods and forces them to purchase inferior items that cost more. As consumers in a society that restricts foreign trade, they face the prospects of seeing shoddy products break down faster and an inability to buy as much because of higher prices—all of which lowers their standard of living.

Protection also adversely affects the performance of producers that are competitive. For example, an otherwise competitive steel industry that is denied access to cheaper and higher-quality foreign iron ore or coal because domestic producers of iron ore and coal are protected from imports will find itself making inferior and higher-cost steel. In turn, the shipbuilding, construction, and auto industries that must use locally produced steel will produce goods that are themselves expensive but inferior, and those who use these ships, buildings, and motor vehicles will in turn suffer. Moreover, protection tends to channel capital in the "wrong" direction. Instead of locating their money in industries that seek to innovate and make new and better products, investors are encouraged to move toward industries that appear less risky and more secure because they are protected, thereby harming a society's long-term prospects for growth and development. Finally, a country that is too vigorous in its pursuit of protection can close itself off from the new ideas and values that often accompany the international interactions associated with trade. Lack of access to such information can seriously damage the economic well-being and national security of the affected country.

The United States and Free Trade

In the late eighteenth century, many of the leaders who guided the newly formed United States found free trade theory eminently compatible with the ideals that motivated their revolt against Great Britain. Capitalism's rejection of mercantilism appealed to revolutionaries who based their actions on their desire to escape from the regulations and limitations imposed on the colonies by the British in the name of mercantilism. Because Americans had chafed so much under the British system, early influential politicians such as Benjamin Franklin, Thomas Jefferson, and Thomas Paine welcomed a sound theoretical basis for rejecting a system that had kept the American colonies in commercial shackles. Moreover, free trade preached the values of limited government and the need to provide people with the freedom to employ their talents to the fullest in order to compete effectively in the marketplace. Such ideas coincided closely with the role that many Americans felt government should play in society and with the emphasis they placed on individual liberty. Finally, free trade complemented the popular yeoman farmer ideal of the time, which was based on the premise that democracy functioned best in an agrarian society. According to this view, the growth of the manufacturing sector enhanced the probability that combinations of special interests would form and attempt to overrule the will of the people. Many felt the United States could avoid this threat to democracy by retaining an agriculture-based economy and trading with other countries for the manufactured goods it required. Free trade, then, tied in neatly with the preservation of democracy.

These views of free trade, however, were not universally accepted. For one thing, the new government needed revenue. Thus one of the first acts of Congress in 1789 was passage of a tariff that averaged just over 8 percent of the value of imports. In addition, Congress responded to demands for a protective program to build industry to increase national strength and safeguard national security by constructing the American system just described.

By the mid-1800s, the debate surrounding trade was focusing most intensely on how high a tariff was needed to guarantee the proper protective framework for American business while ensuring that domestic consumers would not be gouged by unnecessarily high prices. Throughout the second half of the nineteenth century, Republicans consistently favored high tariffs to protect American producers from an invasion of their home markets by imports. Indeed, Republican-sponsored protection sometimes went so far as to advocate tariff barriers for industries that did not even exist and for which American firms expressed little interest, maintaining that the duty would induce domestic production.[7] The Democrats generally argued against what they saw as Republican excesses over the tariff. They pointed out that the Republican approach was designed to cut off imports almost entirely, that many of the American firms receiving protection neither needed it nor wanted it,[8] that industrialization was unfairly taking place on the back of common consumers who were burdened with excessive expenses because of high tariffs, and that tariff rates should be more closely pegged to the government's need for revenue, coming down in times of budget surpluses and increasing in times of deficits.

By 1900, the forces opposing protection had two new weapons in their arsenal. The first was the growing threat of monopolies and trusts, stemming from the ability of excessively large corporations to snuff the life out of their competitors and gain control of entire industries. The Standard Oil empire of John D. Rockefeller was the epitome of this breed of corporate giant. A second weapon was found in the increasingly accepted belief that the more two countries engaged in trade, the less likely they would engage in war.

The relationship between protection and the threat of monopolies stemmed from high tariff barriers. Because of these barriers, large American firms that succeeded in overcoming or buying out their domestic rivals were assured that they would face virtually no competitive pressures from foreign producers in their attempts to dominate the home market. In effect, then, the American system of protection was preventing American consumers from having choices when making purchases. Many Democrats and some progressive Republicans, such as William Howard Taft, who was elected president in 1908, sought to revise the tariff to prevent such situations. When he assumed office in 1913, President Woodrow Wilson called for a substantial reduction of the tariff as part of his New Freedom assault on the special interests. Wilson believed such interests, by forming trusts, were conspiring against the general public to benefit the privileged.[9]

The connection between trade and war was built on the growing belief that the extensive commercial interactions that evolved naturally from free trade and an international division of labor would operate to prevent the sort of conflict between trading partners that produced wars. In part, the mutual reliance, or **interdependence,** resulting from trade would render war too costly from a commercial point of view. Countries with high levels of trade simply would be unable to fight because if they went to war they would be killing their best customers and suppliers and thereby would wreak as much damage on themselves as on their enemies. Widespread trade would ensure that all countries that engaged in war would be losers, for their economies would go into tailspins, creating unemployment and domestic discontent. In the end, then, anyone accepting the premise that rising levels of international economic interdependence produced prosperity for all countries could also easily conclude that trade made war irrational because it threatened the economic well-being that governments valued so highly.

Advocates of lower tariffs also pointed out that interdependence fostered peace by promoting the rise of a middle class and spreading the liberal values that would lead to democratic forms of government. Democracy in turn would serve as a powerful force for peace because it would limit the influence of the small but powerful social cliques that many believed promoted war to further their self-interests. Furthermore, democracy would give a strong political voice to those who hated war the most: the common people who fought and died in the conflicts.

The arguments relating trade to peace took on an extreme sense of urgency during the First World War. The toll of human suffering and the slaughter that accompanied the fighting provided convincing reasons for favoring any plans that might help avoid such calamities in the future. The use of trade to promote peace attracted the attention of many influential Americans. Among the most prominent was Cordell Hull, a Democratic member of the House of Representatives from Tennessee who later served as secretary of state. As Hull recounts in his memoirs,

When war came in 1914, I was very soon impressed with two points. The first was its terrific commercial impact on the United States. I saw that you could not separate the idea of commerce from the idea of war and peace. You could not have serious war anywhere in the world and expect commerce to go on as before. And the second was that wars were often largely caused by economic rivalry. . . . I thereupon came to believe that . . . if we could increase commercial exchanges among nations over lowered trade and tariff barriers and remove international obstacles to trade, we would go a long way toward eliminating war itself.[10]

In a move designed to spur the movement toward freer trade and therefore a more peaceful world, Hull proposed in April 1917 that an international trade conference be convened in Washington at the first possible moment after the conclusion of World War I. Although the trade conference did not materialize, Hull did have the satisfaction of noting that a call for free trade was the third of the Fourteen Points that President Wilson hoped not only would serve as the basis for the settlement ending the First World War, but also would constitute a giant step toward ending all war.

Thus by 1920, the proponents of free trade could point to both the economic and political reasons for its enactment. Economically, free trade promoted efficiency in production and superior products at lower prices. Politically, it offered the possibility of reducing and potentially eliminating international conflict. The opponents of free trade, however, had a different point of view and suggested that those favoring the dismantlement of protection were excessively idealistic and willing to risk America's economic future in pursuit of untested theories about the supposed benefits of trade. It would be far better, nationalists asserted, to stick to a protectionist system that promoted economic development and reserved American markets for American producers.

The Realist View

In the years after the First World War, another line of argument—the realist view of international relations—emerged to question the value of free trade as a means of promoting international peace and prosperity.[11] For realists, the most prominent features of the international system were its division of the world into independent countries, or states, and the absence of any international agency able to assume the role of a government and regulate their conduct. These features combined to create an international climate of anarchy in which all countries were free to formulate their own goals and to pursue their interests as they pleased. Indeed, as realists saw it, the freedom countries had to define and implement policy—and inevitably to develop diverging interests—virtually guaranteed that conflict would be a characteristic of international relations.

Because clashes between international actors could occur without the restraining influences that a world government might be able to impose, they could escalate to warfare. In fact, many realists regarded the international arena as one in which war was a normal state of affairs among countries. In such an environment of violence and the potential for violence, no state was safe and all countries had to struggle constantly to protect their security.

Living in a world without security, however, is unacceptable to most international actors. States attempt to reduce their insecurity by pursuing policies of self-interest designed to provide them with a margin of safety in the event another country poses a threat. For example, a country may build its military capabilities to the point that it can withstand assaults from other international actors. But such a prescription for managing security contains an inherent problem, because moves by one actor to increase its security assets will promote anxiety in others, prompting countermoves and renewed feelings of insecurity for the country making the initial move. One move can thus lead to another, and the search for security can simply breed insecurity and distrust among all international actors—a phenomenon known as the "security dilemma."[12]

For realists, the implications of the security dilemma extended beyond the buildup of armaments; simply put, the competitive and conflictual environment of the international system made cooperating with others difficult. When one actor lowered its guard and trusted another actor, it would run risks, and caution demanded that it avoid risks because of the terrible consequences it might confront given the strength and resources other actors possessed and the danger that they might resort to violence and warfare. As a result, governments would be forced to base their policy on their calculations of their own best interests, taking into account the best ways to protect their people and territory. In acting on such calculations, countries might even have to violate international agreements they pledged to uphold. Such violations may be morally wrong from the point of view of other international actors, but governments must live according to a morality that dictates that they protect their people and other national interests before they concern themselves with how other countries view their conduct.

For opponents of free trade, this new and increasingly popular view of international relations provided two avenues for assaulting proposals for more open commercial arrangements with other countries. The first was built on the doubt that in itself free trade would produce the international peace its advocates envisioned. According to realist theory, conflict was a product of the combined effects of anarchy and the power in the possession of international actors. Because expanding international commerce would do little to change these characteristics of international politics, realists believed that the incidence of international conflicts, including wars, would be unaffected by free trade.

The second realist argument centered on the fact that free trade required countries to cooperate in lowering their trade barriers, something realists doubted could be arranged. In the absence of such cooperation, there was the fear that the United States might dismantle key restrictions on imports and open its domestic market to foreign competition while others would not. Under such circumstances, some American producers would be confronted with an avalanche of foreign-made goods that might undermine their ability to stay in business, but there would be no compensation in the form of opportunities for other American firms to do business in markets abroad. For those who believed in the American system of protection, this would be a fool's bargain. Because trust was in such short supply in the international arena, and because a mistake could mean the ruin of American corporations and the loss of jobs for American workers, it was far better to forsake the obvious risks of free trade in favor of protection.

Beyond this, nationalists pointed to the geographic realities confronting the United States. Separated from Europe and Asia by the Atlantic and Pacific Oceans, Americans enjoyed a unique degree of security because those great oceans made military assaults on the United States nearly impossible. Most nationalists, then, believed that the wisest course for the United States was to forego contacts, including trade, that might draw America into foreign conflicts. By isolating itself both politically and economically from those across the high seas, many nationalists believed that the United States could remain at peace and American businesses could prosper. Thus in the minds of many American political and business leaders, realist notions about how the international system operated reinforced nationalist ideas about the need to limit foreign trade.

CONGRESS AND TRADE

In the U.S. Congress, trade and the tariff were among the most hotly contested issues of the first 150 years of American independence. The preeminence of Congress in matters pertaining to trade and the tariff is mandated by the U.S. Constitution. Article I, section 8, empowers Congress "[t]o lay and collect Taxes, Duties, Imposts [customs duties] and Excises" and "[t]o regulate Commerce with foreign Nations." These grants of authority provide Congress with the right to make the rules by which Americans trade and engage in other forms of commercial activity with other countries. Congress also is entitled to set tariff levels and any other customs duties it might deem necessary. By contrast, the president has little authority in this area; under Article II of the Constitution the president has only the power to negotiate treaties, some of which may relate to trade issues. However, treaties require the consent of two-thirds of the members of the Senate. Given Congress's vast scope of authority over commerce and the president's circumscribed role, it is not surprising that right up to the Second World War Congress served as the battleground for those seeking to dominate American trade policy.[13]

The nature of Congress itself had profound implications for the direction of trade policy. For one thing, members of Congress are elected by and responsible to relatively small constituencies or to individual states. As a result, members of Congress tend to treat trade as a local issue, evaluating the impact of trade legislation in terms of its effect on those living in their own district or state instead of looking at how the legislation might affect the nation as a whole. After all, members who forget local needs in an attempt to deal with national problems may lose their seat in Congress even while gaining prominence on the national scene.

Beyond this, the undisciplined and relatively decentralized nature of Congress, with its weak political parties and members who jealously guard their independence, allows special-interest groups to play a substantial role in the legislative process. All interest groups, however, do not affect the formation of trade policy equally. Those adversely affected by imports tend to have a far louder voice than do those who benefit from more open trade, such as consumers and businesses that aspire to participate more vigorously in international commerce. The louder voice of import-sensitive actors stems in part from their stronger incentive to seek from Congress a policy favoring their needs. After all, trade may threaten their very existence, sparking a drop in profits and perhaps even bankruptcy unless protective policies are enacted. These concerns provide powerful reasons for such actors to organize and to bring the maximum possible pressure to bear on congressional decision makers.

Another factor working to amplify the voice of the adversely affected is that such industries often are concentrated geographically, and therefore they have the ear of specific members of Congress who represent the districts or states in which they are clustered. These members may then be counted on both to lend their own support to protectionist legislation and to pressure or bargain with other members of Congress for their support as well. In fact, members often engage in logrolling or horse trading—that is, trading votes to help each other out on the issues important to their constituents. Finally, members of Congress are aware that those who fear imports may see the issue as so important that they will base some kinds of political behavior such as voting and contributing funds to political campaigns on how politicians respond to their trade needs. Members who ignore these realities put their political careers at risk.

By contrast, consumers and exporters are much less likely to share the sense of political urgency and commitment characteristic of import-sensitive interests. These groups rarely believe that trade barriers, whether up or down, pose any clear and present danger to their economic existence. Indeed, many consumers are unaware of trade barriers or may not fully understand how they are affected by those barriers, though they may display sympathy toward those who stand to lose jobs in industries unable to compete with imports. Moreover, consumers tend to be poorly organized for political action and usually base their votes and other forms of political behavior on issues other than trade. For their part, exporters frequently eschew political action as a waste of time that could be better spent handling an already profitable business. Besides, exporters tend to define their political problems not in terms of congressional action on U.S. trade policy, but in terms of the restrictive practices of foreign governments.

In the late nineteenth century, all these factors culminated in a policy-making process that strongly favored creating and maintaining trade barriers. Adding fuel to the protectionist fire, tariffs were set on an item-by-item (sometimes labeled product-by-product) basis that facilitated and encouraged congressional vote trading. For example, a member from Massachusetts could obtain a high tariff for the shoe industry by promising members from Louisiana and Michigan to vote for high tariffs on sugar and automobiles. And so it would go, until nearly every producer that wanted protection received it. The tariff-setting process, in fact, was so fraught with horse trading and exchanges of favors that it almost defied control. Indeed, when describing the system one distinguished observer noted that "in tariff making, perhaps more than in any other kind of legislation, Congress writes bills which no one intended."[14]

The excesses found in the tariff system did not end with vote swapping; they also included attempts by Congress to compensate industries hurt by tariffs with their own high tariff because "the political logic of protection leads to 'protection all around.'"[15] For example, when tariffs on sugar made candy makers vulnerable to imports, they received protection in the form of a tariff on foreign-made candy. If tariffs on wood hurt the furniture industry, Congress placed a tariff on imported furniture. The auto industry was compensated for tariffs on glass, steel, and paint, and the clothing industry was recompensed for tariffs on wool, cotton, and silk. And so it went. Businesses came to regard protection as a God-given right that Congress reconsidered only at the risk of a full-scale political outcry, even when any economic justification for protection, such as the need to safeguard a newly formed industry from more established foreign competitors, no longer existed.[16] Under these circumstances, "a vote for lowering trade barriers [was] . . . an unnatural act."[17] By early in the twentieth century, Congress was finding it increasingly difficult to withhold protective tariffs because "the sentimental basis of the protection system [was] nationalism, [and] all who desire[d] protection [came] within this set of loyalties equally." Under such circumstances, Congress found it "vastly more easy to grant the plea than to deny it."[18]

Table 2-1 Party Control of Congress and the Presidency and Average Tariffs as a Percentage of Dutiable Imports in Years of Major Tariff Legislation, 1870–1930

Year	House	Senate	President	Tariff
1870	R	R	R	44.2
1872	R	R	R	42.3
1883	R	R	R	45.3
1890	R	R	R	48.9
1894	D	D	D	41.6
1897	R	R	D/R	47.3
1909	R	R	R	40.8
1913	D	D	D	28.3
1922	R	R	R	38.2
1930	R	R	R	52.8

Source: Judith Goldstein, *Ideas, Interests, and American Trade Policy* (Ithaca: Cornell University Press, 1993), 95–96, 125. Reprinted by permission of the publisher Cornell University Press.

Note: D = Democratic, R = Republican. In March 1897 Democratic president Grover Cleveland yielded the White House to the Republican president William McKinley.

This Congress-centered policy-making framework presented free trade advocates with formidable obstacles and greatly favored the nationalist approach inherent in the American system. Reinforcing these domestic forces was the fact that until World War II the United States faced no serious international threats that might have forced it to develop close political and economic ties with other countries. With the exception of the very brief and easily won Spanish-American War in 1898 and the First World War in 1917–1918, America's geographic isolation and near self-sufficiency allowed Congress and the American people to insist on maintaining a substantial degree of political and economic separation from the rest of the world. Congress could therefore regard the tariff as a primarily domestic affair and continue to play its protectionist game.

Table 2.1 reveals that after the Civil War the Republican Party, which billed itself the party of protection, almost always controlled both Congress and the presidency in the years when major tariff bills were passed. The result was tariffs that were uniformly high, exceeding 40 percent every year except in 1913 and in 1922, the year Republicans regained control of Congress from the Democrats and began reversing the lower tariffs the Democrats had initiated in 1913. But even when the Democrats were in the driver's seat, as in 1894 and 1913, there hardly was an attempt to move to free trade. In 1894, the Democrats did lower the tariff from 48.9 percent to 41.6 percent, but this reduction, even though substantial, still left American rates at very high levels.

Table 2-2 Average Tariffs as a Percentage of Dutiable Imports, United States and Major European Trading Countries, 1875 and 1913

Country	1875	1913
Austria	17.5	18.0
Belgium	9.5	9.0
France	13.5	20.0
Germany	5.0	13.0
Italy	9.0	18.0
Netherlands	4.0	4.0
United Kingdom	0.0	0.0
United States	42.3	28.3

Source: Judith Goldstein, *Ideas, Interests, and American Trade Policy* (Ithaca: Cornell University Press, 1993), 95. Reprinted by permission of the publisher Cornell University Press.

Even when rates were cut to 28.3 percent in 1913, they still were much higher than the comparable rates among the major trading countries of Europe—see Table 2.2. In fact, in 1875 American rates were up to ten times higher than European rates. While the lower American rates and somewhat higher European duties in 1913 narrowed this difference, American tariffs were still nearly 50 percent higher than the highest European rates (those in France) and vastly exceeded the lowest duties found on the other side of the Atlantic.

Tables 2.1 and 2.2 are revealing in other ways as well. For one thing, the congressional system for handling trade led to the strong political pressures that produced high tariffs, and even the Democratic Party, which professed to favor low tariffs, had a hard time resisting these pressures. For another, through 1930 the ideals associated with free trade made little impression on those who made American policy, even during and after World War I when the horrifying costs of the fighting in Europe brought appeals for freer trade as a means of eliminating the threat of future wars. In the United States, such appeals apparently carried little weight, because when the dust settled after the war Republicans, who had regained control of Congress in 1918, immediately called for higher tariffs. The American system of protection was so firmly entrenched, and the special interests that profited from it had such a strong voice in Congress, that nothing seemed able to sidetrack it, not even the prospect of using trade as a weapon to prevent war.

CHAPTER SUMMARY

Throughout the first century and a half of American history, Congress dominated U.S. trade policy making, and special-interest groups had easy access to the policy process. Congress focused on the tariff, which served as both a source of revenue for the U.S. government and a means for protecting American businesses from foreign competition. Through the use of high tariffs, Congress attempted to encourage the growth and development of the American economy with an eye not only to guaranteeing American prosperity, but also to promoting democracy and the American way of life. The major political parties split, however, over how high tariffs should be and how long protection should last. The more nationalist Republicans favored higher and longer-lasting tariffs; the more free trade Democrats branded themselves the party of consumers and called for the lowest possible tariffs. For most members of both parties, free trade represented a set of ideals that to a large degree were precluded by the realities of domestic and international politics.

Developments in the international and domestic arenas had almost no effect on these attitudes or on the process of trade policy making. Internationally, the costs of war and the possibility that trade might be used to prevent war made little impression on Congress, especially its conservative Republican members. Domestically, the increasing might of American industry and its potential ability to handle challenges from any part of the world also did virtually nothing to change the general protectionist thrust of trade policy. Beliefs in protectionism and isolationism, together with special interests' desires to remain shielded from international competition, drove Congress toward a restrictive trade policy. Even when it became evident that these beliefs and special-interest needs were counterproductive, they continued to drive policy, as we will see in the next chapter.

NOTES

1. Quoted in Raymond A. Bauer, Ithiel de Sola Pool, and Lewis Anthony Dexter, *American Business and Public Policy: The Politics of Foreign Trade* (New York: Atherton Press, 1964), 16.

2. Tariffs might be thought of as an unseen sales tax, because importers almost always incorporate the value of the tariff into the final price of a good. That way, consumers usually do not realize they are paying yet another tax when they purchase the good.

3. Governments valued bullion for the uses they could put it to and not because they simply wanted huge quantities of precious metals as an end in itself.

4. Mercantilists also promoted any industries, such as those producing armaments, or other economic activity that they thought might increase their country's strength. See Stephen D. Cohen, Joel R. Paul, and Robert A. Blecker, *Fundamentals of U.S. Foreign Trade Policy: Economics, Politics, Laws, and Issues* (Boulder: Westview Press, 1996), 56.

5. Capitalists have long accepted qualifications to their arguments about government intervention. From the beginning, they accepted the need to promote industries related to safe-

guarding national security. In addition, they recognized that intervention might be appropriate for new or infant industries, provided that the protection did not exceed the limited time required for those industries to become internationally competitive. More recently, some capitalists have accepted the argument that governments should intervene to maintain the public's health, to limit damage to the environment, and to prevent any other business practices that might be injurious to the public. However, most capitalists consistently have opposed government interventions to manipulate the competitive outcomes associated with operation of the marketplace—that is, capitalists generally believe that businesses should be allowed to fail if they are unable to produce goods that others wish to consume.

6. In some circumstances, those actors calling for protection may not fully realize the degree to which they could dominate in a truly competitive system of unrestricted trade and that they could in fact be better off if protection was eliminated. American farmers were in just this situation in the early twentieth century because many did not realize how much more efficient they were than their counterparts around the world. As a result, many farm organizations, such as the Grange, favored protection when farmers would have been better off with a system of free trade in agricultural goods.

7. The duties on tin plates are a good example. See F. W. Taussig, *The Tariff History of the United States* (New York: Augustus M. Kelley Publishers, 1967), 272–273.

8. By the early twentieth century, many American commercial enterprises (for example, the iron and steel industry and some areas of agriculture) had become as strong or stronger than their foreign counterparts and hardly needed protection from imports. Indeed, some, such as the automobile and petroleum industries, were moving aggressively into the export field and regarded high American tariffs as a hindrance because they prompted foreigners to retaliate with high tariffs of their own.

9. Thomas J. Knock, *To End All Wars: Woodrow Wilson and the Quest for a New World Order* (New York: Oxford University Press, 1992), 23.

10. Cordell Hull, *The Memoirs of Cordell Hull*, Vol. 1 (New York: Macmillan, 1948), 84.

11. The following discussion is based on material from John M. Rothgeb Jr., *Defining Power: Influence and Force in the Contemporary International System* (New York: St. Martin's Press, 1993), 52–64; Hans Morgenthau, *Politics among Nations* (New York: Knopf, 1948); and Kenneth N. Waltz, "The Origins of War in Neorealist Theory," *Journal of Interdisciplinary History* 18 (spring 1988).

12. For a more complete discussion of the security dilemma, see John H. Herz, "Idealist Internationalism and the Security Dilemma," in *The Nation-State and the Crisis of World Politics*, ed. John H. Herz (New York: David McKay, 1976), 72–73.

13. Not only do presidents have a very small constitutional role in the area of foreign trade, but most presidents of the nineteenth and early twentieth centuries were content to accept these limits and made few attempts to acquire more authority or to intervene to any great extent in the congressional consideration of trade. See Cohen, Paul, and Blecker, *Fundamentals of U.S. Foreign Trade Policy*, 28–29.

14. E. E. Schattschneider, *Politics, Pressures, and the Tariff* (New York: Prentice-Hall, 1935), 13.

15. Ibid., 86.

16. Bauer, Pool, and Dexter, *American Business and Public Policy,* 12.

17. I. M. Destler, *American Trade Politics* (Washington, D.C.: Institute for International Economics, 1995), 5.

18. Schattschneider, *Politics, Pressures, and the Tariff,* 87.

3 From Protection to Reciprocal Trade

When the First World War ended on November 11, 1918, the United States possessed an impressive array of political and economic strengths that placed it in an enviable international strategic position. The political strength of the United States stemmed in part from its previous isolation from international politics and from President Woodrow Wilson's Fourteen Points plan for ending the war. Because of its isolation, the United States was unencumbered by the kind of historical baggage that weighed on postwar Britain, France, Germany, and other European countries and that led many observers to harbor suspicions about their motives. The United States had a limited history as an imperial power, and, unlike the British and French who scrambled to use the war to obtain new colonies, Americans claimed they had entered the war simply to "make the world safe for democracy" and to create a new international system that would be free of war. In a world sickened by the carnage of war, such messages offered the hope that many longed for.

President Wilson's Fourteen Points were built on the liberal principles that he believed would provide a foundation for a new world order. They called for national self-determination, democracy, collective security, disarmament, and free trade. Each principle addressed a force that was thought to have caused the First World War. National self-determination was the answer to the assassination of the heir to the Austrian throne, the 1914 act that had sparked the war. In the future, such nationalist actions would be unnecessary because all people who wanted independence would have it. Democracy would put power in the hands of the common people who had paid the price of war, ensuring that the selfish elites who benefited from international violence could not ignite conflicts. Collective security and disarmament would prevent war both by guaranteeing the safety of all countries through a pledge that aggression would be met by a worldwide response and by allowing potential aggressors to have fewer weapons to use when starting trouble. Finally, free trade would intertwine countries in commercial networks that would bind them so closely that war would be impossible.

Reinforcing Wilson's message of peace were America's enormous economic resources, which not only allowed it to play a prominent role in international strategic and political affairs, but also positioned many American producers to dominate international commerce. By the early 1920s, the United States possessed 106 million consumers, a prosperous population that was 70 percent bigger than that of Germany, the next largest great power. Moreover, American production far outstripped that of any other country. For example. American mills were producing over 36 million metric tons of steel a year, or 57 percent more than all the other great powers put together. America's petroleum production of 76 million metric tons was fourteen times greater than the combined efforts of the other great powers. Meanwhile, 3.6 million cars and trucks a year were rolling off of America's assembly lines—a number over ten times greater than that produced by the rest of the world.[1] In fact, to a large degree the enormous industrial and agricultural output of the United States had laid the foundation for the defeat of the Central Powers in World War I; American exports to the French and British had increased from $40 million in 1914 to nearly $2 billion a year by the end of the war. U.S. exports to other European countries also grew dramatically during the war. In addition, private American banks and the federal government played a major role in financing the war, loaning America's European allies approximately $7 billion during the war and another $3.3 billion for relief afterward.[2]

Thus as it moved into the post–World War I era, the United States was well positioned strategically and commercially within the international community. Its immense military and political advantages could protect American interests around the globe, and its economic base appeared to point toward a new open trade policy so that American dominance in the steel, automobile, petroleum, and dozens of other industries could be fully exploited. In other words, the United States was poised to break with its isolationist past and dismantle its system of protection in favor of freer trade.

These changes in policy never came about, however, because the majority of Americans persisted in their belief that international involvement was unwise and that protection from imports was the bedrock of American prosperity. Indeed, as described in the rest of this chapter, in the decade that followed the end of the First World War the faith in protection became more pronounced than ever and even reached the point where many Democrats pushed to redefine their party's position on trade in order to attract the support of voters favoring the American system.

The decision to reject an internationalist course also stemmed from the feeling among many political leaders, especially Republicans in Congress, that by pursuing Wilsonian ideals they might erode the constitutional role reserved for Congress in the conduct of foreign affairs and in the formation of trade policy. They were particularly concerned about Wilson's proposal that the United States join the League of Nations, because Article X of the League Covenant called for all members to protect the territorial integrity and independence of other members. This provision appeared to imperil the right of Congress to determine when the United States went to war and to shift authority to the new international organization and to the president who would manage American membership in the League. In addition, Wilson's ideas about freer trade implied that the president would receive the power to enter into international agreements to set tariffs, a job that Congress perceived to be within its jurisdiction and that its members were loath to give up.

Beyond this, special-interest groups favoring protection were exceedingly active in the months after the war. Many American producers had benefited immensely from the increased sales and the reduced foreign competition that had accompanied the wartime interruption in imports. When peace brought a return to normal international commercial activity, business leaders demanded that Congress raise tariffs to protect them from financial losses at the hands of foreign competitors. A majority in Congress was receptive to these cries for assistance because they meshed with generally held beliefs about the importance of protection for guaranteeing prosperity, because acting on the tariff was a useful way to reaffirm congressional authority, and because members welcomed the opportunity to help influential constituents in their battle against imports.

Accordingly, when they regained control of Congress in November 1918, the Republicans reasserted congressional power. They began by demanding that the Treaty of Versailles, the agreement that Wilson negotiated to end World War I and that included the Covenant of the League of Nations, be amended to modify American commitments to the League. When Wilson refused, the Senate defeated the treaty by a 53–38 vote.[3] The election of Republican Warren G. Harding to the presidency in 1920 paved the way for increases in American tariffs. With these developments, the United States appeared set on returning to the political isolation that most Americans found comfortable and to the system of protection that so many found profitable.

The decision to erect commercial barriers ignored, however, the links among American trade policy, the health of the European economies, and the ability of the United States to obtain repayment of the war loans made to the Europeans. U.S. political leaders also refused to accept the possibility that decisions by a dominant international economic force such as the United States could have serious implications for international stability and could even undermine America's prosperity. As a result, American economic isolation did not last as long as its proponents expected. By the early 1930s, an economic calamity had shaken the United States to its foundations. The shock was so great that political leaders were prepared to try almost anything to right the floundering economy, including a new law that gave the president the authority to negotiate tariff reductions with other countries. Although this grant of power was modest, it represented a new way to conduct trade policy and set a course that transformed the international commercial relations of the United States.

This chapter examines America's return to commercial isolation after World War I, explores some of the consequences of that isolation, and describes how the Great Depression created the climate that led to changes in trade policy.

COMMERCIAL ISOLATION

At the end of World War I, most Americans called for renewal of the American system of protection.[4] Among other things, the war illustrated the value of economic self-sufficiency as a guarantee that the United States would never be susceptible to economic coercion by hostile powers. Many Americans also wanted to protect the new industries set up to meet America's wartime needs and that now needed assistance to survive in the competitive postwar world. In addition, peace brought with it the fear of a downturn in an economy still flush from the wartime demand. With the fighting over, American exports might drop and Europeans would likely rebuild their economies by exporting to the United States, thereby crushing American prosperity under a flood of imports.

These fears of a postwar depression were soon felt in the agricultural sector, where the wartime demand for American products disappeared almost overnight, and the return of European producers led to a glut on the market. The effect on American farmers was stark: the gross farm income fell from $17.7 billion in 1919 to $10.5 billion in 1921, and mortgage foreclosures on farms rose from 3.2 per thousand farms during the war years to 10.7 per thousand farms after 1921.[5]

The Fordney-McCumber Tariff

Republicans, who controlled both Congress and the White House after the 1920 election, argued that tariff increases were the most appropriate remedy for economic problems. As Herbert Hoover, the new secretary of commerce, put it, "No measure . . . [is] more vital to the American working man and the farmer today than the maintenance of a protective tariff."[6] In January 1921, the House Ways and Means Committee, which had jurisdiction over tariffs, began work on an emergency tariff bill designed to avert a recession by limiting imports. Congress first passed the bill in early March, only to have it vetoed by President Wilson as one of his last acts in office. The bill was passed again and signed on May 21, 1921, by the new president, Warren Harding.

Within weeks of enactment of the emergency bill, the Ways and Means Committee began putting together a more complete package of tariffs. During this process, the demands of industries seeking higher tariffs easily overshadowed the arguments of those opposing increases. The interest groups against new tariffs were either politically weak, such as the Consumers Committee of Women; divided, such as farmers (the opposition of the more export-oriented American Farm Bureau Federation was countered by support for tariffs from the nearly million-member National Grange); or ignored, such as wholesalers and retailers, who were represented by the Wholesale Dry Goods Association and the National Garment Retailers Association.[7]

During the congressional hearings on the tariff increases, especially persistent demands for protection were heard from the industries born during the war. Time and again, lobbyists for these industries argued that they had taken up the slack to meet the demand for vital goods when the war was on and that they now deserved payback in the form of protection. Such claims might have made some sense when applied to the industries vital to national security, such as certain types of chemical or metals producers, but this argument was advanced by all kinds of producers, ranging from toy makers to jewelry firms to the perfume and cosmetics industry.[8]

Proving that they were ever gullible when it came to dispensing tariff increases, the Republicans controlling the tariff-making process handed out one increase after another to such companies. The only significant departure from this exercise in protection was their refusal to grant the newly formed synthetic dye industry the outright ban on imports it demanded. Instead, dye makers had to settle for a substantial tariff because textile makers convinced the House of Representatives that a dye import ban would increase the price of clothing and hurt the textile industry. In the process, dye makers learned a lesson about the nearly unmatched political clout of textile manufacturers.[9]

Congress employed the principle of the **scientific tariff** in devising the new bill—that is, tariffs would be used to ensure that foreign producers could not undercut the prices U.S. firms charged for their goods. Advocates of this approach argued that they were not antitrade; they just wanted a competitive environment that would give American companies a chance to compete with imports. Opponents of the scientific approach noted that equalization of costs eliminated any reason to trade, because the purpose of trade was to allow consumers to buy goods produced more cheaply abroad. Nevertheless, Congress based the new bill on the scientific approach and empowered the president to raise or lower duties by as much as 50 percent if the **Tariff Commission** recommended such a change.[10]

Under the Republican presidents of the 1920s, virtually all of these adjustments were upward.

The new tariff law had two other interesting protectionist features. The first was the use of a device called the **American Selling Price (ASP),** which allowed the president to calculate some duties not on the price foreign producers wished to charge but instead on what it cost American producers to make the goods. When used, the ASP resulted in higher tariffs and a much greater degree of protection, which outraged America's trading partners because the calculations reflected American-imposed prices.

The second protectionist feature was stiff tariffs on raw materials that, while found in the United States, were in short supply and had been imported before World War I. The avowed purpose of the duties was to protect American national security by ensuring the continued mining of certain ores. The tariffs did, in fact, favor short-term mining interests, but the long-term effect on national security was questionable; the domestic supply of the ores was limited, and encouraging production accelerated their depletion. In the end, then, the desire to protect domestic producers led to a curious logic that called for stepping up domestic production of nonrenewable resources in the name of national security when it made better sense to use imports and to conserve domestic resources for an emergency.

The new tariff bill, dubbed the Fordney-McCumber Tariff, was approved by Congress and signed by President Harding in September 1922.[11] The foreign protests were immediate. Cuba held demonstrations over increased sugar duties, Argentina threatened retaliation, and Spain observed that the United States appeared intent on a trade war. More ominous was the comment by a Japanese diplomat visiting Washington when the new bill became law: "A tariff war may breed an armed war."[12] Several European countries also complained that the new American tariffs were so high that it would be impossible to pay the war debts they owed the United States for they would be unable to earn the necessary income by exporting to the American market.

At home, bankers too immediately realized that high tariffs might reduce the ability of Europeans to repay their war debts. Exporters in industries such as petroleum, automobiles, machinery and equipment, steel, and tobacco also were alarmed, fearing that increased American rates would invite foreign retaliation. Democratic House member Cordell Hull expressed these concerns when he said, "Our foreign markets depend both on the efficiency of our production and the tariffs of countries in which we would sell. Our own [high] tariffs are an important factor in each. They injure the former and invite the latter."[13]

By 1927, the fear of foreign retaliation had become a reality. France raised its tariff on American automobiles from 45 percent to 100 percent, Spain announced increases of 40 percent on the rates charged for U.S. goods, and Germany and

Italy hiked their duties on wheat.[14] Republicans in Congress responded to these moves by stating that American tariffs were a domestic issue that would not be affected by foreign pressures.

THE FARM PROBLEM AND THE SPLIT AMONG DEMOCRATS

As the 1928 election approached, economic troubles at home and abroad swung public attention to America's trade policy. In Europe, the war loan repayment question exacerbated relations that already were sensitive because of American tariffs. As Europeans saw it, because high American tariffs made it difficult for them to earn the money needed to repay war debts through trade, the key to meeting their debt obligations was Germany's payment of the war reparations owed the Allies. The U.S. government disputed the validity of connecting tariffs, reparations, and war loans, but there was little it could do to change the European approach. Instead, the situation lurched from crisis to crisis.

The first crisis came in early 1923 when Germany suspended its reparations payments, claiming that the Allies were demanding such excessive payments that Germany was experiencing sky-high levels of inflation.[15] The French responded by invading Germany's Ruhr region. The result was a general strike throughout Germany and the almost complete collapse of the German economy. This threat to debt repayment prompted the former Allies to restructure German reparations and to arrange emergency loans for Germany in 1924.

This solution was temporary, however, because by 1928 Germany was once again in dire economic straits. German reparations were restructured a second time and more loans followed in 1929. Yet despite these arrangements, American bankers and their political allies feared that the reparations problem might be unsolvable. As a result, the American tariffs became all the more controversial; if European debtors could not get the cash for loan repayments from Germany, then the only logical alternatives were raising money through exports to the United States or cancellation of the loans. Because cancellation was politically unacceptable, doing something about U.S. tariffs became a priority.

Adding to these foreign sources of controversy were the economic problems at home. American farmers in particular were a source of concern, for the economic tailspin that began with the end of the war continued unabated throughout the 1920s. In 1926, the U.S. Census Bureau reported that 75,000 farms were abandoned between 1920 and 1925, and the American Farm Bureau Federation noted that the purchasing power of the farmers' dollar had dropped by 40 percent since the end of the war. The foreclosure rate on farms also increased, from 3.2 per thousand farms between 1913 and 1920, to 10.7 per thousand from

1921 to 1925, to 17.0 per thousand from 1926 to 1930.[16] Moreover, the farmers' misery spread to other parts of the economy, affecting the industries, such as textiles, housewares, and machinery, that commonly sold to those who tilled the soil.

The central question was what to do. Cordell Hull proposed lowering tariffs to reduce the prices farmers paid for the goods they consumed and to induce foreign nations to lower their own barriers to American agricultural goods, thereby providing farmers with additional markets.[17] Republicans responded that the problem was not that the tariff was too high, but that it was not high enough. They argued that the farm problem stemmed from excessive imports of foreign food. Endorsing the Republican position, the Grange called for a high tariff on agricultural goods to compensate farmers for the tariffs they paid on imported manufactured goods.[18] Once higher tariffs were in place, it was expected that farmers' purchasing power would return.

Another plan was developed by George Peek, a machinery manufacturer who later became an adviser to President Franklin D. Roosevelt. Peek proposed using tariffs to keep foreign agricultural products out of the United States and having the federal government buy farm surpluses, which would then be sold on world markets. The plan was introduced in Congress by Sen. Charles McNary, R-Ore., and Rep. Gilbert Haugen, R-Iowa. Congress passed the McNary-Haugen bill in 1927 and again in 1928, but it was vetoed both times by President Calvin Coolidge.[19]

The debate about the economic problems of the late 1920s created divisions within the Democratic Party. The party had traditionally supported low tariffs and freer trade, but by the 1920s the forces represented by the scientific tariff, the prospect of using tariffs to solve the nation's economic problems, and the desire to divorce the United States from many of the world's troubles persuaded many Democrats to accept higher tariffs. For this faction of the party, the **competitive tariff** became a rallying cry. When these Democrats spoke of competition, they meant using tariffs to guarantee that imports would not sell for less than American producers charged for like products. As some Democrats saw it, imports were unacceptable if they harmed American firms and cost American workers their jobs. In taking this stand, these Democrats moved close to the Republican position. As F. W. Taussig, a former chairman of the Tariff Commission, put it, "The Republicans wished to be sure of keeping imports out; the Democrats wished to be sure of letting some in"—but not many.[20]

Low-tariff Democrats vigorously protested the competitive tariff, but to no avail. When the party held its presidential nominating convention in 1928, it adopted a trade platform calling for a competitive tariff that would "equalize the difference between the costs of production abroad and at home." Cordell Hull and his supporters argued in vain that such a position was virtually identical to the Republican approach. As Hull said later:

> What [most delegates] failed to see was that such a policy actually meant an embargo on imports. If our tariffs were to make up the difference between cost of manufacture abroad and . . . at home, no manufactured products could ever come into the United States . . . because the importers would still have to pay the cost of transportation, insurance . . . and the like.[21]

In November 1928, the stage was set for an upward revision of American tariffs: Republican Herbert Hoover was elected president and the Republicans retained control of both the House and the Senate. Tariff increases were thought to be the best solution for the country's economic maladies, and, with some exceptions, leading Democrats jumped aboard the high-tariff bandwagon. In December 1928, the House Ways and Means Committee announced that hearings on new tariffs would begin in January 1929. As he watched these developments, Cordell Hull felt helpless: "The year 1929 was perhaps the nadir of my Congressional career. We had again lost the national elections; I was disturbed by those Democrats who had swung toward high-tariff ideas; my fight of two decades to reduce tariffs was failing . . . [and] a new movement to boost them still higher was successfully underway in Congress."[22] No one realized that forces were at work that would make the new tariff hearings the last such hearings in American history. Congress was about to write its final tariff bill.

The Smoot-Hawley Tariff

As the House Ways and Means Committee began deliberating a new tariff bill in early 1929, the U.S. economy seemed to be sound. The only weak spots were in the agricultural sector and in selected areas of manufacturing, such as the textile industry. Accordingly, President Hoover requested only limited tariff revisions to help just those parts of the economy that required aid. Republican Willis Hawley of Oregon, chairman of the House Ways and Means Committee, promised Hoover that the new bill would follow the recommended course.

After the hearings opened, however, they quickly spun out of control. One reason was the subcommittee structure used for conducting hearings. Each subcommittee was chaired by a member with an interest in that portion of the tariff schedule examined by the subcommittee—an arrangement that facilitated vote trading. The chairs pushed to increase rates on products from their districts while agreeing to hike rates on products of interest to everyone else.[23] As a result, the hearings often degenerated into sessions in which subcommittee members accepted at face value statements made by industry lobbyists about tariff increases.

Indeed, members rarely pressed for information about the operating costs of domestic industries and frequently accepted without question comments about the production capacity, costs of production, and export plans of foreign producers.[24] The result was that committee members caved in to almost all industry demands.

The Republicans may have taken the lead in pledging tariff increases to one industry after another, but the Democrats were not far behind. In fact, when Ways and Means sent the tariff bill to the House floor, the minority report from the Democrats was signed only by Cordell Hull. As Hull wrote later, "When the bill was reported by the Committee to the House, I felt constrained to write a minority report on it. I signed it alone because, amid this atmosphere of greed and privilege, I feared the Democrats would split so widely that it would be better not to seek other signers. There were many in the party willing to go along with the idea of higher tariffs."[25] In his report, Hull argued that higher tariffs were not the answer to the problems confronting farmers. Expanding foreign markets was the key, he asserted; tariff increases would only cause foreigners to retaliate with their own trade barriers.

Not only was Hull's view ignored, but so was the evidence supporting it. After all, agricultural imports made up only a fraction of the American market. For example, in 1927 barley production was 265.9 million bushels, of which 38 million was exported; only 713 bushels were imported. And it was the same story for rye: 58 million bushels were produced, 36 million bushels were exported, and only 16 bushels were imported.[26] If farmers had a problem, it was excess production at home, not imports. And if there was a solution, it would be found in exports, not tariffs.

When the tariff bill reached the floor of the House, it was greeted with consternation because many felt its coverage was too narrow. Member after member offered amendments to raise tariffs on goods produced in their districts. Representatives from agricultural states were angered both because farm rates were not high enough and because rates for manufactured goods had been increased. This set off the cry for "parity" between the rates for agricultural and manufacturing products so that the average rates for each category of goods would be the same.[27]

When the House finished with the tariff bill, the proponents of limited revision of the tariffs hoped the Senate would roll back rates. But these hopes were dashed almost immediately. The chairman of the Senate Finance Committee, Republican Reed Smoot of Utah, was "an out-and-out protectionist of the most intolerant stamp."[28] His goal was to protect the interests of the people in his own region and the beet sugar raised there. He knew that to achieve his protectionist goal he had to allow his colleagues to achieve theirs. As a result, vote trading continued in the Senate. In addition, the desire to aid campaign contributors became an ingredient in tariff calculations. Cordell Hull noted that "Senator Grundy of

Pennsylvania . . . was open and avowed in his methods, stating in effect that the interests which put up the money for campaigns should be compensated . . . by high tariffs."[29]

If anything, then, the Senate was more extreme than the House. Industries that pleaded for caution were ignored. For example, the auto industry, smarting from the sting of severe French tariff increases in 1927, implored Congress without effect to show moderation.[30] When the bill reached the Senate floor, another controversy erupted over agricultural rates; senators from the northwest and mountain states were upset because they felt farmers had been short-shrifted.[31] Finally, the disputes became so contentious that the Senate adjourned in late November without passing the bill.

In the meantime, there was shocking news from Wall Street. On Thursday, October 24, investors went on a selling spree that drove down the price of one stock after another. At one point, the tumult was so alarming that police were dispatched to keep the peace. By afternoon, a group of influential bankers had calmed investors by purchasing selected stocks. All concerned hoped the trouble was temporary and that the worst was over.[32] Unfortunately, this hope was misplaced.

On Monday, October 28, a new wave of panic selling hit the market, but the bankers who had saved the day on October 24 no longer had the wherewithal to stave off disaster. Investors greeted the opening of the market on Tuesday, October 29, with a sense of impending doom—a sense justified when the market almost immediately went into a free fall. At times, there were no takers at any price for some stocks. The vast fortunes of the wealthy and tidy nest eggs of the middle class were suddenly worthless. Some were so horrified by their misfortune that they committed suicide. "Black Tuesday," as it was called, was the "most devastating day in the history of the New York stock market."[33] From this day forward, it was apparent that the limited economic problems that had prompted the call for restricted tariff revisions were now widespread and serious.

When Congress reconvened in January 1930, confusion reigned. Many members were unsure about the economy; some argued that things would correct themselves soon, and others called for strong action. Questions surrounded the tariff as well. Free trade Democrats asserted that reducing tariffs and promoting exports were the best way to right the economy. Republicans insisted that high tariffs were the answer. Some observers, such as F. I. Kent, director of Bankers Trust Company, said doubts about the tariff were the problem and that any tariff bill, whether it increased or decreased rates, was the best medicine just so long as it eliminated the uncertainty.[34]

In the Senate the fight continued. Farm belt members argued vehemently that rates were not high enough, with Republican William Borah of Idaho vowing to fight on, even if it "shakes the Stock Exchange to the earth."[35] In late March, the

Figure 3-1 U.S. Imports and Exports, 1927–1935

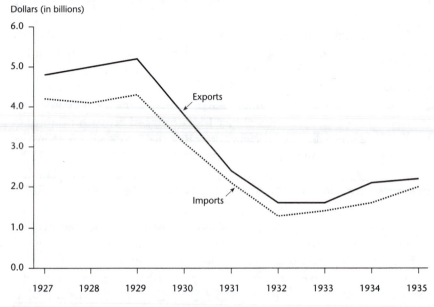

Source: *Statistical Yearbook of the League of Nations, 1936/1937,* 208.

deadlock was finally broken and the Senate passed a tariff bill by a 53–31 vote. Lengthy conference committee sessions followed as the House and Senate ironed out their differences, and in mid-June Congress approved the final version of the bill. When President Hoover signed it on June 17, 1930, the Smoot-Hawley Tariff became law.[36]

Smoot-Hawley was controversial from the start. For one thing, the Great Depression was under way by the time it was enacted, and its opponents, naturally, asserted that it played a role in deepening already terrible economic troubles. Smoot-Hawley's average **ad valorem** rate of 52.8 percent was the highest since the Civil War.[37] When that rate was coupled with the effects of the depression, the impact on trade was profound. In 1929, the United States imported $4.3 billion and exported $5.2 billion in merchandise (see Figure 3.1). After that, the value of both imports and exports fell, so that by 1932 the United States was importing only $1.3 billion in merchandise and exporting approximately $1.6 billion. In other words, by 1932 American imports and exports were running at about 30 percent of their 1929 levels. By any standard, this decline was a disaster. If surplus American production was one reason for America's economic turmoil, as many Democrats argued, and if exports were at least part of the solution, then these export figures were clear evidence of deep trouble.

Table 3-1 Percentage Unemployment, United States, United Kingdom, Germany, and Canada, 1929–1936

	Year							
	1929	1930	1931	1932	1933	1934	1935	1936
United States	12	21	26	32	31	26	23	17
United Kingdom	8	12	17	18	16	14	13	11
Germany	NA	NA	24	30	26	15	12	8
Canada	6	11	17	22	22	18	15	13

Source: Statistical Yearbook of the League of Nations, 1936/37, 53–54.
Note: NA = not available.

Foreign protests of the new law were vehement. The passage of the law just as the Great Depression struck left other countries with the impression that the American tariff was responsible for their difficulties and that the United States was attempting to solve its economic problems by thrusting them on others. Expressions of concern flowed in from Argentina, Australia, Austria, Belgium, Britain, Denmark, France, Japan, Italy, Norway, Spain, Sweden, and Switzerland. In 1931, France countered Smoot-Hawley with a **quota** system that established a numerical limit on imports of American farm products. Italy and Spain increased their duties on American-made autos and auto parts.[38] And Britain, the bastion of free trade, passed the Import Duties Act in early 1932 and took the lead in forming the Ottawa Agreements in July 1932 that set up special trade relations within the British Empire known as the **Imperial Preference System.** As a result, 70 percent of American goods entered Britain duty-free before 1932, but only 20 percent afterward.[39]

Rising unemployment figures in the United States and abroad also exacerbated the concern about Smoot-Hawley. By 1932, unemployment worldwide was at historically high levels (see Table 3.1), generating social pressures so severe that many countries felt them to be a threat to government stability. Indeed, in January 1933 Adolf Hitler came to power in Germany, in part because of the extreme problems associated with the country's 26 percent unemployment rate, which was 5 percentage points lower than the U.S. rate of 31 percent.

RECIPROCAL TRADE

Clearly, a policy change was needed to avert disaster. Because the Republicans, and to a lesser degree the Democrats, had long proclaimed the tariff to be the key to prosperity, it was only natural that an alteration of the tariff would be part of any attempt to dig the nation out of the depression. But would tariffs be raised still higher, as some would have it, or would free traders finally have their chance?

The 1932 Election and Its Aftermath

Coming as it did in the midst of the worst economic calamity in American history, the 1932 election could lead to but one result. The Republicans were swept from power as the Democrats gained the presidency and control of both houses of Congress under the leadership of Franklin Roosevelt. During the campaign, the Democrats split over the tariff issue. Al Smith, the Democratic candidate for president in 1928, and John Raskob, a Smith ally and chairman of the Democratic Party, favored protection as the appropriate answer to the depression. Fearing competition from low-wage foreign workers, labor leaders agreed with Smith and Raskob. Many in Roosevelt's "brain trust," including Raymond Moley, Rexford Tugwell, and Adolf Berle, partially agreed with the protectionists, arguing that the depression was a product of domestic forces. These advisers believed the United States should seal itself off from disruptive international forces while it straightened out its economic mess. Farmers tugged the party in yet another direction, demanding protection from imports and passage of the McNary-Haugen legislation considered by Congress in 1927 and 1928. Finally, free trade Democrats led by Cordell Hull wanted to lower tariffs and to reverse the international tide of higher trade barriers that was destroying America's ability to export.[40]

Feeling he needed support from everyone, Roosevelt waffled. On some occasions, he was vociferous in his attacks on the Smoot-Hawley Tariff; on others, he was more guarded in his comments, indicating that protection was part of his plan for recovery and that there would be no unilateral reduction in American tariffs because other countries might use the United States as a dumping ground in trying to export their way out of the depression. Moreover, in the seventy years since the Civil War it had become widely accepted political dogma that high tariffs and carefully regulated trade were vital to economic success, and Roosevelt hesitated to challenge these beliefs.

In flip-flopping on the trade question, Roosevelt first signaled his interest in reform by asking Cordell Hull to serve as secretary of state. He then moved toward protection by appointing a member of his brain trust, Raymond Moley, as assistant secretary of state. As noted, Moley favored commercial isolation as the way to solve the nation's economic ills, a view that ran counter to Hull's strong desire for lower tariffs. In another protectionist move, the new president presented Congress with the Agricultural Adjustment Act and the National Industrial Recovery Act, both of which would authorize the president to restrict imports. The agricultural legislation was designed to set and maintain agricultural prices above the world market level and allowed for trade restrictions to prevent foreign farmers from taking advantage of these prices by selling in the United States. The industrial recovery proposal attempted to increase prices for manufactured goods and established the National Recovery Administration to advise the president on limiting industrial imports.[41]

This pattern of vacillating between reform and protection continued throughout Roosevelt's first year in office and encouraged in-fighting within the executive branch, especially in the State Department. As he prepared for the World Economic Conference scheduled for London in June 1933, Secretary of State Hull believed he had Roosevelt's full support for trade reform and that a bill to that effect would soon be submitted to Congress. In fact, in a radio address on May 7 Roosevelt indicated that his goals at the conference included reducing trade barriers and stabilizing currency exchange rates, both vital ingredients of any trade reform package.[42] In addition, Roosevelt invited officials from eleven nations to meet in Washington to work on arrangements for the June meeting in London.[43] These actions appeared to be clear signals of Roosevelt's interest in trade reform.

Running contrary to these signs favoring reform, however, was Roosevelt's selection of a weak U.S. delegation to accompany Hull to London; it consisted of protectionists and politicians with little international experience. And this disappointing development was followed by yet another one. On his way to London Hull received word that Roosevelt was reneging on his promise to introduce a trade reform bill and was considering a request for higher tariffs.[44]

The disappointments continued during the conference. For one thing, Roosevelt sent the protectionist-minded Moley to London as a special envoy. The purpose of Moley's presence was unclear, but Hull felt upstaged and threatened to resign. On top of this, in early July Roosevelt shocked the conference by indicating in a message that the United States would not cooperate in firming up currency exchange rates, the stabilization of which was a prime reason for the conference.[45] This last action, which drew sharp criticism from many delegates, especially the British, threw the conference into an uproar and left Hull scrambling to find a formula for winding down the meeting without having Roosevelt stuck with the blame for failure.

Upon his return to the United States, Hull found the president changed. When the two met at Hyde Park, Roosevelt was gracious and anxious to retain the services of his secretary of state. Moley, Roosevelt said, would be reassigned to the Justice Department. Moreover, Hull was assured that Roosevelt would send a trade bill to Congress as soon as it was practical to do so.[46] Once again, the president seemed committed to reform.

Having mollified Hull, Roosevelt again changed course in December 1933 by appointing George Peek as his special assistant on foreign trade. Hull perceived this move as a challenge because Peek disagreed with the trade reforms Hull wished to pursue. One dispute centered on the unconditional **most-favored-nation (MFN)** approach to trade, which Hull favored and Peek opposed. Under such an approach, a nation agrees to conduct trade on a nondiscriminatory basis—that is, agrees to extend to all trading partners covered by the MFN arrangement the same trading privileges that are extended to whatever partner is getting the best deal that is offered. In effect, all countries included in the system are treated as equals. If a country maintains more than one tariff schedule, some with higher rates than others, then the most-favored nations are entitled to the schedule with the lowest tariffs. When MFN is extended on an unconditional basis, then any deal to lower a given set of tariffs with one partner is automatically extended to all other partners with MFN status without any requirement for compensation.

Hull felt that the unconditional MFN was the best way to reduce the trade barriers that by the mid-1930s were choking the life out of international commerce. Peek argued that the MFN approach would force the United States to play the role of sucker by extending better trading terms to countries that sometimes offered nothing in return. Peek's appointment as Roosevelt's trade assistant therefore created anxiety among liberals over the future of trade reform.

Another dispute between Peek and Hull emerged over **barter trade,** which Peek favored and Hull opposed. Peek regarded barter arrangements as opportunities to unload American surpluses in exchange for the overproduced goods of other countries. In this way, the United States benefited because it got something it could use for something it had too much of. For Hull, these bilateral deals represented the breakdown of the trading system. They were cumbersome to negotiate and produced pressures to balance exactly the value of imports and exports between trading partners. At Hull's request, the Commerce Department calculated that such attempts to balance trade could cost the United States up to one-third of its already low level of trade.[47] Hull also was wary of barter arrangements because they were discriminatory and created ill will between the United States and countries that might feel cheated by being left out of the barter deals.

Believing Peek to be a threat to trade reform, Hull attempted to limit his role in the administration. At first, he was only partially successful, for when the Export-Import Bank was created in February 1934 Roosevelt named Peek president of the bank. Peek also was appointed head of the Office of the Special Adviser on Foreign Trade when it was created in March 1934. There, he was charged with gathering data, advising the president, looking into barter arrangements, and helping cabinet departments with trade.[48] At this point, though, Roosevelt again displayed his tendency toward pursuing policy on multiple tracks by agreeing in February 1934 to send Hull's proposals for trade reform to Congress.

The Reciprocal Trade Agreements Act

As Hull prepared his trade reform legislation, he realized he had to deal with certain political realities. Protectionist sentiment remained strong in Congress and in the public at large. Indeed, many people agreed with Republican representative Everett Dirksen of Illinois that by lowering its protectionist guard, America would be inviting other nations to sell manufactured goods in the U.S. market. According to Dirksen, such a move would "retard instead of aid recovery."[49] Hull also knew that there was powerful opposition to trade reform within the administration and that he could not count on Roosevelt's total support. He decided, then, to seek legislation that would involve as little controversy as possible, that would short-circuit the interest group involvement that produced the Smoot-Hawley fiasco, and that, once through Congress, would promise a chance for steady success.

These considerations led Hull to the concept of **reciprocity.** Instead of lowering American tariffs in the hope that other countries would follow suit, as many economists and liberal internationalists wished to do, the legislation would allow the president to negotiate tariff reductions with other countries. Under this approach, American tariffs would be reduced only if other countries agreed to do the same. And the president would only give as good as he got—that is, the value of American tariff reductions would be matched to the value of foreign reductions so there could be no cheating.[50]

As for specifics, negotiations would be on a product-by-product (or item-by-item) basis so that the United States could offer to lower tariffs on goods, such as automobiles, that American companies excelled at producing and that could withstand foreign competition. Products more likely to suffer from competition simply would not come up for negotiations and would remain protected by the high Smoot-Hawley tariffs. In fact, Hull did not seek to change the Smoot-Hawley rates through legislative action; he knew that presidential negotiations would take care of that problem over time. Finally, Hull asked Congress to give the president the power to change tariff rates without any additional congressional action, thereby restricting the ability of special interests to short-circuit the process.[51] To make his proposals more palatable for Congress, Hull included a three-year time limit on the president's authority to cut trade deals. After that, the president would need renewed congressional authorization.

In pursuing the reciprocal approach to trade negotiations, Hull was turning to a technique that Congress had included in one form or another in tariff bills for nearly forty years. Even protectionist Republicans recognized the useful role that reciprocal agreements could play in opening foreign markets for surplus American production. Past reciprocity legislation, however, had almost never produced tangible results because Congress so jealously guarded its power to set tariffs and to play a role in the treaty ratification process. Yet that process had been rife with the strident demands of the special interests.[52] Hull's proposal to allow the president to negotiate and to put changes into effect by proclamation was designed to avoid these problems.

When presenting the trade bill to Congress, Hull played down free trade, emphasizing that his bill provided the president with a weapon to use in the fight to gain markets and to create jobs for American workers. As a supporter later said, "The trade agreements program is not in any sense a free trade program. It is merely an attempt to remove the causes of retaliation and to restore thereby to American enterprise its natural markets abroad and to retain at the same time reasonable protection for domestic industry."[53] Smoot-Hawley and the resulting acts of foreign retaliation were described as major causes of the depression, and the trade reforms were deemed a suitable cure. After the **Reciprocal Trade Agreements Act (RTAA),** as the reforms were known, was passed, Hull explained in a speech that "the appalling repercussions of the 1930 [Smoot-Hawley] tariff act upon our own domestic prosperity bring home the lesson that . . . the tariff is no longer a purely domestic issue. We learned that a prohibitive tariff is a gain that recoils upon ourselves . . . slamming the door shut against foreign products, we have found the door shut against our own products."[54]

When considering the reforms, Congress was encouraged to broaden its definition of protection to include farmers and workers who would have jobs only if the goods they produced could be exported. Hull explained to Congress that protection that looked after only those who faced competition from imports while ignoring the needs of those who exported was unfair. After all, why should one type of worker receive help while another does not? A Ways and Means Committee report from March 1934 reveals that Congress bought these arguments. It speaks of the need to look after the "millions of farmers and working men who would normally be engaged in agriculture and industry to produce goods for our foreign trade. Can a policy be called protection in any true sense which does not protect such farmers and working men also?"[55]

Finally, the trade reformers warned Congress that many foreign governments had the authority to conduct reciprocal negotiations and that if the United States failed to get into the game, then other governments could work out trading arrangements that would hurt American interests, making it all the more difficult to climb out of the depression. The Reciprocal Trade Agreements program was, in effect, a tool the president could use to safeguard America's national economic security.[56]

As they considered the trade reform program, members of Congress were concerned about both the national emergency produced by the depression and the sordid spectacle of special-interest manipulation associated in the public mind with Smoot-Hawley.[57] By March 1934, the depression was entering its fifth year with no end in sight. Unemployment was still above 25 percent, and trade was running at less than half of its pre-depression levels. Many in Congress felt the situation was desperate and were amenable to almost any proposal to pull the country out of the doldrums, especially if it simply involved the three-year experiment Hull requested.

Moreover, there was a lot to be said for the reforms. Tariff reductions would be negotiated on a limited basis and only for industries that could stand foreign pressure. Congress, then, could have it both ways; protection could be maintained where needed while trade was expanded to create jobs for exporters. In addition, by giving the president negotiating authority Congress would be able to divert some of the pressure of special interests to the executive branch and away from Congress. Actually, most members could see the need to give the president the negotiating authority Hull proposed. Given Congress's past track record on the tariff, few foreigners would bargain seriously if they knew Congress could reverse any deal the president made.

Keeping these considerations in mind, the House of Representatives passed the Reciprocal Trade Agreements Act on March 20, 1934, by a vote of 274–111. The bill passed the Senate on June 4 by a vote of 57–33, and President Roosevelt signed it on June 12 much to the delight of the secretary of state. Although no one realized it at the time, the United States was embarking on a course that would not only transform the way America handled its trade relations, but also lead to fundamental international changes.

Implementing the Reciprocal Trade Agreements Act

In the years after its passage, the Reciprocal Trade Agreements Act of 1934 was credited with producing a revolution in the way American trade policy was made. The essence of the revolution was found in the grant of authority to the president to negotiate tariff reductions without any further congressional action. For the first time in history, American tariffs were more than a "domestic" issue; the executive branch could now bargain with other countries to reduce tariffs. Moreover, access to the American market could be exchanged for entry into foreign markets, and American businesses that wished to export would have the incentive to lobby as a counterbalance to those seeking protection.

For all the fanfare about RTAA, a closer look at its provisions reveals an apparently modest law (see box). It carefully set limits on the tariff changes the president could make, the procedures for conducting negotiations (product-by-product), the issues the president could address (only tariffs), and the length of time during which the president could negotiate (three years). The president also was required to seek many opinions in conducting any negotiations, including those of the Tariff Commission, four cabinet departments (State, Treasury, Agriculture, and Commerce), and any private interests affected by negotiations.

Provisions of the Reciprocal Trade Agreements Act of 1934

Conditions for Trade Negotiations

- Negotiations are to be conducted on a product-by-product basis.
- Any agreements reached with foreign governments can take effect without any further action by Congress.
- Agreements may be terminated after three years with six months' notice.
- Negotiations are to be conducted using the unconditional most-favored-nation approach.
- The president must provide public notice of the intent to negotiate and allow for input from interested members of the public.
- When negotiating, the president must seek the advice of the Tariff Commission and the Departments of State, Treasury, Agriculture, and Commerce.
- The president's authority to negotiate is limited to three years.

Tariffs

- The president may negotiate on a reciprocal basis to lower or raise American tariffs by up to 50 percent of their Smoot-Hawley levels.
- The president may not eliminate the tariff on any good.

Foreign Debts

- The president may not negotiate foreign debts owed to the United States.

Note: The provisions of the RTAA are discussed in Edward S. Kaplan, *American Trade Policy, 1923–1995* (Westport, Conn.: Greenwood Press, 1996), 45; Robert A. Pastor, *Congress and the Politics of U.S. Foreign Economic Policy, 1929–1976* (Berkeley: University of California Press, 1980), 89; and Carolyn Rhodes, *Reciprocity, U.S. Trade Policy, and the GATT Regime* (Ithaca: Cornell University Press, 1993), 61.

The president's authority to negotiate on a reciprocal basis to lower or raise American tariffs by up to 50 percent of their Smoot-Hawley levels differed from the one in Fordney-McCumber. The latter allowed the president to change rates to equalize production costs. RTAA permitted the president to negotiate decreases (although the law allowed for increases, such negotiations did not occur) in American rates in return for reductions in foreign rates. Under RTAA, equalizing production costs was not a consideration in changing rates. The most important concern was inducing foreigners to lower rates.

To comply with the requirements for consultation, Roosevelt set up a Trade Agreements Committee that included officials from the Departments of State, Treasury, Agriculture, and Commerce and from the Tariff Commission. The committee was chaired by the State Department representative. Roosevelt also established the Committee for Reciprocity Information to gather information from the public and made provisions for publicizing negotiations.[58]

The State Department conducted negotiations for the president using the "principle supplier" approach—that is, it focused on the goods that constituted the bulk of each trading partner's exports to the United States. For example, negotiations with Cuba centered on sugar, with Brazil it was coffee, and so on. Such an approach allowed the United States to secure the greatest reductions in foreign tariffs. All deals were extended to others on an unconditional most-favored-nation basis. Allowing the benefits of any single deal to apply to all trading partners was criticized by opponents of the program, but Hull noted that advantages flowed in both directions, for the United States gained from any later deals its partners might make. For example, an American deal with Belgium on typewriters called for a reduction in duty from 2,012 to 1,500 francs. When Belgium later cut a deal with Germany to lower the duty to 1,150 francs, American exporters secured the new rate as well.[59]

The first RTAA bargain was negotiated with Cuba in August 1934. The result was a lower U.S. sugar tariff in exchange for lower Cuban duties on U.S.-made textiles, automobiles, and farm products. Additional agreements followed in 1935 with Belgium, Brazil, Canada, Colombia, Haiti, Honduras, the Netherlands, and Sweden, and in 1936 with Costa Rica, Finland, France, Guatemala, and Switzerland. The agreement with Canada represented a distinct change from 1932 when Canada took the lead with the British in establishing the Imperial Preference System. By 1939, the United States had negotiated twenty-one agreements lowering tariffs on over one thousand items. When the law was renewed in 1937, Hull pointed out that it was responsible for a $1 billion increase in exports.[60]

In addition to securing passage of RTAA, Hull achieved important victories in 1934 and 1935 in his bureaucratic battles with George Peek. The first step came in November 1934 when Roosevelt cancelled a barter deal Peek had arranged between the United States and Nazi Germany. Two months later, Peek's authority over trade was further reduced when Roosevelt abolished his position as foreign trade adviser. Peek left the administration altogether in November 1935 after publicly attacking the reciprocal trade agreement with Canada.[61] Thus by 1936, Hull and his free trade allies were well positioned to dominate trade policy.

Despite Hull's diligence in negotiating trade agreements and winning bureaucratic battles, by the time RTAA came up for renewal in 1937 it had achieved only modest success in restoring American trade to its pre-depression levels. Although fifteen agreements had been negotiated and exports had increased by nearly 50 percent, the United States still was exporting merely 60 percent of what it had sold to the world in 1929. With the exception of the one for France, the agreements were with smaller countries, and the biggest prize of all was not yet in place, for there was no agreement with the United Kingdom that would tear down the walls of its Imperial Preference System. Moreover, the gains in the volume of American trade were slowing and, in fact, even reversed somewhat as exports peaked in 1937 at approximately $3.1 billion and then declined to $1.8 billion in 1938 and $1.84 billion in 1939 before increasing again in 1940 to $2.3 billion.[62]

Further complicating matters, by the late 1930s international and domestic political developments had made the prospects for more agreements doubtful. Internationally, acts of aggression were disrupting the stability required for setting up trade agreements. In October 1935, Italy invaded Ethiopia, creating a crisis at the League of Nations and plunging Europe into diplomatic turmoil. Five months later, in March 1936, Hitler ordered the German army into the formerly demilitarized Rhineland, thereby signaling his intent to rebuild the German armed forces and to reverse the Treaty of Versailles. As if these crises were not enough, the Far East became the setting in July 1937 for fighting between Japan and China. In view of these conflicts, Hull redoubled his efforts to negotiate RTAA agreements in the hope that trade might calm the troubled international system, but the turmoil undermined the willingness of many countries to bargain.[63]

At home, complaints began to emerge about the trade reform program. The iron and steel industry disliked the agreement with Belgium, midwestern farmers were angered by the Canadian deal, beet sugar producers were upset about the Cuban sugar accord, and the chemical, watch, and lumber industries were arguing against RTAA renewal.[64] Textile imports from Japan had increased so much that Hull was compelled to suggest strongly in the spring of 1936 that Japan "voluntarily" limit its textile sales in the United States—after World War II such "voluntary" arrangements came to be known as **voluntary export restraint (VER) agreements.** Hull's experience revealed once again the power of the textile lobby and illustrated that while he was an ardent supporter of open trade, Hull was first and foremost a practical politician who knew how to mute criticism of his reform program.[65] Finally, the Republican minority in the House and Senate opposed the RTAA on the grounds that it was an unconstitutional usurpation of Congress's power to regulate trade.

In arguing for renewal of the RTAA, Hull had several cards of his own to play. One was his description of trade reform as the most positive course the United States could take to promote peace. This tactic played off the fears that many in Congress had of another war. Hull also claimed that the RTAA program played an important role in reducing unemployment in the United States from 26 percent in 1934 to 16 percent in 1937.[66] Even though this was a dramatic improvement, the unemployment number was still too high, and renewal could help put more people back to work. RTAA renewal also received the support of several industries, such as the automobile, machine tool, and banking. They argued that they benefited from more open markets, that trade reform allowed them to return to profitability and rehire workers, and that renewal would permit them to continue down these paths.[67]

Curiously enough, the final ingredient in Hull's fight for renewing the RTAA was the relatively limited success of the program in expanding trade. As noted, trade did increase between 1934 and 1937, but the increase was modest, in part because the RTAA program proved a cumbersome way to tear down trade barriers—one country at a time and on a product-by-product basis. The relatively glacial progress of trade reform, however, meant that opposition was not as vocal as it might otherwise have been had trade expanded quickly and more industries had felt pressured by imports. Ironically, the fact that the success of trade reform was limited contributed to the willingness of Congress to renew the program.

Even with the Democrats in control of both houses, Congress insisted on renewing the RTAA for only three more years. Renewal passed the House on February 9, 1937, by a 284–100 vote. On February 25, the Senate did the same, 58–24.[68] Hull's program could continue until 1940, by which time the world would be transformed by war.

CHAPTER SUMMARY

In the years before World War II, Americans believed strongly in protecting U.S. industry and maintaining isolation from the rest of the world, two notions that seemed to complement one another. These convictions were so widely held by the general public and were so frequently presented as the key to prosperity and the American way of life that by the late 1920s and the early 1930s even the Democratic Party, which had advocated lower tariffs and more open trade for decades, had come to embrace the idea of safeguarding American producers and workers by limiting foreign commerce. In this atmosphere, special interests had a field day as they secured high tariffs to limit their exposure to foreign competition.

When the Great Depression struck in 1929, it produced alarm and confusion over what to do about trade. Even as trade declined and unemployment soared, politicians from both political parties clung to the notion that further closing the country to foreign trade might prove to be the best course. After his election, President Franklin Roosevelt was hesitant to pursue a liberal course that would push for open trade, and Roosevelt's caution was more than matched by that exercised by most members of Congress. Thus when Secretary of State Cordell Hull finally sent a trade reform bill to Congress, it was modest and few political leaders believed it would produce major and lasting changes in the way the United States made trade policy.

Although the number of agreements negotiated during its first three years seemed impressive, the Reciprocal Trade Agreements Act had only modest effects on trade and represented an awkward process for pushing both the country and the international arena toward a new commercial system. The most important contributions of the RTAA to the reform effort were its inclusion of increased negotiating power for the president and its new emphasis on opening export markets, which generated special-interest activity in favor of reform by those who wished to export. These were big changes from the congressional domination and protectionist approach that once had marked trade policy making. But the world would never know how far reform might have gone because yet another global calamity was on the horizon—World War II. Its effect on trade is the subject of the next chapter.

NOTES

1. These figures are based on data from the *Statistical Yearbook of the League of Nations, 1931/32,* various tables.

2. Edward S. Kaplan, *American Trade Policy, 1923–1995* (Westport, Conn.: Greenwood Press, 1996), 10.

3. Thomas J. Knock, *To End All Wars: Woodrow Wilson and the Quest for a New World Order* (New York: Oxford University Press, 1992), 263–264.

4. The discussion in this section is based on Edward S. Kaplan and Thomas W. Ryley, *Prelude to Trade Wars: American Tariff Policy, 1890–1922* (Westport, Conn.: Greenwood Press, 1994), chap. 5; Kaplan, *American Trade Policy,* chap. 1; E. E. Schattschneider, *Politics, Pressures, and the Tariff* (New York: Prentice-Hall, 1935), chaps. 1–2; and F. W. Taussig, *The Tariff History of the United States* (New York: Augustus M. Kelley Publishers, 1967), chap. 10.

5. Kaplan, *American Trade Policy,* 1. Also see Kaplan and Ryley, *Prelude to Trade Wars,* 99; and Stefanie Ann Lenway, *The Politics of U.S. International Trade: Protection, Expansion, and Escape* (Boston: Pitman Publishing, 1985), 62.

6. Quoted in Kaplan, *American Trade Policy,* 2.

7. Ibid.; and Kaplan and Ryley, *Prelude to Trade Wars,* 106, 111.

8. Taussig, *Tariff History,* 468–469.

9. Ibid., 475. Textile manufacturers have so much clout because they are found in nearly every state and in many congressional districts. Thus textile companies can turn to most senators and many representatives when they need help.

10. The Tariff Commission was established in 1882 to investigate the practices of America's trading partners and to provide Congress with information. The commission expired in 1913 but was revived in 1916. The Tariff Commission was renewed from that point forward and evolved into the International Trade Commission. See Judith Goldstein, *Ideas, Interests, and American Trade Policy* (Ithaca: Cornell University Press, 1993), 98–99, 114. The congressional grant of authority allowing the president to raise or lower tariffs by up to 50 percent was challenged in 1928 in the case of *Hampton and Company v. United States.*

The plaintiff argued that this grant violated the Constitution, which gave Congress the power to set tax rates. The Supreme Court ruled that Congress could grant such authority to the president, provided that it set specific boundaries and conditions under which the authority could be exercised. This Congress did in the tariff law that was contested. See Louis Henkin, *Foreign Affairs and the U.S. Constitution* (New York: Oxford University Press, 1996), 401–402; and Goldstein, *Ideas, Interests,* 145–146.

11. Traditionally, tariff laws were named after the chair of the House Ways and Means Committee and the chair of the Senate Finance Committee, in that order. In 1922, Republican Joseph Fordney of Michigan chaired the Ways and Means Committee and Republican Porter McCumber of North Dakota chaired the Finance Committee. The new law became the Fordney-McCumber Tariff.

12. Kaplan and Ryley, *Prelude to Trade Wars,* 105–106.

13. Cordell Hull, *The Memoirs of Cordell Hull,* Vol. I (New York: Macmillan, 1948), 126.

14. Kaplan, *American Trade Policy,* 14.

15. A critical analysis of the reparations in the Treaty of Versailles is found in John Maynard Keynes, *The Economic Consequences of the Peace* (New York: Penguin Books, 1988).

16. Kaplan, *American Trade Policy,* 1, 6.

17. Hull, *Memoirs,* 126.

18. Schattschneider, *Politics, Pressures,* 94.

19. Kaplan, *American Trade Policy,* 4–5.

20. Taussig, *Tariff History,* 421.

21. Hull, *Memoirs,* 130–131.

22. Ibid., 132.

23. Taussig, *Tariff History,* 492.

24. Schattschneider, *Politics, Pressures,* 72–75.

25. Hull, *Memoirs,* 132–133.

26. Schattschneider, *Politics, Pressures,* 87.

27. Kaplan, *American Trade Policy,* 23–24; and Taussig, *Tariff History,* 495.

28. Taussig, *Tariff History,* 496.

29. Hull, *Memoirs,* 132.

30. Kaplan, *American Trade Policy,* 27.

31. Taussig, *Tariff History,* 496; and Kaplan, *American Trade Policy,* 27.

32. John Kenneth Galbraith, *The Great Crash of 1929* (Boston: Houghton Mifflin, 1988), 88, 98–99.

33. Ibid., 109, 111.

34. Kaplan, *American Trade Policy,* 37; Alfred E. Eckes Jr., *Opening America's Market: U.S. Foreign Trade Policy since 1776* (Chapel Hill: University of North Carolina Press, 1995), 111.

35. Quoted in Eckes, *Opening America's Market,* 111.

36. For some reason the popular name of this particular tariff does not follow the normal pattern for naming tariff laws (see note 11). It should be the Hawley-Smoot Tariff.

37. An ad valorem tariff is calculated as a percentage of the value of the imported good. See Eckes, *Opening America's Market,* 107, for a comparison of Smoot-Hawley rates with those of other tariff laws.

38. These restrictions on American cars and parts reveal that trade restrictions often are aimed at industries that actually oppose the trade-limiting practices of their own governments. Recall that the auto industry urged Congress to show moderation during the Smoot-Hawley debate.

39. Kaplan, *American Trade Policy,* 33–35.

40. Michael A. Bailey, Judith Goldstein, and Barry R. Weingast, "The Institutional Roots of American Trade Policy: Politics, Coalitions, and International Trade," *World Politics* 49 (April 1997): 316–317; and Stephan Haggard, "The Institutional Foundations of Hegemony: Explaining the Reciprocal Trade Agreements Act of 1934," *International Organization* 42 (winter 1988): 104–106.

41. Haggard, "Institutional Foundations," 107–108; and Goldstein, *Ideas, Interests,* 139, 154–155.

42. Stable currency exchange rates are important to trade because businesses need to know the values of foreign currencies in relation to their own so they can set prices for the goods they sell abroad. In the absence of stability, trade breaks down because businesses are uncertain of the value of foreign currencies.

43. Hull, *Memoirs,* 246.

44. Ibid., 249–251; and Michael A. Butler, *Cautious Visionary: Cordell Hull and Trade Reform, 1933–1937* (Kent: Kent State University Press, 1998), 35–36, 44.

45. Butler, *Cautious Visionary,* 63.

46. Ibid., 78.

47. Ibid., 99.

48. The Export-Import Bank is a U.S. government agency that provides loans and credits to encourage the export of American products. See ibid., 99–100.

49. Quoted in Carolyn Rhodes, *Reciprocity, U.S. Trade Policy, and the GATT Regime* (Ithaca: Cornell University Press, 1993), 59.

50. These negotiations to lower trade barriers were very different from the barter deals George Peek favored. In barter deals, the negotiations by two trading partners center on the direct exchange of given items. The negotiations Hull envisioned would have revolved around lowering tariff barriers, and achieving balance in reciprocity negotiations would have centered on how much each party lowered its trade barriers.

51. In *Hampton and Company v. United States* (1928), noted earlier in this chapter, the Supreme Court ruled that Congress could delegate such power to the president.

52. Goldstein, *Ideas, Interests,* 111–115; and Rhodes, *Reciprocity,* 23–33.

53. Henry Grady, "The New Trade Policy of the United States," *Foreign Affairs* (spring 1936): 295; quoted in Rhodes, *Reciprocity,* 60.

54. Cordell Hull, *International Trade and Domestic Prosperity,* U.S. Department of State Commercial Policy Series no. 3, Washington, D.C., 1934, 5; quoted in Rhodes, *Reciprocity,* 55.

55. Quoted in Rhodes, *Reciprocity,* 58–59.

56. Haggard, "Institutional Foundations," 111; and Lenway, *Politics of U.S. International Trade,* 65.

57. I. M. Destler, *American Trade Politics* (Washington, D.C.: Institute for International Economics, 1995), 14; Goldstein, *Ideas, Interests,* 133, 143; Robert A. Pastor, *Congress and the Politics of U.S. Foreign Economic Policy, 1929–1976* (Berkeley: University of California Press, 1980), 82–83; and Rhodes, *Reciprocity,* 53.

58. Susan A. Aaronson, *Trade and the American Dream: A Social History of Postwar Trade Policy* (Lexington: University Press of Kentucky, 1996), 19–20; Goldstein, *Ideas, Interests,* 153; Hull, *Memoirs,* 366; and Rhodes, *Reciprocity,* 62.

59. Hull, *Memoirs,* 361.

60. Raymond A. Bauer, Ithiel de Sola Pool, and Lewis Anthony Dexter, *American Business and Public Policy: The Politics of Foreign Trade* (New York: Atherton Press, 1964), 26; Rhodes, *Reciprocity,* 65; Kaplan, *American Trade Policy,* 48; and Hull, *Memoirs,* 368.

61. Butler, *Cautious Visionary,* 135; and Hull, *Memoirs,* 371–374.

62. These figures are from the *Statistical Yearbook of the League of Nations, 1941/42,* 178.

63. E. F. Penrose, *Economic Planning for the Peace* (Princeton: Princeton University Press, 1953), 22.

64. Wayne S. Cole, *Roosevelt and the Isolationists, 1932–1945* (Lincoln: University of Nebraska Press, 1983), 109; and Kaplan, *American Trade Policy,* 47, 49.

65. Butler, *Cautious Visionary,* 161–162.

66. These figures are from the *Statistical Yearbook of the League of Nations, 1941/42,* 76.

67. Cole, *Roosevelt and the Isolationists,* 109.

68. Kaplan, *American Trade Policy,* 49.

4 From Neutrality to Bretton Woods and the GATT

In the years between the First and Second World Wars, one of the most hotly debated issues in American foreign policy centered on the relationship between trade and war. On one side of the debate, liberal internationalists, such as Secretary of State Cordell Hull, believed that extensive trade contacts would prevent war by creating international interdependence. The reciprocal trade agreements program created in 1934 was designed to promote such interdependence by lowering tariffs (see Chapter 3). Liberals also maintained that wars could be avoided if all countries promised to sever trade with any country that started a war for the threat of suspended trade would create the prospect of such economic pain that potential aggressors would reconsider violence.

The opposing view was presented by isolationists who believed that promoting trade increased the chance of war and that limiting trade with those who started wars would guarantee American involvement in the fighting. Increasing trade enhanced the probability of war because it created special interests that profited from trade and that would seek to pull the United States into war to preserve those profits when trading partners got into conflicts. And suspending trade to isolate aggressors was even more dangerous for the aggressor might lash out at the countries interrupting trade.

For isolationists, the better course was to limit trade during peacetime and to terminate it with all combatants when a war broke out. Limiting trade would mean there would be no special interests to push for participation in wars to protect their profits. At the same time, limited trade would maintain the American system of protection that guaranteed American workers their jobs and American businesses their markets. And when war came, a prohibition of trade, especially in munitions, would ensure that the United States would not be pulled into unnecessary conflicts.

The disagreements between liberals and isolationists over how trade affected the chance of war reflected their differing beliefs about the strategic situation confronting the United States. For liberals, one of the lessons of World War I was that modern warfare tended to spread, drawing in even countries that wished to remain at peace. And that is precisely what had happened to the United States in 1917. Given this characteristic of twentieth-century international conflict, liberals argued, no country could hide from large-scale warfare, no matter how distant the battlefields might seem. They felt it made sense therefore to band together with other countries to restrict trade to punish those who disturbed the peace.

Isolationists saw things differently; they believed the United States was beyond the reach of countries with the power to threaten American national security. The United States faced few problems in the Western Hemisphere, and the Atlantic and Pacific Oceans seemed insurmountable barriers to invasion from across the seas. Beyond this, isolationists believed that Britain and France, both of which were democracies and former allies in the First World War, had the strength to counterbalance any international aggressors that might emerge in the future. For isolationists, the wisest course for the United States was one that steered the country clear of foreign wars.

As this debate played out in the decade between 1935 and 1945, the isolationists held the upper hand—that is, until war came to Europe in 1939. During this period, the isolationists in Congress passed laws limiting American commerce with nations at war. One characteristic of this legislation was limited presidential discretion when applying the law for Congress worried that the executive branch might use any leeway in the law to involve the United States in foreign conflicts.

In the late 1930s, however, isolationists' beliefs about averting war by regulating trade, the strategic invulnerability of the United States, and the need to tie the president's hands were called into question by the unfolding of international events. Among the difficulties confronting isolationists were wanton acts of violence by international aggressors, the surprising weakness of the Western democracies as they grappled with international crises, and the growing fear among Americans that advances in military science might negate the security advantages the United States derived from its geographical location. Each of these problems undermined the isolationist approach. The viciousness of the aggressors turned the conflict into a contest between good and evil, which in turn made U.S. **neutrality laws** seem inappropriate. Moreover, a U.S. refusal to trade with the weakened European democracies during a war might doom America's former allies and permit the totalitarian countries to turn their war machines toward the Western Hemisphere.

As a result, by 1940 isolationism had become less and less viable as a policy option, and the United States devoted its energies to helping the victims of aggression without running the risk of belligerency. For both the president and

Congress, trade became a vital ingredient of the U.S. effort to extend aid and slow the march of violence. In successive steps, the years 1939, 1940, and 1941 saw the emergence from Congress of legislation that permitted countries acting in the defense of freedom to obtain supplies from the United States, that financed the acquisition of those supplies, and that allowed the president to terminate trade with countries that threatened international stability. Most Americans hoped this combination of trade-related measures would be adequate for winning the war against the German, Italian, and Japanese Axis alliance. In the end, though, these hopes were in vain, and the United States was forced to join the war.

The legislation of 1939–1941 represented more than a change in American attitudes about trade and war; the new laws expanded the powers of the executive branch as Congress granted the president unprecedented authority to handle the challenges of war. At the urging of Secretary of State Hull and Treasury Secretary Henry Morgenthau, President Roosevelt used this power not only to respond to military dangers, but also to build important new international institutions to promote trade. Because these institutions were being constructed while war raged, the Roosevelt administration found it convenient to encourage American participation by arguing that increased trade would guarantee postwar peace and prosperity and that the absence of such institutions after World War I was in part responsible for the Great Depression and for World War II. These arguments found acceptance in an America that wanted to believe it was fighting its last war.

But the public's willingness to accept liberal arguments proved ephemeral because postwar conflicts brought disillusion. For many Americans and members of Congress, the onset of the Cold War demonstrated that trade would not eliminate conflict. Instead, the Cold War taught many the realist lesson that violence is inherent in international politics. At the same time, the end of the Second World War brought renewed demands from special interests for protection. When doubts about the value of trade for promoting peace were combined with the decades-old American faith in protection, the result was a near halt in the establishment of new international institutions for encouraging trade.

This chapter examines the transformation of American trade policy during the period 1935–1948. The discussion illustrates how this transformation was in part a product of the changing international strategic environment confronting the United States and the effects that this new environment had on American beliefs about the relationship between trade and war. These revised attitudes about trade combined in turn with the wartime authority Congress gave the president to pave the way for dramatic and permanent alterations in how the United States handled its trading relations with other countries.

TRADE AND WAR

The U.S. attempt to avoid war by restricting trade began with a 1935 act of Congress that required a mandatory arms embargo against all combatants in a war, banned loans to belligerents, and forbade American vessels to transport weapons to nations at war.[1] The law, which would expire in six months, gave the president only a limited degree of leeway in its application: he could determine when war began, what arms to embargo, and when the embargo would extend to countries that joined the war later.[2]

The Neutrality Laws

The Neutrality Law of 1935 was the product of a year-long investigation into the relationship between trade and war by a special Senate committee chaired by Republican Gerald Nye of North Dakota. After its sensationalist reviews of America's entry into World War I and the big profits earned by U.S. arms exporters during the war, the Nye Committee confronted little congressional opposition when it proposed restrictions on commerce as a way to keep the United States neutral during foreign wars. Large banks, shipping interests, and munitions makers such as DuPont, Colt, and Remington opposed the law, but support among the general public was so widespread that even President Franklin Roosevelt, a committed internationalist, felt compelled to state that "we seek to isolate ourselves completely from war . . . [and] if we face the choice of profits or peace, the nation will answer—must answer—'we choose peace.'"[3]

On October 3, 1935, the new legislation received its first test when Italy invaded Ethiopia. In response, the president proclaimed American neutrality, instituted an arms embargo, cut off bank credits to the belligerents, and warned American ships about transporting munitions. The State Department also called for a "moral embargo" to halt the sale of oil and other vital natural resources that were not included in the legal embargo.

In enforcing the law, Roosevelt stressed that it applied equally to Ethiopia and Italy. But, in fact, there was strong public sentiment against Italy, for the Italians were brutal aggressors, using modern weapons against a primitive foe. This situation created a moral controversy, because as written the law failed to distinguish the helpless victim from the fascist aggressor. The law also did not include any legal controls over the export of important raw materials. Accordingly, when the law was considered for renewal in early 1936, the State Department suggested a revision to allow for presidential discretion to include limits on exports of raw materials and to restrict trade only with aggressors. Members of Congress, however, were reluctant to accept these changes, suspecting that the White House was angling for a law that would allow the president to involve the United States in foreign conflicts. In addition, a storm of protest descended on Congress from business interests incensed by the realization that they would lose valuable commercial opportunities if trade restrictions on raw materials were enacted. As a result, Congress simply extended the current law with no changes until May 1, 1937.[4]

The next act in the neutrality drama came in July 1936 in Spain when the fascist military forces under Gen. Francisco Franco revolted against the republican government. Within weeks, the Spanish Civil War expanded as Italy and Germany aided Franco and the Soviet Union helped the Spanish government. Volunteers from around the globe, including Americans, flocked to the war, which became a symbol of the international confrontation between fascism and democracy.

Initially, the fighting in Spain created a dilemma for American policy makers for the neutrality law applied to international wars, not to civil wars. In early 1937, Congress remedied this omission with legislation that extended trade restrictions to civil wars. In the meantime, American internationalist critics complained that the neutrality laws made the United States appear uninterested in the fate of any democratic country that was facing a fascist challenge. These criticisms increased as the evidence of German and Italian intervention in the Spanish conflict mounted and the republican forces suffered defeat after defeat. Even the staunchly isolationist senator Nye was so moved by the fate of the republican forces that he called for an end to the embargo.[5] In the end, the trade restrictions were not lifted, but during the 1937 renewal debate the fighting in Spain called the wisdom of neutrality laws into question.

That debate was shaped by the concept of **cash and carry,** which was proposed as an alternative to the previous neutrality legislation. Under the cash and carry system, during war the United States would sell anything except arms to countries that were prepared to pay for the goods immediately and transport the goods in their own ships. This approach was designed to allow American firms to continue exporting during conflicts, thereby safeguarding American jobs, an idea that had appeal during the depression. At the same time, through the cash and carry approach Congress could prevent the United States from entering wars by outlawing loans to belligerents and forbidding American ships from transporting goods on the high seas. Essentially, then, the idea was that the United States could enjoy the benefits of commerce without running the risks of war. Congress found the idea worth a two-year experiment and passed legislation to that effect in mid-1937.

The flaws with cash and carry became apparent in July 1937 when Japan attacked China. As Roosevelt realized immediately, invoking the new law favored the aggressor. Japan produced its own arms, could finance trade, and had a merchant marine to transport goods, but China had none of these things. Once again, then, legislated neutrality threatened to put the United States on the wrong side of the moral equation. To sidestep the issue, Roosevelt refused to recognize a state of war between China and Japan, neither of whom had declared war. Because most Americans sympathized with China, the public accepted this policy, for it allowed the United States to continue supplying that country with aid.

Concerns about the viability of cash and carry also extended to Europe, where crises in 1938 and 1939 convinced many in Congress that war was only a matter of time. In March 1938, Germany absorbed Adolf Hitler's native Austria, thereby violating agreements dating to the end of the First World War. In September and October 1938, Germany demanded the Sudetenland region of Czechoslovakia. For a time war seemed unavoidable, until an agreement was reached to give Germany the Sudetenland in exchange for German pledges to seek no further territory. These German promises were short-lived, however; within five months Hitler ordered the occupation of the rest of Czechoslovakia. At this point, it became clear that Hitler's next target was Poland.

It was in this gloomy environment that Congress considered renewing the cash and carry law that would expire May 1, 1939. To further complicate matters, Roosevelt told Congress in January 1939 that the United States must be prepared to use "many methods short of war" to oppose aggression.[6] Some members of Congress, believing the president's message to be an attempt to side with Britain and France in the event of war, became warier than ever of legislation that would allow the president to push the United States toward such a conflict. Others in Congress were convinced of the moral necessity of helping the democracies in their struggle with Hitler and Italy's dictator, Benito Mussolini. Congress, then, was stalemated; the divisions among its members made it impossible to either revise or extend the cash and carry policy, which finally expired. Even a White House conference with congressional leaders in mid-July failed to break the logjam.

As a result, when Germany invaded Poland on September 1, 1939, there were no cash and carry provisions in American law. After Britain and France declared war two days later, World War II was under way. Roosevelt declared American neutrality and an arms embargo, but most Americans were shocked by the savagery of the German assault and were receptive to calls for a new cash and carry law. A presidential request for new legislation met with congressional consent, and by early November the United States was able to export goods, including weapons, to the democracies on a cash and carry basis.

The American neutrality laws that passed Congress in the fall of 1939 reflected new attitudes in the United States toward the nature of conflicts around the world. The laws enacted in 1935 and 1936 had been based on abstract thinking about wars and how they might affect the United States, but by 1939 reality had set in and the American people tended to see conflict more in terms of black and white—good and evil. Under these conditions, impartial trade restrictions became unacceptable to Americans. After all, it was wrong to act as though the wars that raged were the equal responsibility of all belligerents. In the Far East, a militant Japan appeared to be bullying China. In Europe, the Germans and Italians seemed bent on a war designed to destroy democracy, snuff out individual liberty, and shatter entire nations. While Americans were still determined to stay out of war, they also were willing to express their distaste for totalitarianism by changing American trade policy so that American goods could flow to the victims of aggression. Beyond this, Americans were beginning to realize that American national security was tied to the fate of the European democracies.

The year 1940 brought additional reasons for American concern. Hitler struck at Denmark and Norway in April. Both countries succumbed quickly, and the British and French met with defeat when they tried to give assistance. Worse news came in May when the Germans invaded the Netherlands, Belgium, Luxembourg, and France. Although most military analysts expected a rerun of the trench warfare and stalemate of the First World War, in actuality the Germans were devastating the Allied forces. Within a week the British and French armies were sliced in half, and by the end of the month the British were forced to evacuate France at Dunkirk. In late June the French surrendered, leaving the depleted British to face the victorious Germans alone.

While these events took place, Congress debated the **National Defense Act of 1940,** which would allow the president to "prohibit or curtail" the export of any products when the president determined such an action was "in the interest of national defense."[7] This act complemented the new cash and carry policy: cash and carry allowed the United States to export goods to aid the democracies; the National Defense Act empowered the president to prohibit exports to aggressors in an attempt to curb their reckless behavior. Just a year earlier, such a law would have had no chance of passage by Congress amid suspicions that Roosevelt would use it to involve the United States in a war. But in 1940 the legislation passed easily, by a vote of 392–1 in the House on May 24 and without opposition in the Senate on June 11.[8]

The president's new power was put to use against Japan in July after Roosevelt learned that the Japanese were buying large amounts of aviation fuel and scrap metals from U.S. producers. Export of these items was first restricted and then prohibited after Japanese forces entered Indochina.[9]

Lend-Lease Act

In the meantime, the British were facing mounting problems in their war against Hitler. Since almost all of their weapons were lost in France during the disastrous battles of May and June, the British had to import supplies as never before. The American cash and carry policy required immediate payment upon the receipt of goods and that goods be shipped to belligerent ports only on foreign ships. Britain, then, had to transport its supplies across an Atlantic teeming with Nazi submarines. To help the British with their transportation problem, Roosevelt agreed to exchange fifty aging American destroyers for British naval bases in Bermuda and the West Indies. This arrangement helped Britain, but it did little to solve British financial problems.

Throughout the fall of 1940, Roosevelt contemplated the British financial situation while he campaigned successfully for an unprecedented third term. Shortly after the election, British prime minister Winston Churchill wrote Roosevelt about his country's payment problems:

> The more rapid and abundant the flow of munitions and ships which you are able to send us, the sooner will our dollar credits be exhausted. . . . Indeed . . . the orders already placed . . . many times exceed the total exchange resources remaining at the disposal of Great Britain. The moment approaches when we shall no longer be able to pay cash for . . . supplies.[10]

Roosevelt realized that Congress would hesitate to extend loans to Britain even though America needed to keep Britain in the war. To solve the conundrum of how to aid the British without loaning them money, Roosevelt decided to refer to the transfer of the equipment itself as a loan. At a press conference on December 17, 1940, Roosevelt used a homey analogy to explain the concept:

> Suppose my neighbor's house catches fire and I have a length of garden hose four or five hundred feet away. If he can take my garden hose and connect it up with his hydrant, I may help him to put out the fire. Now what do I do? I don't say to him before that operation, "Neighbor, my garden hose cost me fifteen dollars; you have to pay me fifteen dollars for it." No! What is the transaction that goes on? I don't want fifteen dollars—I want my garden hose back after the fire is over.[11]

Several days later, Roosevelt reinforced this example by arguing that the European dictatorships of Hitler and Mussolini aimed at world conquest, that Britain stood between the United States and a war with Hitler, and that aiding Britain decreased, rather than increased, the chances the United States would have to fight. The president also pointed out that if the United States did not lend or lease Britain the equipment it needed, it would be forced to surrender. The United States, Roosevelt argued, could not put a fellow democracy in such a position. The **Lend-Lease** bill was submitted to Congress in January 1941 and passed the House 260–165 on February 9 and the Senate by 60–31 on March 11. The new law authorized the president, "notwithstanding the provisions of any other law," to "sell, transfer title to, exchange, lease, lend, or otherwise dispose of" any "defense article" to any country "whose defense the President deems vital to the defense of the United States."[12]

Eventually, the president did use this power to help the British, as well as Canada, China, the Soviet Union, and France. In addition, as we shall see later, lend-lease was used to nudge the British toward cooperating in the construction of the postwar international commercial structures that the United States favored.

Freezing Assets

By 1941, the United States was struggling to use trade policy to slow aggression on two fronts. In Europe, lend-lease was the centerpiece of the effort to aid the British, and in the Far East Roosevelt employed his authority under the National Defense Act of 1940 to deny Japan such vital supplies as aviation fuel and scrap metal. While these moves upset and inconvenienced Japan, they fell far short of stopping Japan's rush toward hegemony.

In the summer of 1941, Japan posed a new threat by advancing farther into Indochina. At a late July cabinet meeting, Roosevelt contemplated two possible American responses to the Japanese move. The first was to use the National Defense Act of 1940 to stop the flow of American oil to Japan. The second was to rely on a 1933 amendment to the Trading with the Enemy Act of 1917 that permitted the president to freeze a country's assets in the United States. Roosevelt favored the second course, for he feared the first would provoke a Japanese move against the oil fields of the Dutch East Indies. Because the United States was not prepared for such an attack, Roosevelt proceeded cautiously. On July 26, the U.S. government announced that Japanese funds in the United States would be frozen and that licenses would be required before Japan could purchase American goods. Roosevelt hoped this step would slow the flow of oil and other essential goods to Japan while avoiding unnecessary friction.[13]

Whatever Roosevelt's intentions, the State Department officials issuing licenses refused to let Japan purchase oil. As a result, Japanese officials felt increasingly hemmed in, because Japan produced no oil of its own and yet needed it for military operations. Indeed, American, British, and Dutch companies owned almost all of the world's oil concessions, and Japanese leaders had little doubt that the British and Dutch companies would follow the example of the U.S. government and deny Japan the oil it needed.[14]

By September 1941, the Japanese felt they had but two choices: either seize the oil they needed by means of a military attack or call off their acts of aggression. Because the latter course meant giving up any pretense of great-power status—an intolerable alternative for the Japanese—they decided to attack the

Dutch East Indies to obtain oil, as Roosevelt feared.[15] Yet another problem remained, however; U.S. military bases in the Philippines were astride the routes needed for shipping the conquered oil to Japan. Japanese leaders therefore concluded that a move to take the Dutch East Indies would require an attack on the Philippines, which would mean war with the United States. And if war was inevitable, the Japanese decided they also should strike at the American naval base at Pearl Harbor in Hawaii.

Throughout the fall of 1941, the Japanese attempted to negotiate an agreement with the United States that would turn the oil spigot back on. In the meantime, they prepared to attack. In late November, with negotiations at an impasse, Japanese forces moved. On Sunday, December 7, the Japanese struck at Pearl Harbor, the Philippines, and other targets. The next day, President Roosevelt requested and received from Congress a declaration of war on Japan. Three days later, the Germans declared war on the United States. The war that many had hoped to avoid by regulating trade was now a reality.

In any assessment of both the efforts of the 1930s to keep the United States out of war and the forces that eventually entangled America in World War II, it is plain that trade policy played a key, and perhaps decisive, role. From 1935 to 1939, isolationists fought to curtail American trade with those involved in a war. But as war came first to Asia and then to Europe, it became impossible to retain these limitations because the American public and most political leaders, both Democratic and Republican, regarded the contests that raged as battles between freedom and a totalitarian way of life. Under these conditions, the American people accepted a policy that used American exports to help the democracies and restricted American trade with aggressors. In following this course, the United States allowed its trade policy to draw it ever closer to war, for American lend-lease assistance angered the Germans, and the termination of oil and other shipments to Japan left that country believing it had to attack the United States. Thus trade policy was an important determinant of when and how the United States entered World War II. That conflict would now become a vital force in shaping American trade policy in the postwar world.

TRANSFORMING THE WORLD TRADING SYSTEM

When the United States entered World War II in 1941, the debate over the American trade agenda took on a new tone. Isolationists had been discredited by the events of recent years, and within the Roosevelt administration liberal internationalists were now in a dominant position. As tragic as the war was, it presented liberals with an opportunity to reshape international political and economic structures. Contemplating the changes they wished to make, leaders such as Secretary of State Hull, Treasury Secretary Morgenthau, and Secretary of War Henry Stimson were sure of two things. First, they were determined to avoid the errors that had undermined peace after 1919. And, second, they wanted to begin planning for peace even during the war, for they realized how quickly the spirit of wartime cooperation would disappear once the emergency was over.

In assessing mistakes, internationalists could point to the U.S. refusal to join the League of Nations, to America's lack of cooperation with fellow democracies in the face of totalitarian aggression, and to its failure to maintain adequate armed forces. In the economic arena, the Fordney-McCumber tariff increases after World War I and American inflexibility over war debts clearly disrupted the economic conditions needed for peace. The sky-high Smoot-Hawley tariffs that followed were hailed as an even greater disaster. They stunted world trade just as the depression was starting, thereby deepening and widening an already terrible calamity that destroyed jobs at home and abroad. The tariffs also paved the way for the rise of Adolf Hitler and the acts of aggression that led to war. No matter how they looked at it, the internationalists believed that many of the problems of the interwar years could be traced directly to misdeeds associated with trade policy, and the United States, as they saw it, had been one of the world's chief sinners.

Making Preparations

To guarantee that past mistakes would not be repeated, cabinet officials created organizational machinery to plan for the postwar world and attempted to mold public opinion to favor more open trade and greater American participation in international affairs. In 1941, Hull asked State Department economist Leo Pasvolsky to head the Division of Special Research, which would explore ideas to promote freer trade. He also assigned Harry Hawkins, director of the State Department's Division of Commercial Policy, to set up a Special Committee on the Relaxation of Trade Barriers. Not to be outdone by the State Department, Morgenthau made his chief economic adviser, Harry White, acting assistant secretary of Treasury in charge of foreign affairs and asked White to prepare a paper on postwar international monetary problems.[16]

Public opinion was shaped through speeches, press conferences, publications, and appearances before Congress stressing the value of freer trade for avoiding another depression, guaranteeing jobs for Americans, and guarding world peace. For example, in a widely publicized speech in July 1944, Morgenthau emphasized the relationship between economic travails and conflict, stating that "all of us have seen the great economic tragedy of our time. We saw the worldwide depression of the 1930s . . . we saw unemployment and wretchedness . . . we saw their victims fall prey, in places, to demagogues and dictators. We saw bewilderment and bitterness become the breeders of fascism, and, finally, of war."[17] On another occasion, Undersecretary of State Sumner Welles declared that "one of the surest safeguards against war is the opportunity of all peoples to [trade] on equal terms."[18] Hawkins's special committee expressed similar sentiments in late 1942, arguing that "a great expansion in the volume of international trade after the war will be essential to the attainment of full . . . employment in the United States . . . and to success of an international security system to prevent future wars."[19]

For all their rhetoric, the would-be architects of a new international economic order realized that two factors might limit their ability to accomplish their goals. The first was Congress, where there was less enthusiasm for open trade than in the executive branch. The second was the willingness of other countries, especially Great Britain, to go along with American designs.

Congressional and British Obstacles

The pressures of world events between 1939 and 1941 forced Congress to change one aspect of American trade policy, the neutrality laws, but those same events had little effect on Congress's willingness to grant the president additional authority to lower American trade barriers. When the Reciprocal Trade Agreements Act, first passed in 1934 and extended in 1937, came up for renewal in 1940 it met strong opposition. One reason was the economic upturn in the United States; exports to war-torn countries had increased production, lowered unemployment, and reduced the need for a law designed to pull America out of the depression. Another reason was the worried noncompetitive industries; they feared lower tariffs would expose them to international pressures. For their part, many farmers continued to believe that protection meant prosperity and that the RTAA reforms would seriously harm them over time. Isolationists also feared that RTAA trade agreements might drag the United States into war. Finally, those favoring a strict interpretation of the Constitution argued that the RTAA improperly shifted the authority over trade policy from Congress to the president.[20]

The result was a surprisingly close vote for renewing the RTAA. The House voted 218–168 in favor of renewal on February 23, 1940. In the Senate, the vote in favor on April 5 was much closer, 42–37.[21] The tally in both chambers was highly partisan; in the House Republicans voted 146–5 against the bill, and the respective vote in the Senate was 20–0.[22]

Even in the midst of war in 1943, renewal of the RTAA was controversial. As in 1940, there were charges that the law was unconstitutional, and disadvantaged interest groups campaigned against the legislation. In the end, the margin of victory for those favoring passage appeared impressive, 342–65 in the House and 59–23 in the Senate. However, the rough and tumble of the debate, the need for the president, the secretary of state, and other administration officials to work hard to secure renewal, and the fact that the act was renewed for only two years, all indicated that Congress was not interested in major efforts to dismantle trade barriers. These hard-fought congressional victories over the RTAA sent a clear signal to internationalists that they would need to remain carefully attuned to Congress's moods as they constructed any new international commercial institutions.

The British were another story. Long champions of free trade, they broke with the practice in 1932 when they set up the Imperial Preference System which provided special trading arrangements within the British Empire and set higher duties for others. Almost from the moment the Imperial Preference System took form, American internationalists set out to dismantle it. In attempting to do so, the internationalists met with determined opposition, for many British leaders regarded the system as a reaction to the Smoot-Hawley Tariff and saw American demands both as an intrusion into imperial affairs and as hypocritical given America's history of high tariffs.

Faced with British recalcitrance and convinced of the need to alter the Imperial Preference System, American negotiators took every opportunity to dent the British creation. They made the first attempts to do so before the war, in 1937, when they sought a trade agreement under the RTAA program. The American goal was modification of the preference system, but the British opposed all attempts to do so. In the end, the November 1938 agreement was modest; the British eliminated duties on wheat and reduced tariffs on a few other goods, and the United States primarily lowered tariffs on textiles.[23]

Although the final RTAA agreement fell short of American hopes, it only whetted the appetite of American officials for additional efforts. When President Roosevelt proposed the lend-lease arrangement for Britain in December 1940, the State Department saw a new opportunity for striking at the Imperial Preference System. As passed by Congress in March 1941, the Lend-Lease Act left it to the president to determine how recipients of aid could repay the United States, whether it be "in kind or property, or any other direct or indirect benefit" that the president found appropriate.[24] Even though it is doubtful that a Congress that barely approved renewal of the RTAA just eleven months earlier would have agreed that lowering trade barriers was an appropriate "benefit," the State Department proceeded to define the British obligations to the United States in precisely this fashion. In effect, the British were told that doing away with the Imperial Preference System and cooperating in the pursuit of more open trade were the price they would pay for lend-lease assistance.

U.S.-British lend-lease negotiations opened in Washington in the summer of 1941. The British team was headed by John Maynard Keynes, the famed economist. Keynes suggested that American aid take the form of a grant, with Britain returning what it could after the war. Assistant Secretary of State Dean Acheson found this proposal unacceptable. Acheson presented Keynes with a seven-part counterproposal, the first six parts of which the British accepted. The seventh part, Article VII, was another matter. It stated that the lend-lease settlement should be "such as not to burden commerce between the two countries, but to promote mutually advantageous economic relations between them and the betterment of worldwide economic relations." In addition, it would "provide against discrimination in either the United States or the United Kingdom against the importation of any product originating in any other country." As Keynes saw immediately, this provision was aimed at the Imperial Preference System, which was based on discrimination against trade with countries, including the United States, that were not part of the British Empire. The British protested Article VII and refused to accept it as the basis for lend-lease compensation. Because the Americans insisted on Article VII, negotiations reached an impasse.[25]

Stymied in its attempt to poke a hole in the Imperial Preference System by way of Article VII, the State Department raised the issue when Roosevelt met Churchill in Newfoundland in August 1941. During the discussion, Undersecretary of State Welles urged the two leaders to make an open trading system a goal of the meeting. Churchill reacted by reminding Welles that the British had for decades pushed for free trade and that the United States had been a major obstacle. He then declared that Britain would not renounce the Imperial Preference System. In the end, Roosevelt decided that preservation of Anglo-American harmony was more important than a fight over trade. The joint statement issued after the meeting, known as the Atlantic Charter, allowed the British to retain preferences.[26]

Negotiations over lend-lease, Article VII, and the Imperial Preference System continued for several months after the Newfoundland meeting. Final agreement came only in early 1942 after a direct appeal from Roosevelt to Churchill.[27] Even then, the final accord created as many obligations for the United States as it did for Great Britain. The agreement stated in part that

> the terms and conditions [of lend-lease repayment] shall be such as not to burden commerce between the two countries, but to promote mutually advantageous economic relations between them and the betterment of world-wide economic relations. To that end, they shall include provision for agreed action by the United States of America and the United Kingdom . . . directed to the expansion . . . of production, employment, and the exchange and consumption of goods . . . to the elimination of discriminatory treatment . . . and to the reduction of tariffs and other trade barriers.[28]

For the Roosevelt administration, the agreement was a means of paving the way for more open trade; the reference to the elimination of discriminatory treatment obligated the British to end preferences. For the British, who emphasized the reduction of tariffs, the agreement spelled the end of the American system of protection and represented an American pledge to fully eliminate the Smoot-Hawley Tariff.[29] The failure to resolve these misconceptions resulted in continuing U.S.-British tensions over postwar trade.

The Bretton Woods Agreements

When American officials looked back on the trading problems of the interwar years, two issues stood out: (1) exchange rate fluctuations among the currencies used by different countries and the balance-of-payments problems that had plagued some nations, and (2) the high tariffs and other trade barriers that countries had erected to shield themselves from the depression. Exchange rate problems bedeviled commerce between the wars by making it difficult for traders to set prices for their international transactions. The inability to finance balance-of-payments deficits forced some countries to practically halt all their international commercial activity. Together with trade barriers, these problems were perceived as harming, rather than helping, efforts to end the depression. As they planned for the postwar world, American decision makers felt that international stability, prosperity, and peace would be elusive unless these problems were solved.

In tackling these issues, the Roosevelt administration put the Treasury Department in charge of solving the exchange rate and balance-of-payments questions and gave the State Department the trade barriers problem.[30] At Treasury, Secretary Morgenthau assigned his assistant Harry White the task of preparing an American plan. As White set about his task, he found that a British team led by John Maynard Keynes also was working on the problem. As it happened, White and Keynes developed rival plans, and the give and take between the two became the basis for what is known as the **Bretton Woods System.**

The Keynes plan had a distinctly British flavor. Keynes realized Britain would face severe international commercial problems after the war. He anticipated an import surge to meet pent-up consumer demand and the need to buy foreign goods to repair the damages of war. He also expected Britain to have a hard time paying for import for many British exporters were in ruins and Britain's links to traditional export markets in Latin America, the Far East, and Eastern Europe had been disrupted by the war. A high demand for imports coupled with an inability to export spelled for Keynes balance-of-payments problems. These problems would be exacerbated by the loss of many of Britain's overseas investments during the war and by the sale of gold to pay for wartime supplies.

Keynes's plans for monetary stability and remedying balance-of-payments deficits reflected the problems Britain faced. He began by proposing the establishment of a new international organization that would loan countries funds to cover balance-of-payments shortfalls and would supervise currency exchange rates. Keynes also proposed the creation of a new international currency for use in settling balance-of-payments deficits. Furthermore, by means of an assessment of interest charges on accounts that ran either a credit or a debit, all nations would be encouraged to maintain an exact balance in their balance of payments. Thus countries with a positive balance of payments would have an incentive to import more goods, and those with a negative balance would be stimulated to find additional foreign markets to absorb exports. Final decisions on exchange rates would remain in the hands of national governments, but for an indefinite period after the war countries would be unable to convert any currency into gold or into another currency. Finally, Keynes envisioned the creation of a second international institution to finance rebuilding from the war and to promote economic growth and development.[31]

The Treasury Department plan prepared by Harry White displayed a different perspective. White agreed with Keynes that currency exchange rates should be stabilized and that a means should be found for financing balance-of-payments deficits. White also felt it was appropriate to create two international organizations, one to deal with exchange rates and balance-of-payments problems and the other with reconstruction and development. But White differed with Keynes over the method for financing balance-of-payments shortfalls, the question of who would decide exchange rate changes, the assessment of charges for the failure to maintain an exact balance in a country's balance of payments, and the creation of an international currency.

White insisted that the new organizations be financed by their members through payments in gold or in their own currencies (these payments were called quotas). Balance-of-payments deficits would be financed by short-term loans from the new organization devoted to that problem in the currency needed to handle the deficit, and adjustments in exchange rates would be permitted only with the consent of the new organization. White argued against setting up a new international currency; he believed Congress would refuse to agree to such a plan. Instead, the dollar would serve as the cornerstone of the new system because the American economy outstripped all others in size. White also asserted that charges should not be assessed for a positive balance of payments, but that those countries that borrowed to finance a deficit would have to pay interest on their loans. Beyond this, White envisioned that voting in the organizations would be weighted according to a member's quota, a formula that would give the United States a greater voice than would a one country–one vote rule.[32]

Extensive negotiations between the United States and Great Britain followed the unveiling of the Keynes and White plans. In late 1943, other countries, including Canada, France, and the Soviet Union, entered the discussions. By 1944, it was clear that a version of the White plan would serve as the basis for the new organizations, which were referred to, at Keynes's suggestion, as the **International Monetary Fund (IMF)** and the International Bank for Reconstruction and Development, or **World Bank**.[33] Delegates from forty-four nations were invited to a conference at Bretton Woods, New Hampshire, in July 1944 to create the new institutions.

In preparing for the conference, Morgenthau and White paid close attention to securing congressional support for the outcome of the negotiations. The American delegation to Bretton Woods included members of Congress, both Republicans and Democrats, prominent bankers, distinguished scholars, and representatives of the executive branch. These delegates were chosen with an eye to co-opting those who had expressed doubts about setting up international financial organizations. Foremost among these skeptics were bankers and isolationist members of Congress.

In an attempt to ensure that reports from Bretton Woods were favorable, organizers of the conference paid special attention to the press. White also took care to manage the conference to avoid controversies that opponents could use later to claim the gathering was flawed. White's managerial techniques were particularly geared toward guaranteeing American dominance of the most important issues. Once again, this was done in part to make sure that the final product was one that key American interest groups and Congress would accept. Finally, both Morgenthau and White insisted that the headquarters of the new organizations be located in Washington, D.C., because the United States would be making the biggest contribution to both the IMF and the World Bank. Again, this move was designed to build congressional support.[34]

During the conference the most important debates focused on the IMF—specifically, the size of members' quotas, the percentage of each member's quota to be paid in gold, voting procedures, how to set and adjust currency exchange rates, and whether countries with a positive balance of payments would be required to import from debtor countries to eliminate imbalances, as Great Britain desired.[35] The negotiations produced agreements that conformed to American wishes. In the IMF, voting was weighted according to quotas. Of the total $8.8 billion in quotas, the United States was to contribute $3 billion. Currencies were pegged to the U.S. dollar, which was set at $35 to an ounce of gold, and members were allowed to make only minor exchange rate adjustments without consulting the IMF. Member countries would finance their balance-of-payments deficits by borrowing from the IMF and would pay interest for such loans. Creditor countries were not required to import from debtors. Members also

agreed not to set multiple exchange rates for their currencies, not to impose currency restrictions after a transition period, and to cooperate to maintain the set
exchange rates.

The International Bank for Reconstruction and Development also was set up
and funded by quotas. The headquarters for both of the new organizations were
located in Washington, D.C.[36]

Once the IMF and the World Bank were established, the Roosevelt administration faced the task of securing congressional acceptance of U.S. membership.
The Bretton Woods agreements went to Congress in early 1945, just weeks after
the Battle of the Bulge, in which the Allies crushed the last German offensive of
the war. In hearings before the House Banking and Currency Committee, Treasury Secretary Morgenthau argued that congressional approval would avert future
wars and depressions. Bretton Woods delegate and bank president Edward Brown
sounded the same theme, stating that "if a fund and bank had been in operation
in the early twenties, the present war would probably not have occurred."[37]

In addition to appearing before Congress, Bretton Woods supporters went all
out to influence special-interest groups and the general public. A New York public relations firm was hired by the Treasury Department to conduct a publicity
campaign, and advocates made dozens of speeches and appearances.[38] At times,
though, they made extravagant claims. In Detroit, for example, Morgenthau
boasted that the Bretton Woods agreements would help trade so much that there
would be "a standing export market for more than a million cars a year," leading
to five million new jobs. Advocates also engaged in some mud-slinging for opponents of the agreements were depicted as isolationists who were unconcerned
about avoiding future depressions and wars.[39]

The banking community led the opposition to the Bretton Woods agreements. It feared the IMF and World Bank would retard the functioning of international finance. The bankers were joined by members of the U.S. Chamber of
Commerce, who worried that the agreements would force American taxpayers to
finance balance-of-payments shortfalls and reconstruction efforts around the
world.[40] Some members of Congress echoed these criticisms and added that membership in the new organizations could mean that the United States would surrender sovereignty over the dollar and that the agreements would fail to stabilize
currencies, promote prosperity, and prevent war.[41]

When Congress voted in the summer of 1945, the agreements passed by large
margins—345–18 in the House and 61–16 in the Senate.[42] By becoming a member of both the IMF and the World Bank, the United States was taking a giant
step toward dominating the postwar world of commerce that it had played a critical role in designing.

Trade Negotiations: Slow Going and Tough Bargaining

The Bretton Woods agreements were important to the construction of a post–World War II trading system designed to bring prosperity and peace to the international arena. Stable currencies would facilitate trade both by eliminating uncertainty about pricing and by ensuring that countries would not manipulate currency values to gain short-term advantages.[43] International financing through the IMF for balance-of-payments deficits would give countries some breathing space as they tried to work their way out of difficulties without facing national insolvency. And long-term loans from the World Bank would allow war-torn countries to purchase imports for rebuilding and poverty-stricken nations to import to promote growth and development.

By themselves, however, the Bretton Woods agreements were not sufficient to meet the international commercial goals of the United States. Stable currency exchange rates, balance-of-payments financing, and long-term reconstruction and development loans would not produce prosperity and peace unless international trade increased. And trade would not increase unless barriers to trade were dismantled. The State Department therefore was determined to push vigorously for arrangements to lower tariffs, eliminate import quotas, and establish rules for conducting international trade negotiations.[44]

As it pressed for new trading arrangements, the State Department found the British a natural partner based on the wartime spirit of cooperation between the U.S. and British governments and the fact that the British Empire and Imperial Preference System controlled a substantial portion of world trade. For their part, the British were prepared to bargain because they feared a repeat of America's post–World War I performance in which isolationism and high tariffs contributed to international instability. The British also realized that America's economic strength would give the United States a commanding role in postwar commerce. Negotiating with the Americans would give the British an opportunity to counter American isolation and to help design any new trading system.[45]

As they talked, the British and Americans disagreed over several issues. The bargaining over lend-lease Article VII revealed one such issue, the Imperial Preference System. A second issue was how to conduct trade negotiations. After some initial confusion, the British suggested the creation of an international trade organization as the best approach to trade bargaining after the war.[46] The State Department was impressed with the idea, but American negotiators wondered whether Congress would accept the British approach. Congressional approval was required for anything beyond the RTAA country-by-country and item-by-item negotiating format, and the hard fight over RTAA renewal in 1940 and 1943 gave American trade specialists reason to pause.[47] As a result, the State Department preferred that any new trade bargaining arrangement be set up within the context of the RTAA program. Meanwhile, the two countries could explore provisional planning on a grander scale.

For the British, the RTAA framework was too slow. Moreover, the British insisted that if the United States wanted freer trade, then it should, as a gesture of good faith, wipe out the remaining Smoot-Hawley rates. The British also asked the United States to adopt an approach that would reduce the tariffs of all countries to the same basic rates. Such a technique for tariff cutting, however, ran counter to the congressionally mandated strategy that called for countries to reduce their rates by the same basic amounts. Thus to the consternation of the British, State Department negotiators insisted that talks stick to the RTAA approach.[48]

Another point of contention between the United States and Great Britain was managed trade and import quotas. For the Americans, managed trade was the antithesis of the open system they favored. American negotiators also opposed import quotas, arguing that they involved discrimination because they usually applied to specific products from individual countries. The State Department therefore insisted on either the elimination of quotas or the conversion of quotas to less-discriminatory trade barriers such as tariffs.[49]

The State Department's position on import quotas was undercut, however, by the insistence of some Americans that managed trade and quotas were acceptable for agricultural goods. The American attachment to managing trade in agriculture grew out of the farm depression in the United States, which by the 1940s was two decades old and had been a key factor in the passage of both the Fordney-McCumber and the Smoot-Hawley Tariffs. Still, for negotiating partners, agricultural quotas indicated that Americans only favored principles if their application benefited the United States.[50]

The British position on managed trade and quotas was a product of the fear that the war would leave the United Kingdom so weak economically that it would be unable to compete in international commerce and would face balance-of-payments problems. The British believed that managed trade and quotas represented an effective way to regulate the imports they needed as they recovered from the war. Thus American arguments met determined British resistance.[51]

When compared with the relatively rapid progress of the discussions that led to the creation of the Bretton Woods institutions, the movement toward an international trade organization was slow. In part, the American and British differences just described were the reason. The planning for the Bretton Woods conference and problems pertaining to the war and to RTAA renewal in 1945 also retarded progress. Moreover, Secretary of State Hull, the champion of freer trade and inspiration for virtually all of the trade reforms of the Roosevelt years, had resigned in

November 1944 for health reasons. Then, in April 1945 President Roosevelt died. Between them, these two events brought such turmoil to the executive branch that advances in trade talks were difficult.

The International Trade Organization and the GATT

At the end of the Second World War in September 1945, State Department trade specialists concluded that the United States should pursue a two-track approach to trade negotiations. On the one hand, they would use their authority under the recently renewed RTAA to set up a framework for conducting multilateral tariff reduction talks. On the other hand, they would work with the British and other countries to create an **International Trade Organization (ITO)** to complement the new IMF and World Bank. By moving along both tracks, the State Department hoped to lower tariffs under RTAA with a large number of countries at a single international gathering, while also attempting to create a trade organization that would play a key role in a new world order.[52]

Thus in 1946, the United States joined other countries in calling for the convocation of a United Nations Conference on Trade and Development with the mandate to draft a charter for the ITO. The conference agreed to begin by drafting the rules for immediate tariff reduction negotiations and then to move on to drafting an ITO charter. A meeting devoted to setting up the rules for tariff bargaining, known as the **General Agreement on Tariffs and Trade (GATT)**, was held in Geneva in the spring of 1947.

As in previous negotiations, American and British differences surfaced immediately. The head of the British delegation, Sir Stafford Cripps, insisted that the United States offer tariff cuts according to formulas favored by the United Kingdom. Will Clayton, the undersecretary of state for economic affairs who led the American team, had only the authority under the 1945 RTAA renewal, which allowed him to cut U.S. tariffs by 50 percent from their 1945 levels. This disagreement produced a virtual stalemate between the two most important trading countries of the time, and few tariff reduction deals were arranged.[53] The Geneva meeting then proceeded to draw up the rules for conducting future trade negotiations. The resulting GATT agreement was signed by the United States and twenty-two other countries in August 1947 and went into effect on January 1, 1948.

The General Agreement on Tariffs and Trade was intended to act as a temporary expedient to coordinate tariff reductions among its signers; GATT rules and procedures would be incorporated into the ITO when that organization was set up. In itself, the GATT was not an organization. Instead, it was both a statement of the basic rules and principles for conducting international negotiations and commercial interactions and a process for achieving tariff reductions.

Four principles were at the heart of the GATT: nondiscrimination, transparency, consultation and dispute settlement, and reciprocity.[54] *Nondiscrimination* meant that every country subscribing to GATT would grant unconditional most-favored-nation status to every other subscriber. This stipulation reflected a strong American preference for this approach to trade negotiations and was based on the way RTAA discussions were conducted. **Transparency** referred to open trade relations between GATT parties; secret trade barriers and secret trading arrangements were ruled unacceptable. To provide an equitable, competitive arena for trade, subscribers also were required to publicize their trade rules and procedures for complying with those rules. Manipulative trade rules and secrets designed to slow imports would be inappropriate. *Consultation and dispute settlement* reflected the belief that the parties to the GATT should resolve their differences through direct negotiations. If direct negotiations between parties were not possible, then a panel made up of other GATT subscribers could hear a case and offer an opinion. In the end, however, the GATT had no authority to order anyone to do anything. Instead, it was up to the parties involved to stop unacceptable behavior or to offer compensation. The final principle, *reciprocity,* stemmed from the agreement's insistence that all subscribers incur balanced obligations. Every trade concession offered by a party to GATT had to be matched by equal concessions from other GATT subscribers. This principle was based on the way the United States conducted trade negotiations under the RTAA program and reflected Congress's demand that in any trade deal the United States was to give no more than it got in return.

With the GATT preliminaries out of the way, the United States and its negotiating partners turned to creation of the International Trade Organization. Early talks were held in 1946 and 1947 in London and Geneva. The final push was scheduled for Havana in November 1947. The American preparations for these talks got off to a rocky start, however. First, Undersecretary of State for Economic Affairs Clayton, who again was selected to head the American team, resigned his State Department position for personal reasons. Although Clayton agreed to participate in the Havana meeting, this move demoralized the American representatives. A second problem was the selection of the American delegation. Following the practice that had worked so well at Bretton Woods, Clayton attempted to recruit members of Congress. But after several members rebuffed his invitation, he was forced to put together a team with no congressional participants.[55] Thus even before the American delegation left Washington it was handicapped.

When the Havana meeting opened on November 21, 1947, the American delegates found it impossible to replicate their performance at Bretton Woods, where they had set the agenda and dominated the discussion. From the beginning, other countries pressed their own proposals and displayed little deference to

American wishes. The British insisted that the Imperial Preference System be left untouched and that managed trade and quotas be permitted. Latin American representatives demanded that the ITO charter include provisions about the foreign investments of more advanced countries in less-developed societies, special rules governing the trade of poorer nations, and allowances for the creation of trading blocs. Poorer countries also attacked several American proposals as imperialistic and insisted that the United States provide large volumes of economic aid. All in all, the American team found the Havana meeting grueling and unsettling.[56]

By the time the ITO charter was signed by the United States and fifty-two other countries on March 23, 1948, the Americans had been forced to accept many provisions that were politically unpopular back home.[57] Instead of the weighted voting scheme the United States preferred and that would have given it a commanding voice in the ITO, the American delegation accepted a one-vote-per-member rule. Also in the charter were provisions related to the regulation of direct foreign investments, special trade rules for developing countries, the creation of regional trading blocs, the acceptability of quotas for agricultural products, balance-of-payments problems, national security, and economic development. One issue not in the charter, however, was the elimination of the Imperial Preference System, which was allowed to continue during a transition period.[58]

In addition to the political controversy that surrounded these provisions of the ITO charter, there were problems related to timing. For one thing, the RTAA was due to expire in June 1948. For another, the 1948 elections were only eight months away, and the Republicans were confident they would capture both the White House and Congress. Under these circumstances, several of President Harry Truman's advisers, including Secretary of State George Marshall and Undersecretary of State Robert Lovett, recommended postponing the submission of the ITO charter to Congress. Instead, they urged the president to focus on securing RTAA renewal. When Congress renewed the RTAA for only one year, Truman and his advisers decided to hold off on the ITO until after the 1948 election.[59]

The Democrats' surprise victory in the 1948 election gave temporary hope to ITO proponents that the charter would win quick congressional approval in 1949. This hope faded, however, when RTAA renewal was again given priority. In addition, national security issues, such as pushing U.S. membership in the newly formed North Atlantic Treaty Organization through the Senate, crowded the ITO off the congressional agenda.

It was not until April 1950 that Congress opened hearings on the International Trade Organization. From the beginning, things went poorly. By 1950, there was less enthusiasm for international organizations than there had been five years earlier when the Bretton Woods agreements were considered by Congress.

Few in Congress believed any longer that promoting world trade would ensure peace. Indeed, many felt that opponents of the United States were using international organizations to launch political attacks denouncing America. Beyond this, Republicans were hostile to an organization that was the product of Democratic diplomacy.[60] Business leaders also refused to support what they regarded as a flawed charter. After the Korean War broke out in June 1950, congressional attention once again shifted from the ITO. Finally, in November 1950 the Truman administration decided to withdraw the ITO charter from Congress. In essence, the International Trade Organization was dead.[61]

But the end of the ITO did not leave the world without a set of principles and rules for handling trade and conducting tariff negotiations; there was still the GATT. It, however, was not an international organization nor would it ever become one, because doing so would require congressional approval for American participation, which in the prevailing climate was unlikely. And because there was little point in forming a trade group without the United States, it was in the interest of all parties to avoid making the GATT a formal organization. Instead, the GATT was treated as the equivalent of a contract among its adherents, with everyone agreeing to observe certain mutually beneficial forms of conduct in international trade. Indeed, the signers of the GATT agreement were not referred to as "members" but as "contracting parties."

The United States participated in the GATT under the authority granted to the president by RTAA legislation and under the president's ability as chief executive of the U.S. government to make executive agreements.[62] In Congress, the GATT was tolerated but not accepted. Some claimed it was an international organization and denounced American participation. Others felt the GATT served a useful purpose. Congress's willingness to renew the RTAA time and again through 1962, however, indicated that it hesitated to rock the trade boat that the GATT represented. Still, on almost every occasion that the RTAA was renewed after 1948 a statement was inserted in the legislation that read, "The enactment of this Act shall not be construed to determine or indicate the approval or disapproval by Congress of the Executive Agreement known as the General Agreement on Tariffs and Trade."[63] This attitude did eventually change, however, as the GATT's value in opening markets became more apparent over the years.

CHAPTER SUMMARY

The Second World War had a dramatic impact on American trade policy. For one thing, it demonstrated that trade policy could not be used to keep the United States out of war. Early on, such efforts centered on legislated neutrality that restricted American trade with belligerents. But as events between 1935 and 1940 revealed, such legislation establishes a moral equivalence between combatants that rarely is appropriate. Furthermore, the policy actually did little to keep the United States out of war, for those who started the war were able to overwhelm their enemies and began casting hungry eyes in new directions that threatened American national security.

After 1940, American policy shifted and trade became a method for avoiding war by assisting one party over the other. At first, cash and carry and then lend-lease schemes appeared to be a means of aiding the victims of German and Japanese aggression. In addition, the U.S. government placed restrictions on American trade with aggressor countries in an attempt to hamper their ability to wage war. But this approach proved hazardous for it drove Japanese leaders toward further aggression to secure new sources of the supplies no longer available from the United States. In the end, this approach led to the Japanese attack on Pearl Harbor and to war.

A second effect of the war on American trade policy was the change in the U.S. attitude toward international economic organizations and statements of principles. Before World War II, it was inconceivable that the United States would join anything of the sort. After all, the United States had rejected the League of Nations and had not hesitated to disrupt the London Economic Conference in 1933. The war, however, affected American attitudes toward international organizations and created opportunities for the United States to construct and join them. Lend-lease negotiations offered an opportunity to begin talks on creating some badly needed economic organizations and the Bretton Woods conference was cleverly scheduled for the summer of 1944, a time when America's influence with its allies was at its peak and many Americans were optimistic that a new world order could be constructed. The result was American leadership in creating the International Monetary Fund and the World Bank.

But a trade organization was another matter. Here, the issues were more politically charged and members of Congress were concerned that American membership would threaten that body's role in setting trade policy and would endanger members' abilities to watch out for the interests of their constituents. In addition, other countries were less willing to allow the United States to dominate negotiations. The result was what many Americans regarded as a badly flawed International Trade Organization. Moreover, by the time the charter was ready for congressional consideration, the blush was off the promise of using international organizations to promote peace, and Congress balked at ITO membership.

But this development did not spell the end of American participation in international ventures to set rules for conducting trade and for lowering trade barriers; the General Agreement on Tariffs and Trade filled the void left by the end of the ITO. The GATT was patterned on the RTAA legislation that Congress repeatedly renewed. Thus through the GATT, the United States could continue to push for open trade and for new rules to regulate trade.

NOTES

1. This section draws on Wayne S. Cole, *Roosevelt and the Isolationists, 1932–1945* (Lincoln: University of Nebraska Press, 1983); Robert Dallek, *Franklin D. Roosevelt and American Foreign Policy, 1932–1945* (New York: Oxford University Press, 1979); Robert Divine, *The Illusion of Neutrality* (Chicago: University of Chicago Press, 1962); and William L. Langer and S. Everett Gleason, *The Challenge of Isolation, 1937–1940* (New York: Council on Foreign Relations, 1952).

2. Cole, *Roosevelt and the Isolationists,* 179.

3. Quoted in Divine, *Illusion of Neutrality,* 164.

4. Dallek, *Franklin D. Roosevelt,* 117–120; and Divine, *Illusion of Neutrality,* 137–152.

5. Dallek, *Franklin D. Roosevelt,* 158–160.

6. Divine, *Illusion of Neutrality,* 234.

7. Cole, *Roosevelt and the Isolationists,* 354.

8. Ibid.

9. Dallek, *Franklin D. Roosevelt,* 240–242.

10. Winston S. Churchill, *Their Finest Hour* (New York: Bantam Books, 1977), 482.

11. Ibid., 483–484.

12. Cole, *Roosevelt and the Isolationists,* 421; and Dallek, *Franklin D. Roosevelt,* 258.

13. In 1940 the United States was the world's largest exporter of oil and was Japan's primary source of refined and unrefined petroleum. See Dean Acheson, *Present at the Creation: My Years in the State Department* (New York: Norton, 1969), 23; and Waldo Heinrichs, *Threshold of War: Franklin D. Roosevelt and American Entry into World War II* (New York: Oxford University Press, 1988), chaps. 4–5.

14. Acheson, *Present at the Creation,* 25–27; and Heinrichs, *Threshold of War,* 32–36.

15. Charles A. Kupchan, *The Vulnerability of Empire* (Ithaca: Cornell University Press, 1994), 330–339.

16. Susan A. Aaronson, *Trade and the American Dream* (Lexington: University Press of Kentucky, 1996), 24; Richard N. Gardner, *Sterling-Dollar Diplomacy in Current Perspective* (New York: Columbia University Press, 1980), 101; Armand Van Dormael, *Bretton Woods: Birth of a Monetary System* (London: Macmillan, 1978), 40; and E. F. Penrose, *Economic Planning for the Peace* (Princeton: Princeton University Press, 1953), 38.

17. Quoted in Van Dormael, *Bretton Woods,* 1.

18. Gardner, *Sterling-Dollar Diplomacy,* 8.

19. Ibid., 101.

20. Cole, *Roosevelt and the Isolationists,* 110–111, 516.

21. Edward S. Kaplan, *American Trade Policy, 1923–1995* (Westport, Conn.: Greenwood Press, 1996), 50.

22. Raymond A. Bauer, Ithiel de Sola Pool, and Lewis Anthony Dexter, *American Business and Public Policy: The Politics of Foreign Trade* (New York: Atherton Press, 1964), 27.

23. Michael A. Butler, *Cautious Visionary: Cordell Hull and Trade Reform, 1933–1937* (Kent: Kent State University Press, 1998), 153–155.

24. Dallek, *Franklin D. Roosevelt,* 258.

25. Acheson, *Present at the Creation,* 29–30.

26. Winston S. Churchill, *The Grand Alliance* (New York: Bantam Books, 1977), 369–375; and Gardner, *Sterling-Dollar Diplomacy,* 41–49.

27. Acheson, *Present at the Creation,* 33.

28. Penrose, *Economic Planning,* 25–26.

29. Gardner, *Sterling-Dollar Diplomacy,* 64–67.

30. Van Dormael, *Bretton Woods,* 81.

31. Alfred A. Eckes Jr., *A Search for Solvency: Bretton Woods and the International Monetary System, 1941–1971* (Austin: University of Texas Press, 1975), 65–71; Gardner, *Sterling-Dollar Diplomacy,* 77–80; Penrose, *Economic Planning,* 41–45; and Van Dormael, *Bretton Woods,* chap. 4.

32. Eckes, *Search for Solvency,* 46–52; Gardner, *Sterling-Dollar Diplomacy,* 71–77; Penrose, *Economic Planning,* 41–45; and Van Dormael, *Bretton Woods,* chaps. 5–6.

33. Van Dormael, *Bretton Woods,* 110.

34. Ibid., chap. 16.

35. Ibid., 170–171.

36. Joan Edelman Spero and Jeffrey Hart, *The Politics of International Economic Relations* (New York: St. Martin's Press, 1997), 10; and Van Dormael, *Bretton Woods,* chap. 16.

37. Van Dormael, *Bretton Woods,* 254.

38. Aaronson, *Trade and the American Dream,* 42.

39. Gardner, *Sterling-Dollar Diplomacy,* 136, 140.

40. Eric Helleiner, *States and the Reemergence of Global Finance: From Bretton Woods to the 1990s* (Ithaca: Cornell University Press, 1994), 40–42; and Van Dormael, *Bretton Woods,* 240–241.

41. Van Dormael, *Bretton Woods,* 258–265; and Gardner, *Sterling-Dollar Diplomacy,* 129–143.

42. Van Dormael, *Bretton Woods,* 262, 265.

43. A country can incur a trade advantage by devaluing its currency. When the value of the country's currency falls in relation to that of other currencies, foreigners, who thus can buy more for less money, have an incentive to buy more goods from the country that devalued, thereby increasing that country's exports, which leads to more jobs in industries that export. Because governments are sensitive to job creation and losses, they tend to react unfavorably when another country devalues its currency.

44. Van Dormael, *Bretton Woods,* 63.

45. Penrose, *Economic Planning*, 96–97.

46. Ibid., 95–97.

47. Aaronson, *Trade and the American Dream*, 39–40; and Penrose, *Economic Planning*, 87.

48. Gardner, *Sterling-Dollar Diplomacy*, 151; and Penrose, *Economic Planning*, 92–107.

49. Penrose, *Economic Planning*, 100; and Carolyn Rhodes, *Reciprocity, U.S. Trade Policy, and the GATT Regime* (Ithaca: Cornell University Press, 1993), 65–66.

50. Aaronson, *Trade and the American Dream*, 31; and Penrose, *Economic Planning*, 107–108.

51. Gardner, *Sterling-Dollar Diplomacy*, 145.

52. Aaronson, *Trade and the American Dream*, 62.

53. Gardner, *Sterling-Dollar Diplomacy*, 354–359.

54. This discussion of GATT principles draws on Rhodes, *Reciprocity*, chap. 4; and Kaplan, *American Trade Policy*, 54–56.

55. Aaronson, *Trade and the American Dream*, 87; and Steve Dryden, *Trade Warriors: USTR and the American Crusade for Free Trade* (New York: Oxford University Press, 1995), 14.

56. Dryden, *Trade Warriors*, 16–24; and Gardner, *Sterling-Dollar Diplomacy*, 361–368.

57. Aaronson, *Trade and the American Dream*, 66.

58. Aaronson, *Trade and the American Dream*, 5; Dryden, *Trade Warriors*, 23–24; and Gardner, *Sterling-Dollar Diplomacy*, 375–376.

59. Dryden, *Trade Warriors*, 25–27.

60. Gardner, *Sterling-Dollar Diplomacy*, 372–373.

61. Dryden, *Trade Warriors*, 25–30.

62. Gardner, *Sterling-Dollar Diplomacy*, xxv–xxvi; and John H. Jackson, *The World Trading System: Law and Policy of International Economic Relations* (Cambridge: MIT Press, 1997), 35–40.

63. Quoted in Kaplan, *American Trade Policy*, 54.

5 Cold War Trade: Protection from Imports and from Communism

When the Second World War ended in September 1945, Americans hoped they had seen their last worldwide conflict. In the future, they believed, wars would either be prevented by the economic linkages the Bretton Woods institutions were designed to foster or be managed by the new United Nations. Few Americans were willing to police the world and guarantee the security of other nations. Indeed, most people felt the primary task of the United States in the immediate future was to return to a peacetime economy that would provide for American consumers and ensure that the specter of the depression would not reappear.

As the trade debate shaped up in 1945, liberals believed that continued efforts to open up world markets were essential for world peace, and conservatives longed for the American system of protection. For liberals, increased trade was the best way to avoid another depression, jump-start the International Monetary Fund, the World Bank, and the United Nations, and guard against a return to isolationism. For conservatives, protection would preserve the American way of life, maintain jobs, and ensure that the United States would not be drawn too deeply into international politics.

The unfolding of international events, however, short-circuited this debate and put trade in a new strategic context. Serious disputes between the United States and the Soviet Union, a former ally in the war against Germany, convinced Americans that communism represented a threat to world peace and that the Soviet Union sought world domination. In these circumstances, national security factors became a key to trade policy. Liberals treated the market opening they favored as part of the struggle between the United States and the Soviet Union, arguing that freer trade would create a close working relationship among members of the noncommunist world and promote the economic security American allies needed to resist communism.

The postwar international competitive environment also favored the promotion of liberal trade. Because of the wartime destruction in Europe and the Far East and the immense American buildup in industrial production as the United States supplied materials to the anti-Axis alliance, many American producers faced no credible international challengers. As a result, many American industries clamored for lower trade barriers so they could take advantage of business opportunities abroad. Interestingly, these special-interest demands for more open trade dovetailed with the American strategic interest in using trade to rebuild Europe and Japan and to promote Western solidarity in the face of potential communist aggression.

The liberals' ability to tie trade to national security put protectionists, most of whom were anticommunist, in an uncomfortable position, faced with two of their basic political beliefs, protection and anticommunism, in conflict. Backing away from protection meant placing noncompetitive American industries in jeopardy and accepting continuation of the RTAA program. But pushing for protection might facilitate the spread of communism. Thus, although many political leaders in the decade after the Second World War remained committed to protection, they found it difficult to act on that belief and to work together as a unified coalition. Despite these problems, from the mid-1940s through the 1950s protectionists fought an effective rearguard action and were able to slow the dismantling of trade barriers.

One way in which protectionists did that was by constructing legal processes that hard-pressed industries could use to shield themselves from foreign competition. These processes were designed to replace the all-encompassing protection offered by the high tariffs of the pre-depression era. As tariffs were steadily lowered by RTAA and GATT negotiations, more and more noncompetitive American special interests felt pressured by imports and looked to Congress for help. But because the struggle against communism and trade agreements with other countries foreclosed sweeping tariff legislation, Congress responded with laws meant to provide assistance without upsetting the general thrust of an approach to trade that successive presidents claimed was essential to American national security. In this way, protectionists sought to balance their anticommunist values with their desire to help local producers.

National security considerations also interacted with trade in another way. Congress passed legislation giving the president the authority to restrict trade in order to prevent communist countries from importing strategically important goods from the West. One characteristic of these laws was the discretion the president could exercise in their application. This discretion was granted in part because Congress recognized that as a legislative body it was ill suited for determining the conditions under which trade limitations might best serve American national interests. In addition, members of Congress realized that America's allies did not uniformly agree with American views about restraining trade with communist countries and that negotiations would be needed to iron out a common approach. As the person who would conduct these negotiations, the president needed the legal authority to bargain. In the end, then, the national emergency associated with the Cold War resulted in a substantial grant of power to the president for regulating trade.

This chapter examines American trade policy during the decade immediately after World War II. It looks at, among other things, how trade contributed to American attempts to build a Western coalition to restrain communism and at the new forms of protection that emerged to aid selected American producers. The discussion will illustrate how liberals used anticommunist rhetoric to continue the march toward freer trade even though many in Congress were reluctant to go down that path. Indeed, one of the most important features of this period was liberals' ability to maintain the momentum toward freer trade at a time when the White House and Congress were, after many years, in Republican hands and when many Americans remained uncertain about whether increased trade would benefit their country.

THE COMMUNIST THREAT

The most prominent feature of the post–World War II period was the collapse of the U.S.-Soviet alliance and the emergence of the Cold War. Tensions between the wartime allies stemmed primarily from the question of how occupied Europe would be handled after the war. Americans expected national self-determination and democracy to serve as guideposts for liberating Europe, but the Russians feared that the application of these principles could lead to anti-Soviet governments that might eventually threaten Soviet national security.

These differences in U.S.-Soviet perspectives manifested themselves in arguments about the fate of the Eastern European countries the Soviets liberated from the Germans. Despite Soviet pledges to hold free elections and to respect self-determination, in one country after another noncommunist political organizations were abolished and totalitarian dictatorships were set up under Soviet tutelage. By 1947, rigged elections in Romania, Bulgaria, and Poland had subverted the will of the people and led to the installation of pro-Soviet governments. The Soviet policy toward Germany also was a source of concern; American leaders found the Soviets uncooperative, determined to prevent German democracy, and bent on leaving the country crippled. Beyond this, the Soviets threatened the independence of Czechoslovakia and Hungary, commanded the obedience of the

French and Italian communist parties, and seemed poised to take advantage of discord in Greece and Turkey. All in all, many Americans began to wonder if they had fought in World War II to free Europe from the menace of fascism only to have a communist threat emerge in its place.

The Truman Doctrine and the Marshall Plan

That was the situation on the afternoon of February 21, 1947, when the British ambassador to the United States delivered two notes to the State Department in Washington from His Majesty's government. One dealt with a communist attempt to seize power in Greece, and the second described a similar situation in Turkey. The notes informed the United States that British assistance to both countries was being terminated, leaving Greece and Turkey at risk of succumbing to communism. The implication was clear: the United States would have to intervene to prevent such an outcome.

President Truman and his advisers were alarmed by the messages. Greece and Turkey were important to the control of the eastern Mediterranean. If communist governments took over, not only could the Soviets dominate the Mediterranean, but they also would be positioned to threaten the Suez Canal, the route for much of the oil bound for Europe. The dire implications of such control for European trade and prosperity seemed obvious. Moreover, Greece and Turkey represented an attempt by the Soviet Union to use a new tactic, internal subversion, to add to their collection of satellites. The stakes were enormous, and the United States had no choice but to give aid.

The problem, however, was whether Congress, now controlled by the Republicans after their 1946 election victory, would provide the funds. The president personally took his case to Congress on March 12, 1947. There, President Harry Truman's appeal for funds was so stirring that it sparked the imagination of the American people and of members of Congress. The heart of his speech was a statement that became known as the Truman Doctrine:

> I believe that it must be the policy of the United States to support free peoples who are resisting attempted subjugation by armed minorities or by outside pressures. I believe that we must assist free peoples to work out their own destinies in their own way. I believe that our help should be primarily through economic and financial aid, which is essential to economic stability and orderly political processes.[1]

Truman then asked Congress to approve money for assistance to Greece and Turkey. The House and Senate quickly complied.

In the meantime, the economic situation in Europe was reaching crisis proportions. Five years of warfare and Nazi rule had left unparalleled devastation.

Across the continent, transportation and communications facilities were severely damaged, factories were unusable, food and fuel were unobtainable, and inflation was out of control. In several countries, communists were poised to take advantage of the misery. Undersecretary of State for Economic Affairs Will Clayton argued that unless something was done quickly, much of Western Europe might fall victim to communist subversion. Gen. Dwight D. Eisenhower, former commander in chief of Allied Forces in Europe during the war, offered similar views.[2]

By April, it was clear that the problem in Europe dwarfed the resources available to the IMF and the World Bank.[3] It also was obvious that, in addition to posing the risk that communists might take advantage of Europe's misery, the crisis threatened to undermine the liberal trading system the State Department was working to build at the GATT/ITO talks under way in Geneva. Liberal trade was imperiled both by Europe's hesitation to bargain while confronting economic disaster and by its growing attraction to barter trade.[4]

Again, American assistance seemed the only answer. The problem was that more aid for Europe was politically controversial. For one thing, would Congress consent? For another, to whom would the aid go, how would the aid be dispensed, and what would be the relationship of the aid to the ongoing trade negotiations?

Truman and his advisers realized the need for a carefully orchestrated public campaign. The campaign opened in Texas with a speech by Truman reminding his audience that as the world's most powerful country the United States had responsibilities that included providing both political and economic leadership. A month later, Secretary of State George Marshall, who believed the Soviets intended to use economic problems to their advantage, graphically described the European situation to the American people in a radio address.[5] Finally, in May Undersecretary of State Dean Acheson warned a Mississippi audience about the impending disaster in Europe and emphasized the importance of American action to avoid a catastrophe that could have devastating strategic consequences. This speech caught the attention of a prominent former isolationist, Sen. Arthur Vandenberg, R-Mich., who agreed to support the administration's aid proposals in Congress.[6]

While the public campaign continued, State Department planning moved forward. Three principles underlay these plans. The first was that any aid program would target all of Europe, east and west, communist and noncommunist. As Marshall later said in his speech outlining the American proposal, "Our policy is not directed against any country or doctrine, but against hunger, poverty, desperation, and chaos."[7] Most State Department analysts feared that anticommunist sentiment was so fierce in Congress that it would refuse to finance any assistance that included the Soviet Union, yet they also were concerned that aid offered only to democratic countries would leave the United States vulnerable to the charge that it was dividing Europe.[8]

The second principle was that the aid program would be employed to induce Europeans to lower trade barriers. Two reasons were behind this objective. First, many of the items Europeans needed would have to be imported from the United States. Maintaining import barriers under such conditions made no sense. Second, American officials were convinced that intra-European trade would be essential to any scheme for rebuilding and that obstacles to trade would hinder progress. In addition, for aid to work the United States would have to eliminate its own trade barriers in order to provide the markets Europeans would require for the goods they produced as they recovered. But because Congress insisted on the reciprocal reduction of trade barriers, Europeans also would have to tear down their walls to trade to gain entry into the American market.[9] Interestingly, these efforts to tie trade liberalization to an American aid program were no more effective in 1947 than they had been six years earlier during the lend-lease negotiations. The Europeans in general and the British in particular were reluctant to accept American arguments, fearing that their already overwhelming reliance on American imports would become unbearable if import restrictions were reduced as requested by American trade negotiators.

The third principle behind American planning was that aid would be conditioned on a cooperative European plan of action for the entire continent. As Truman observed later, "The overriding task that seemed to confront American policy in Europe was to provide an incentive for the Europeans to look at the situation in the broadest possible terms rather than in narrowly nationalistic . . . focus."[10] By 1947, the United States already had spent over $9 billion on bilateral economic aid for Europe. But, instead of spurring European recovery, this aid had had only a marginal effect. American leaders were thus convinced that European collaboration was essential to the success of the new aid program. Such an approach required that former enemies Germany and Italy be rebuilt, because they represented vital parts of the European economic picture. Moreover, American officials hoped that economic cooperation would encourage joint efforts to restrain communism.[11]

The American aid offer came on June 5, 1947, when Secretary Marshall addressed the graduates of Harvard University. Marshall emphasized that assistance was conditioned on a unified European plan for recovery and that the American goals were a decent standard of living and political stability for Europe. After expressing some interest initially, Moscow rejected American assistance, and none of the sixteen nations that assembled in Paris on July 12 to coordinate planning was communist.[12] After two months of work by the group, a European recovery program was presented to the United States.

Congressional consideration of the aid package, now known as the Marshall Plan, continued into 1948. Soviet intransigence in Germany and the violent seizure of power by communists in Czechoslovakia created a grim backdrop to the congressional debate. By March, both the House and Senate had approved funding for assistance, and President Truman signed the aid bill on April 3, 1948. The legislation stipulated that the aid program not be run by the State Department, but by a separate agency, the Economic Cooperation Administration. This stipulation reflected Congress's belief that the State Department would use aid to push for freer trade.[13]

Economic and Political Containment

By mid-1947, American decision makers had concluded that the United States needed a new foreign policy approach. Even though President Truman had rallied the American people to the defense of democracy with his call to help free peoples resist threats to their independence and even though Secretary of State Marshall had organized a program of economic assistance, many observers believed that the country needed a general policy framework. This framework was the doctrine of containment.

Containment was largely a product of the thinking of George Kennan, a State Department specialist on Soviet affairs. In a cable sent to Washington from his diplomatic post in Moscow and in an article in the July 1947 issue of *Foreign Affairs,* Kennan argued that the best American response to Soviet intransigence would be a firm stance against further Soviet advances. If denied the opportunity for expansion, the Soviets would, according to Kennan, be forced to attend to their mounting domestic problems. As they did this, Soviet society would change, subtly at first but more dramatically over time, until communism would no longer be the virulent threat that so concerned policy makers. This assessment was the essence of containment.

Kennan's arguments were widely accepted in Washington and became the guidepost for the new American foreign policy. The United States would not engage in a war with the Soviet Union, but would push it toward more acceptable behavior by denying it new conquests. In doing so, the United States could avoid war while remaining confident that any future Soviet threat would be eliminated.

Having adopted containment as its new policy, the United States could then both assist potential Soviet victims, as it was doing with aid to Greece and Turkey and with the Marshall Plan, and use economic resources as levers to restrain the Soviet Union and encourage changes in behavior. Indeed, several approaches to the use of economic leverage were debated even during World War II. One called for placing few limits on U.S.-Soviet commerce in an attempt to use trade as a means of liberalizing Soviet society. Former vice president Henry Wallace favored this approach, believing that the Soviet Union was a natural market for American goods. Some business executives, such as Armand Hammer of Occidental Petroleum, agreed, but Wallace's arguments did not fit the increasingly anticommunist political climate in Washington.[14]

A second, more coercive policy attempted to link access to American economic resources to Soviet behavior.[15] In early 1945, Averell Harriman, the U.S. ambassador to the Soviet Union, wrote that one way to advance American interests was to tie "our economic assistance directly into our political problems with the Soviet Union."[16] President Truman agreed that such a tactic might be valuable, noting in a memorandum that the Soviet Union "was susceptible to . . . economic pressure, which could be used to control, discipline, and punish it."[17]

Despite U.S. hopes that economic linkages might moderate Soviet behavior, the strategy fell flat. Attempts to use lend-lease shipments to this end met stubborn Soviet resistance, including a statement that the Soviets would sooner do without lend-lease than permit the United States to use the program to pressure them.[18] A Soviet request for a $6 billion postwar loan also provided little leverage because the Soviets again made it clear they would not succumb to such tactics.[19] Thus by late 1946, most American officials believed a linkage strategy would not work.

While the Truman administration grappled with how to conduct economic relations with the Soviet Union, members of Congress, especially Republicans, called for terminating U.S.-Soviet trade and adopting what amounted to **economic warfare.** These demands presumed that an east-west military confrontation was likely and that trade would help the Soviet military.[20] In early 1947, Republican John Thomas of New Jersey, chairman of the House Un-American Activities Committee, urged the suspension of U.S.-Soviet trade to prevent the Soviets from acquiring American technology. House members Leon Gavin, R-Pa., and Alvin O'Konski, R-Wis., noted that American exports of natural resources to the Soviet Union also should be curtailed. In the Senate, Republican Ralph Flanders of Vermont introduced a resolution seeking cessation of American trade with the Soviet Union until it respected national self-determination.[21]

As they considered their options in 1947, administration officials concluded that a **strategic embargo** was preferable to the economic warfare favored by Congress. A strategic embargo would forbid only trade that might help the Soviet military; trade judged irrelevant for military uses would be permitted.[22] Accordingly, in the spring of 1947 President Truman announced he would use his authority under the National Defense Act of 1940 to control the sale of military equipment, munitions, and other military-related goods to the Soviet Union. Truman believed that by regulating strategic sales he could hamper the Soviets' ability to prepare for war while permitting the West to continue purchasing essential raw materials such as manganese.[23]

During congressional testimony later that year, Undersecretary of Commerce William Foster pointed out that any American trade restrictions would require cooperation with Europeans. Otherwise, they might provide the very goods on which the United States had placed limits. Foster also noted the historical pattern of European trade with the Soviet Union and argued that disrupting that trade might hinder the recovery the United States was assisting with the Marshall Plan.[24]

Officials in the State, Defense, and Commerce Departments began to implement the president's decision to control strategic trade by drawing up lists of regulated items. By 1948, there were two lists. List 1A included items of direct military significance and advanced technology that could be used to produce strategic goods. These items could not be exported to communist countries. List 1B contained goods of indirect strategic importance that might strengthen the Soviet economy. Export licenses were required to sell these goods to communist nations.[25]

As noted, American decision makers realized that the success of the trade restrictions depended on cooperation from America's allies. By 1948, the French and British were considering export controls, but they faced problems that Americans did not have. For one thing, many Western European businesses had conducted lucrative trade with Eastern European countries, including the Soviet Union, before the war and opposed trade restrictions. Few American firms had engaged in such trade.[26] Another concern was the possibility that French and British trade limitations would open export opportunities for others. The French and British, then, wanted their restrictions to be part of a general pattern adhered to by all Western nations. Finally, the British and French informed the United States that because trade restrictions would cost them markets in the east, they would need more access to American markets.[27] This request echoed previous American attempts to link cooperation on aid and other matters to lower trade barriers.

As time passed, Belgium, Italy, Luxembourg, and the Netherlands joined Britain, France, and the United States in their discussions of export limitations. In November 1949, the group took the formal step of establishing a **Coordinating Committee for Multilateral Export Controls,** or CoCom, to facilitate export controls on east-west trade. Canada, Denmark, Norway, and West Germany joined the group in 1950, Japan and Portugal in 1952, and Greece and Turkey in 1953.[28] From the beginning, CoCom acted informally and confidentially because of the controversy surrounding export controls in Europe. To this end, it shunned publicity and some members refused to admit they belonged to the group. CoCom decisions did not have treaty status and were nonbinding, and the group did not issue penalties for violations.[29]

Despite its organizational characteristics, the United States found CoCom valuable; it provided a forum for coaxing allies to observe trade restraints against the communists. But from the start, American representatives to CoCom were hard-pressed to overcome European doubts about export controls because of the historical pattern of trade between Eastern and Western Europe. In addition, with the exception of a short period during the Korean War, Western Europeans tended to disagree with American assessments of the probability that the Soviet Union might initiate a war. CoCom was thus the scene of ongoing arguments about the kinds of export controls that should be maintained.

Congressional Trade Restrictions and the Korean War

Congressional concern over east-west trade grew steadily in the late 1940s and into 1950 as many members became convinced that war was only a matter of time. One ominous event stoking these anxieties was the Soviet blockade of Berlin beginning in June 1948. The Soviets refused to allow ground traffic between the American, British, and French zones of occupation in Germany and the portions of Berlin controlled by the Western allies. The Soviet decision to take this move was widely interpreted in the United States as a possible forerunner to more forceful military action and created the atmosphere in Congress that led to approval in 1949 of U.S. membership in the North Atlantic Treaty Organization (NATO) and to passage of the **Export Control Act of 1949.**

The Export Control Act gave the president the authority to restrict exports in peacetime, even if there was no national emergency, and considerable discretion in its application. In passing the law, Congress sought to encourage the executive branch to prohibit trade with communist countries. Mindful that American allies were reluctant to restrain east-west trade, President Truman refrained from taking the tough stance members of Congress had in mind, although he did set up a Commerce Department licensing system to review restricted exports.[30]

Congressional worries about trade with the communist bloc reached new heights in the summer of 1950 after the Korean War broke out. The attack by communist North Korea on South Korea caught the United States by surprise and sparked the fear that a general communist offensive might be in the making. Observers were further alarmed by the obvious Soviet sponsorship of North Korea and by the dawning realization that U.S. troops would have to stop the communist advance. The congressional reaction was immediate and strident. Several members called for terminating all trade with the Soviet Union; others condemned America's European allies for trading with the communists while receiving Marshall Plan aid.[31]

In response to these problems, members introduced resolutions in both houses of Congress calling for a punitive end to American aid and trade for those countries doing business with the Soviet Union. Although President Truman was able to have most of these proposals killed, a relatively moderate amendment to the Foreign Assistance Act of 1948 was proposed by Rep. Clarence Cannon, D-Mo., and passed in September 1950. The **Cannon Amendment,** which applied whenever American forces fought under the command of the United Nations, as in Korea, gave the president the authority to halt trade with any country whose trade with the Soviet Union undermined American national security. In addition, the Cannon Amendment placed restrictions on credit and financial transactions with communist countries.[32] Given the degree of presidential flexibility contained in the amendment, its passage was mostly symbolic. Still, America's allies found the legislation repugnant.

In view of the growing hostility in Congress toward east-west trade, President Truman ordered a cabinet review of the subject in 1950. The review found the Defense Department pressing for tight controls on trade, the State Department concerned about how trade restrictions affected the solidarity of NATO, and the Commerce Department favoring a better licensing system. Each cabinet department, however, recognized the need for consultation with America's European allies. Thus Truman approved new CoCom negotiations to work out more stringent controls to support the military effort in Korea. This approach proved successful, and by early 1951 CoCom members had accepted most of the trade limits suggested by the United States.[33]

When communist China joined the fighting in Korea in November 1950, Congress began to worry about trade with the communists yet again. For many in Congress, the entry of the Chinese into the war was conclusive evidence that the United States faced a coordinated campaign directed by a Soviet Union that could order any communist country to do its bidding. Under these circumstances, it seemed appropriate to halt trade that helped the communists. This sentiment favoring additional trade restrictions resulted in two pieces of legislation, the **Battle Act** and the **Trade Agreements Extension Act of 1951.**

The Battle Act, named for Democratic House member Laurie Battle of Alabama and formally titled the Mutual Defense Assistance Control Act of 1951, was proposed in March and passed by Congress in August. The law allowed the president to prohibit exports of strategic goods to communist countries and to terminate aid to countries that did not go along with American restrictions. The president received the authority to enact these limits on trade during times of war or peace. In effect, the act was an extension of the power granted under the Cannon Amendment, which pertained to trade only in wartime. The new law also gave the president a degree of discretion—that is, he could issue exemptions when he believed it was in the national interest to do so. The Battle Act superceded an attempt by Sen. James Kem, R-Mo., to pass legislation that would have given the president no choice about cutting aid.[34]

The Trade Agreements Extension Act of 1951 renewed the president's authority to negotiate trade agreements under the RTAA program. As a part of the legal package reauthorizing the RTAA, Congress stipulated that all tariff concessions previously granted under the RTAA program to the Soviet Union and other members of the communist bloc must be withdrawn. This stipulation cancelled the Soviet Union's most-favored-nation status, leaving it and other communist countries subject to the prohibitively high Smoot-Hawley tariff rates. This termination of most-favored-nation privileges all but ended communist exports to the United States.[35]

Eisenhower's New Look in Trade

The 1952 election brought the Republicans back to power in Washington; they captured both houses of Congress, and former general Dwight Eisenhower was elected president. For conservative Republicans, this victory was an opportunity to push for more restrictions on east-west trade. Eisenhower, however, was a liberal on trade questions and believed that trade overtures to smaller communist countries could be used to drive a wedge between the Soviet Union and its satellites. Eisenhower therefore was determined to continue special trade exemptions for communist countries such as Yugoslavia that displayed a degree of independence from the Soviet Union.[36]

Two events in 1953 reinforced Eisenhower's inclination to ease trade restrictions: the death of Soviet leader Joseph Stalin in March, which was perceived as creating the possibility for better U.S.-Soviet relations, and the end of the Korean War in July. To prepare the groundwork for a possible shift in policy, Eisenhower obtained congressional approval for a trade study by the Commission on Foreign Economic Policy headed by Clarence Randall, president of Inland Steel. Between September 1953 and February 1954, the bipartisan **Randall Commission,** composed of ten members of Congress and seven private citizens, analyzed all aspects of American trade policy. On east-west trade, the commission recommended that American policy be coordinated with CoCom and that strategic trade controls be tightened. But the commission also argued that trade in peaceful goods was desirable, both because the Soviet Union was a source of several vital raw materials and because trade might lessen Cold War tensions and liberalize Russia.[37]

By early 1954, America's allies also were calling for an easing of east-west trade limits. In February, British prime minister Winston Churchill observed that "the more trade there is between Great Britain and Soviet Russia and the satellites, the better still will be the chances of our living together in increasing comfort . . . [and] the more the two great divisions of the world mingle in . . . commerce, the greater is the counterpoise to purely military calculations."[38] Businesses in Europe and the United States with an interest in Soviet markets endorsed Churchill's sentiments.

After a series of meetings stretching into August 1954, CoCom members, including the United States, revised export controls for the Soviet Union and its European satellites. But American policy diverged from that of its CoCom partners over trade with communist China, because the United States, stung by the fighting against China in Korea, refused to ease controls on Chinese trade even though most of the rest of CoCom did so.[39]

The next year brought still more reasons to reduce east-west trade barriers. In July 1955, U.S., British, French, and Soviet leaders emerged from a summit conference in Geneva with a new attitude, coined the "Spirit of Geneva," which many observers believed was a prelude to the end of the Cold War. One consequence of this new attitude was demands by businesses and farmers for more opportunities to export to the Soviet bloc. Within the Eisenhower administration, the Agriculture Department argued that sales to communist countries would mean profits for American exporters and would drain Soviet reserves of gold and Western currency, thereby reducing the Soviets' ability to purchase strategic goods. When Eisenhower loosened American trade restrictions, many officials, particularly in the Defense Department, protested that such a move would help the Soviets provide consumers with food and other goods whose supply was limited.[40]

By early 1956, the relaxation of American controls on east-west trade had reached the point where Congress became concerned it was going too far. In February, the Senate conducted hearings on the matter and concluded that sensitive goods were finding their way to the Soviet Union. Although Eisenhower disputed the findings and noted the futility of retaining tighter controls than other countries, the White House decided not to remove additional barriers to trade with communist countries.[41] In the end, then, even though prohibitions against Soviet bloc trade were reduced substantially after 1953, as Eisenhower entered his final years in office several important limits remained, including those found in the Battle Act, the Export Control Act of 1949, and the denial of most-favored-nation status in the Trade Agreements Extension Act of 1951.[42]

PROTECTION FROM IMPORTS

The post–World War II era also ushered in new ways to protect American producers from imports. As described in earlier chapters, until the Reciprocal Trade Agreements Act was passed in 1934 the preferred method of protection was the sweeping tariff legislation passed by Congress about every five years. The last of these laws was the Smoot-Hawley Tariff of 1930. Passage of the Reciprocal Trade Agreements Act in 1934 introduced a new method for setting tariffs based on negotiations between the president and America's trading partners. As a result, tariff legislation became a thing of the past.

Protectionism was not dead, however; rather, protectionist measures appeared in new forms. One was the specific-industry tariff, set by Congress to protect a particular American producer from imports. A postwar example was the Wool Act, which Congress passed in the spring of 1947 while the Geneva talks establishing the General Agreement on Tariffs and Trade were under way. American trade negotiators recognized that if tariffs on wool were raised, several countries would walk out of the GATT negotiations. Alarmed, Will Clayton, the lead American delegate in Geneva, appealed to President Truman, who vetoed the bill.[43]

In general, most specific-industry measures have suffered the same fate over the years, often because they have threatened to upset ongoing trade negotiations.[44] But the mere congressional consideration of such bills has contributed to a second, more informal type of protection in which foreign producers, or their governments, or both agree to restrict sales in the American market. This form of protection, known as a voluntary export restraint agreement (see Chapter 3), usually appears when foreigners fear they will confront some form of specific-industry legislation unless they limit exports to the United States. These agreements, which are labeled "voluntary" because they are not based on formal action by the United States, are far from voluntary, however. They are set up to prevent the restrictive legal action that might occur if there were no VER.

In the years after the RTAA reforms were first passed, VERs became increasingly popular as a means of placating industries facing foreign competition. The basic idea in the executive branch was to use a VER to limit imports and to prevent affected industries from pushing for legislative barriers that might upset progress toward more open trade. The textile industry, for example, benefited from this kind of protection in the mid-1950s.

In addition to VERs, Congress created administrative machinery that American producers could use to obtain assistance when imports posed problems. These procedures fell into two categories depending on whether the problem pertained to fair or unfair trade. Congress defined **unfair trade** as a situation in which a foreign producer or its government seeks to manipulate normal market mechanisms to its advantage and to the detriment of an American business. Most unfair trade law originated before World War II and was designed to provide the affected American producer with relief from unacceptable foreign practices. Problems related to fair trade occurred in a normal market context. Here, the procedures set up by Congress were designed to allow American companies to adjust to shifts in international competition. In effect, fair trade protection provides American firms with an opportunity to catch their breath and to regroup so that they could survive unanticipated events. These forms of protection are described in the sections that follow.

Protection from Unfair Trade

At the start of the Second World War, American trade law recognized three forms of unfair trading: (1) **dumping,** (2) **subsidies** provided by a government to its exporting industries, and (3) infringements on the patents, copyrights, and trademarks of American corporations.[45] In each case the remedy created by Congress presumed that the activity in question either violated the normal functioning of free markets or was a foreign attempt to cheat an American firm out of its place in the market. Americans had been concerned about inappropriate foreign practices since the early nineteenth century, but Congress took action on the problem only at the start of the twentieth century as trade began to play a more important role in the American economy.

Dumping occurs when foreign producers offer products for sale in the United States at prices below **normal value,** which can be defined in several ways. Such a pricing policy can put so much pressure on American firms producing the same types of goods that they are forced out of business, leaving the foreign producer well positioned to dominate the American market and to raise prices in the future. A 1919 Tariff Commission report recommended that Congress adopt legislation to protect against this problem. Congress acted on this recommendation in 1921 when it passed the **Anti-Dumping Act.**[46]

Under the 1921 law, an American firm that suspected it was a victim of dumping could petition the Customs Bureau of the Treasury Department to conduct an investigation. If the Customs Bureau found a probable violation, it would refer the case to the Tariff Commission for further investigation. If the Tariff Commission also found a violation that injured an American firm, it would report the violation to the Treasury secretary, who would authorize the Customs Bureau to collect duties equal to the price differential between the normal value price and the actual price. If the Tariff Commission investigation indicated that no dumping had occurred, then it had the authority to set aside the initial Customs Bureau finding.[47]

Several problems were associated with application of the anti-dumping law. One was how to determine the normal value price of a product. The most direct way was to compare the price of a product in its home market with its price in the United States. This comparison sometimes proved difficult, however, because a foreign firm may not have supplied the information needed for the calculations, or the firm may not have sold the product in its home market. When these problems emerged, one of two other procedures was used. The first called for comparing the price of the good in the American market with the price in other export markets. The second involved constructing a normal value price by calculating the cost of production and adding the cost of transportation and a reasonable profit. These alternative methods for assessing normal value were problematic, however, because appropriate information was sometimes difficult to acquire and even small changes in the nature of the available data could lead to different conclusions.[48]

Another problem with the anti-dumping law was conceptual—liberals questioned a policy that punished foreign firms for charging too little for their exports. These critics argued that American businesses that lowered their prices were usually praised. Why then should foreign corporations be damned for the same behavior? Two other problems were related to the absence of any limits on the duration of dumping determinations and to the lack of presidential discretion in determining when duties should be assessed. Once the Tariff Commission ruled that dumping had occurred, the collection of duties was automatic under the law. Presidents had no authority to change a ruling they believed conflicted with the national interest. And once the collection of duties began, there was no procedure for deciding when they should be terminated.[49]

The second type of unfair trade took the form of the subsidies sometimes paid by foreign governments to their exporters so that goods could be sold in the United States at prices below those charged by American firms. Congress had expressed concerns about subsidies since the 1890s, and the tariffs of 1890 and 1897 contained provisions to counter such practices.[50] Additional arrangements for handling subsidies were included in tariff bills passed in 1909 and 1913 and in the Smoot-Hawley Tariff of 1930. The 1930 law set up procedures for dealing with subsidies that were nearly identical to those for dumping: after a complaint by an affected American corporation, the Customs Bureau would conduct a preliminary inquiry, followed by an investigation by the Tariff Commission. If subsidies were found, the Treasury Department would collect **countervailing duties** to offset the subsidy and boost the price of the good in question to the level it would sell for without the subsidy.[51] Like dumping, however, subsidies presented the problem of obtaining adequate information; foreign governments were reluctant to cooperate with American investigations.

The third type of unfair trade, violations of American intellectual property rights, including patents, copyrights, and trademarks, were addressed in **Section 337** of the Smoot-Hawley Tariff. This section empowered the Tariff Commission to conduct inquiries into a broadly defined category of unfair trade. In practice, enforcement of this part of the law was applied to intellectual property rights. In these cases, the injured party, an American firm, petitioned the Tariff Commission, which then conducted an investigation and reported any infringements to the president. The president was authorized to exclude the offending product from the American market.[52]

Protection from Fair Trade

In the 1940s and 1950s, Congress moved to assure U.S. industry that any threats posed by the increased trade resulting from the RTAA agreements would be minimal. Two mechanisms were created to do this: the **escape clause** and the **peril point.** The escape clause allows any party to withdraw from or modify an agreement if a domestic producer is harmed by the changes in trade resulting from the accord. For example, if an agreement with another country leads to an increase in bicycle imports, the United States can use the escape clause to give bicycle manufacturers a chance to adjust to the foreign competition.

After its introduction in 1942 in a RTAA deal with Mexico, the escape clause was often used to appease Congress by promising that injured industries would receive special consideration. When the RTAA was renewed in 1945, President Truman promised that all future trade agreements would have an escape clause, and he signed an executive order to that effect in February 1947. When Congress renewed the president's authority to negotiate under the RTAA in 1951, it wrote the escape clause into law for the first time. In addition, the United States insisted in 1947 that an escape clause be included as Article XIX of the GATT. Thus the escape clause has a basis in both U.S. and international law.[53]

Because the escape clause is part of the GATT, its application must conform to the principles of nondiscrimination and reciprocity. Nondiscrimination means that escape clause protection cannot be directed at some GATT contractors but not others. Any trade barriers erected under the escape clause must apply to all trading partners. Under reciprocity, when the escape clause is invoked to protect an industry from a previously offered American trade concession, then other parties to the agreement can withdraw concessions they made. And the concessions that others withdraw need not be related to the product the United States is protecting. Thus, if the United States decides to invoke the escape clause to shield its bicycle market worth $5 million from imports, then other GATT parties can withdraw previously offered concessions equal to their share of the $5 million U.S. market they have lost. For example, if the French estimate they could have exported $1 million in bicycles to the United States, then France can withdraw a promise to reduce trade barriers on $1 million in American machine tool exports. Other GATT contractors can take similar action. The escape clause, then, must be applied with care, because an attempt to help one American industry may damage others.

The process for handling escape clause cases differs from the procedures for unfair trade cases in that petitioners must meet a different standard of proof and presidential discretion is allowed. The 1951 law called for the process to begin with a petition to the Tariff Commission for an investigation. The request for an inquiry could come from an affected business, the president, the House Ways and Means Committee, the Senate Finance Committee, or it could be self-initiated by the Tariff Commission. During the investigation, the Tariff Commission's job was to determine whether the American industry was harmed by an increase in imports stemming from an American trade agreement. The standard set in 1951 was that the harm from imports had to be "not less than any other cause" of whatever trouble the industry might face—that is, if an industry was experiencing problems for several reasons, imports had to be at least as responsible as any other cause for the industry's woes. If the Tariff Commission felt this standard was met, it could recommend a protective remedy. This recommendation then went to the president, who could accept it, reject it, or modify it, depending on how he viewed national interests. If the president did not accept the Tariff Commission's recommendation, Congress could override the decision with a joint resolution. When granted, escape clause protection had a five-year limit, with a possible three-year extension.[54]

As noted earlier, a key difference between unfair trade protection and the escape clause related to the role of the president, who had the authority to overrule Tariff Commission recommendations. To a large degree, the president was granted this power because a decision to allow escape clause protection could lead to the withdrawal of trading concessions by America's trading partners. In other words, the attempt to help one American industry might cost another American industry an export market. It was essential, then, that the president act as custodian of the national interest by determining which was the lesser of the two evils— the harm to the import-sensitive industry or the harm that might befall the exporting industry. Tariff Commission investigations did not touch on the question of balancing the needs of different industries; it was charged solely with determining whether the petitioning industry was harmed and what the source of the harm was. Although Congress had the authority to overrule presidential decisions to change Tariff Commission recommendations, it never did so under any version of the law.[55] This reluctance reflected a congressional aversion to disputing the president's assessment of the national interest.

The peril point, another protective device devised by Congress after World War II, first became law in the 1948 renewal of the president's RTAA negotiating authority. Under the law, the Tariff Commission established the minimum tariff level (or peril point) below which American producers would be harmed by imports. The procedure began with the president publishing a list of goods for which tariff reductions might be negotiated. The Tariff Commission then investigated to determine peril points for those goods. If the president disagreed with the peril points, he was required to report his disagreement to the House Ways and Means Committee and the Senate Finance Committee.[56]

The peril point had a bumpy history. Introduced in 1948 by a Republican Congress, it was cancelled in 1949 when the Democrats regained control of Congress and then resurrected in 1951. It remained in effect into the 1960s, when it was repealed once and for all. Throughout its existence, the peril point was a nuisance to trade negotiators but did little to slow the move to freer trade, in part because Congress was reluctant to challenge presidents when they disagreed with Tariff Commission findings about peril points.[57]

THE COLD WAR AND FREER TRADE

In the late 1940s, Americans favoring freer trade began to offer Cold War arguments to further their cause. The idealism that tied trade to international peace and prosperity and that was used so deftly to promote the Bretton Woods System gave way to views of trade as a key to Western solidarity in the face of communism. Liberals depicted trade as vital to the economic growth needed for stable democracies and a proper national defense and to the postwar recovery of Western Europe and Japan. Within the executive branch, these arguments favoring freer trade were bipartisan; they were made first by the Truman administration and then by Eisenhower when he became president.

Congress was another story, however, because old-line Republican protectionism lingered in both the House and Senate. The interest in protection was spurred by the effects of previous market-opening moves made under the RTAA program and during GATT negotiations. As American trade barriers fell, some special interests experienced problems and demanded that Congress halt or reverse moves toward freer trade. When combined with the Republican attachment to protection, these special-interest pressures turned every RTAA renewal into a battle and forced the Eisenhower administration to appoint a special commission on trade policy and to urge foreign producers to limit their exports to head off moves by Congress to restrict trade.

Trade and National Security

Early signs of the end of the idealism of the mid-1940s linking trade to peace and prosperity were the strained debate over the International Trade Organization and the discussion of the Marshall Plan. As described earlier, attempts to convince Congress to accept American ITO membership by tying it to peace and prosperity fell on deaf ears. In fact, by 1948 such arguments often were associated with communist propaganda.[58] Under these conditions, advocates of liberal trade began depicting trade as a weapon against communism. The presentation of the Marshall Plan to Congress reflected this shift, for even though the State Department saw the plan as a vehicle for promoting open trade, the House and Senate heard State describe American assistance to Europe as a device for preventing the spread of communism. In the end, such anticommunist arguments did not save the ITO, but they worked admirably to secure passage of the Marshall Plan.

Two reports prepared for President Truman in 1950 and 1951 described the role American foreign economic policy could play in containing communism. The first, written by Special Assistant to the President Gordon Gray, noted that stable democracies were essential to stopping communism, that sound economics was vital both to the creation of such governments and to their ability to defend themselves, and that an American-sponsored system of open trade and foreign investments and loans would help fill any economic gaps left by programs such as the Marshall Plan. The second report, written by Nelson Rockefeller of the International Development Advisory Board, made the case for the establishment of trade and investment programs for developing countries, which might be susceptible to communism. Moreover, developing countries often were sources of key raw materials and markets for American, European, and Japanese industrial goods. Some of these poor countries were located in strategically important areas, such as the Middle East, which further emphasized the need for American interest.[59]

As a candidate and as president, Eisenhower favored freer trade and agreed that trade was important in the struggle against communism. In fact, one reason Eisenhower ran for president was his belief that the leading Republican contender for the presidential nomination, Sen. Robert Taft of Ohio, was insufficiently internationalist and did not appreciate either the need for Western solidarity or the role trade could play in building cooperation among the democracies.[60] Writing before he became president, Eisenhower stated that "the democracies must learn that the world is now too small for the rigid concepts of national sovereignty that developed in a time when nations were self-sufficient . . . [and that] none of them today can stand alone."[61] For Eisenhower, either nations could work together against communism and trade with one another to build a common base of strength, or they could run the risk of being destroyed one by one by those seeking world domination. Eisenhower took seriously Stalin's prediction of October 1952 that trade disputes among countries would give the Soviet Union opportunities to strike blows for world communism, and he was determined to prevent such problems.[62]

The new president also wished to use trade as an alternative to the Marshall Plan, because many conservatives saw foreign aid as an American giveaway.[63] Eisenhower realized that American, European, and Japanese prosperity were intertwined. The Europeans and Japanese needed to export to earn the dollars to pay for their imports, and Americans could only sell to foreigners if they were willing to buy from foreigners. As Eisenhower noted in his memoirs, in the 1950s the United States was exporting 25 percent of its tobacco, wheat, cotton, and rice and more than 10 percent of its trucks, machinery, diesel engines, oil drilling equipment, printing presses, tractors, and machine tools. Many American businesses relied on exports for their profits and to create jobs, and the only way to maintain this export momentum was to open American markets.[64] Indeed, as *Business Week* reported in late 1952, "President-elect Eisenhower is . . . committed to trying to strengthen the free world through a policy of trade, not aid." [65]

When he assumed office, Eisenhower quickly encouraged Congress to follow his lead on trade. In his inaugural address and his State of the Union message in 1953, he called for the United States to work with its trading partners to open markets around the world. As the leader of the free world, Eisenhower argued the United States had the duty to take the first step, which meant extending and expanding the president's authority under the RTAA program.[66] This being said, Eisenhower recognized there were limits to the pursuit of free trade and that national security required protection for industries that were essential to American defense. As he later said, "To go full out in the direction of free trade . . . the world would need permanent peace." [67] Still, he felt the United States could afford to reduce its trade barriers, and he wanted Congress to cooperate in doing so.

The Congress that considered Eisenhower's trade requests in 1953 was controlled by Republicans, many of whom did not agree with the president about freer trade and preferred protection. For them, trade reform reflected a Democratic agenda that did not deserve Republican support, even if the request for RTAA renewal came from a popular Republican president. On top of this, by 1953 Congress was receiving mounting complaints from businesses that felt pressured by foreign competition and wanted protection. The result was a degree of congressional recalcitrance that frustrated Eisenhower and provoked him to write in his diary in July 1953 of the

> short-sightedness bordering upon tragic stupidity of many who fancy themselves to
> be the greatest believers in and supporters of capitalism . . . but who blindly support
> [protectionist] measures and conditions that cannot fail in the long run to destroy
> any free economic system. . . . Unless the free world espouses and sustains under the
> leadership of America a system of world trade that will allow backward people to
> make a decent living . . . then in the long run we must fall prey to the Communist
> attack.[68]

The Randall Commission and Renewing Reciprocal Trade

In 1953, Eisenhower's top priority for trade was renewal of the RTAA, which was due to expire in June. On April 15, he asked Congress for a three-year extension. His request, however, ran into immediate trouble because the protectionists chairing the House Ways and Means Committee and the Senate Finance Committee moved slowly on the president's proposal. On top of this, Republican Richard Simpson of Pennsylvania introduced a bill calling for import quotas, higher tariffs on selected items, and elimination of the president's discretion in dealing with Tariff Commission findings. The Simpson bill received wide support, and Eisenhower was forced to spend a substantial amount of effort to ensure its defeat.[69]

Because of the maneuvering over the Simpson bill, Congress did not begin hearings on the RTAA until late May. When it became apparent that a three-year extension would not pass, Eisenhower accepted a compromise one-year renewal. At the same time, Congress gave the president the authority to establish the Randall Commission to study American trade policy (see the earlier description of this commission in this chapter).[70]

In appointing the Randall Commission, Eisenhower hoped to co-opt opponents of freer trade by including protectionists such as Eugene Millikin of Colorado, chairman of the Senate Finance Committee, and House members Daniel Reed of New York and Richard Simpson. Eisenhower and the commission chairman, Clarence Randall, believed that by naming these Republican protectionists to the commission and by giving them the facts about American trade and why foreign producers needed access to American markets, they would prompt a change of heart. To promote this change, Randall compromised with the protectionists by convincing the commission to favor the peril point, altering the escape clause to assist import-sensitive producers, and promoting a three-year RTAA renewal instead of the ten-year extension Eisenhower wanted.[71]

In the end, though, the attempt to sway protectionists on the commission was in vain. Millikin, Reed, and Simpson chafed at Randall's style of leadership and wasted little time blasting the commission's report when it was released in January 1954.[72] For his part, Eisenhower accepted the commission's findings and sent a message to Congress in March calling for a three-year RTAA extension and the authority to cut tariffs an additional 15 percent. The president also asked Randall to stay on as his special assistant for foreign trade.[73]

Even with the combined weight of a popular president and a bipartisan trade commission behind it, the proposal for RTAA renewal ran into trouble in Congress. Most Republicans feared special-interest reprisals in the fall elections if they agreed to a three-year RTAA extension. Eisenhower was again pressed to accept a one-year renewal. Commission member Reed, sensing that he held the upper hand, asked Eisenhower to promise that if a one-year renewal was granted he would not actually use his authority to negotiate trade agreements. Eisenhower refused, stating that the communist challenge was too serious to forgo trade bargains that might prevent countries from being overwhelmed by communism. The president noted that he was particularly concerned about Asia, where Japan was vulnerable because of the loss of export markets stemming from the communist revolution in China. Indeed, Eisenhower wrote that American trade policy could "dictate whether these areas remain in the free world or fall within the Communist orbit."[74]

The reference to the communist threat convinced Reed to do an about-face. He told the House in June:

> We know the conditions in the world today. . . . We know the situation in Japan. We know . . . the Communists are working to the best of their ability among these people. We need Japan on our side in this troubled world, and we are not going to gain their support by starving them to death. We have to do at least this much [extend RTAA] for them, at least give them a chance to be heard through trade negotiations. I am not willing . . . to take the responsibility . . . of killing this [renewal] and shutting the door to such negotiations.[75]

Simpson also was won over by the comments about communism, informing the House that "because of the plea made today by the Administration . . . namely that we can, by making an agreement between now and next year effectively prevent the spread of war in Asia, possibly making permanent the peace which we now enjoy, I am unwilling . . . to stand in the way of . . . trade agreements [that] will prevent war."[76]

On June 11, the house passed a one-year RTAA renewal, 281–53. The Senate did the same on June 24 by a 71–3 vote.[77]

Trouble with Textiles

The 1954 midterm elections put the Democrats back in control of both the House and Senate. In the House, the new Democratic Speaker, Sam Rayburn of Texas, made it clear that trade would be his number one priority. Because President Eisenhower shared the belief that trade should be handled expeditiously, everything seemed on track for quick RTAA renewal. Congressional hearings on the subject began in mid-January 1955.

The expected smooth sailing did not materialize, however, because of pressure from the textile lobby, which was upset by rapidly expanding Japanese textile sales in the United States. Even though cotton textile imports had only a 2 percent share of the American market in 1955, the pace at which sales were growing alarmed textile manufacturing associations and unions, who informed the

State Department that they were concerned about talks with Japan to reduce textile tariffs.[78]

While it was expressing its anxiety over trade negotiations, the textile lobby also was organizing a letter-writing campaign that flooded the White House and Congress with messages opposing tariff reductions on textiles.[79] In the State Department, however, Far Eastern specialists regarded an economically strong and democratic Japan as vital to containing communism in Asia and argued that because textile exports were important to Japan the United States had to lower tariffs.[80] The decision was made, therefore, to go ahead with the negotiations.

With the continuation of trade talks with Japan, RTAA renewal became a struggle. In addition to protesting Japanese textile imports, the textile lobby argued that it was adversely affected by the government's sale of surplus American cotton in foreign markets at cut-rate prices. As lobbyists pointed out, foreign producers could buy American cotton at low prices and then sell cheap cotton goods in the United States. In effect, the lobbyists argued, the U.S. government was hurting its own textile industry. Under these conditions, the government owed the industry protection and a halt to pursuing trade agreements that affected American textile manufacturers.[81]

The textile producers' opposition to RTAA renewal and their demand for help made the fight for an extension difficult. In fact, matters became so touchy that Speaker Rayburn was forced to take to the floor of the House to make a personal appeal for support of the RTAA program. After a series of close tactical votes, the House finally renewed the RTAA on February 18 by a 295–110 margin.[82]

When the bill moved to the Senate, the debate was just as tough. Senators added amendments that would make escape clause protection easier to obtain by allowing it to apply to specific products instead of an entire industry and that would allow the president to set quotas on imports to safeguard American national security. Instead of fighting the opponents of renewal, Eisenhower accepted the Senate version of the bill, which passed on May 15, 1955. The new law extended the RTAA for three years and permitted the president to cut tariffs an additional 15 percent from their January 1955 levels.[83]

But RTAA renewal did not stop the fracas over textiles. In June, the State Department announced a decision to cut duties on thirty textile items by 20–48 percent. In response, textile manufacturers demanded that Congress set quotas on imports.[84] The pressure became so severe that Secretary of State John Foster Dulles felt compelled to write Republican senator Margaret Chase Smith of Maine to argue that "import quotas on Japanese textiles would be most unfortunate . . . [because] it would serve to restrict trade at a time when the free world must depend for so much of its strength on the expansion of trade and the economic viability of countries such as Japan."[85] This plea and the promise of a textile voluntary export restraint agreement with Japan was sufficient to head off congressional action.

But setting up the textile VER proved to be no easy task. First, Dulles and Eisenhower had to push the Japanese to take action, pointing out that unless they "volunteered" to limit their exports, Congress was likely to set quotas. Next, they had to assuage an American textile industry that was reluctant to accept a VER instead of legislated quotas. Finally, in December a two-year VER was ironed out to limit Japanese textile exports to the United States. When this agreement did not placate textile representatives, who filed three escape clause petitions in 1956 despite the VER, American trade negotiators arranged in 1957 for a complex five-year VER on cotton products that set a limit on total imports and sublimits on specific types of imports. In addition, when it passed the Agricultural Act of 1956 Congress empowered the president to negotiate further trade restraints to protect textiles.[86]

Other trade battles for the Eisenhower administration included the attempt to convince Congress to allow the United States to join the Organization for Trade Cooperation (OTC) and the 1958 renewal of the RTAA. The OTC was designed to replace the GATT and to offer the additional benefits of enforcement mechanisms and conflict resolution capabilities. Eisenhower sent a proposal requesting American membership in OTC to Congress in April 1955 only to have it draw immediate flak from protectionists. In light of the controversy, the OTC proposal was shelved.[87]

The 1958 RTAA renewal produced yet another fight with congressional protectionists. By 1957, Eisenhower was tired of the bickering that went with RTAA extensions. He therefore asked Congress for a five-year renewal that would permit him to cut tariffs an additional 25 percent. He wrapped the request in Cold War rhetoric, warning of dire consequences if his proposal was rejected. The Cold War approach had worked in the 1954 and 1955 battles over RTAA, but by 1957 the arguments were wearing thin, a point Speaker Rayburn made in a conversation with the president. Beyond this, a recession hit the American economy in 1958, creating further resistance in Congress to imports.

In spite of the obstacles, Rayburn was able to give the president most of what he wanted. When the House passed the renewal bill in June 1958, it included a minor amendment allowing Congress to reverse presidential escape clause decisions by a two-thirds vote in each House. The Senate added additional protectionist amendments to the bill and reduced the extension from five years to three and the tariff-cutting authority from 25 percent to 15 percent. The conference committee deleted most of the Senate additions and split the difference for the renewal period and tariff-cutting power, giving Eisenhower four years and 20 percent. Thus when the president signed the bill in August, he closed the book on his RTAA renewal fights with Congress.[88]

CHAPTER SUMMARY

The period from the mid-1940s to the late 1950s saw a transformation in American foreign policy in general and trade policy in particular. In foreign policy the United States abandoned its isolationist past to assume leadership of the free world and to shoulder the responsibility of containing communism. In confronting the communist challenge, the United States faced a task that had at least two vital economic components.

The first component was the need to assist the Europeans and the Japanese as they recovered from the Second World War. This need was basically addressed in two ways: targeting aid through the Marshall Plan aid and lowering trade barriers. While both approaches were controversial, especially among Republicans, Truman and Eisenhower were able to convince Congress to support them. One key to lowering trade barriers was the use of new forms of protection: the escape clause, safeguards against unfair trade, and voluntary export restraint agreements to provide security for such politically potent industries as textiles. An important feature of these new kinds of protection was that they were recipient-initiated and required that a case be made before the Tariff Commission (at least for unfair trade and the escape clause). This new protection differed significantly from the protection of the past which was based on congressional passage of all-encompassing tariff bills.

The second economic component of containment was organizing a system to guarantee that militarily-sensitive goods were not sold to the Soviet Union and its communist satellites. Such a system required cooperation with Western Europe and Japan, which were reluctant to agree to the stringent controls the United States wished to enforce. Further complicating the situation were the frequent congressional demands for tighter trade controls and punishment of any American ally that refused to cooperate in denying goods to the communists. First Truman and then Eisenhower handled congressional pressures by assuring that body that the best control system possible was being employed and by using their power to exempt countries from congressionally mandated reprisals. At the same time, the United States and its allies established the secretive Coordinating Committee for Multilateral Export Controls, or CoCom, to encourage and monitor cooperation on trade limitations. An interesting side effect of the maintenance of east-west trade restrictions was the request by America's allies that they be given more access to American markets to compensate them for the loss of markets in the eastern bloc.

Thus the onset of the Cold War provided the occasion for the United States to assume a visible role as an international leader. But as a leader, America was forced to backtrack from its protectionist past and to move steadily toward freer trade. In shepherding this process along, presidents had to handle congressional and special-interest trade anxieties carefully, which they did in part by setting up a new rule-based system for safeguarding American producers from excessive imports.

NOTES

1. Harry S. Truman, *Years of Trial and Hope* (New York: Doubleday, 1956), 106.

2. Dean Acheson, *Present at the Creation: My Years in the State Department* (New York: Norton, 1969), 226; and Gregory A. Fossedal, *Our Finest Hour: Will Clayton, the Marshall Plan, and the Triumph of Democracy* (Stanford: Hoover Institution Press, 1993), 216–218.

3. Fossedal, *Our Finest Hour*, 219; and Joan Edelman Spero and Jeffrey A. Hart, *The Politics of International Economic Relations* (New York: St. Martin's Press, 1997), 11.

4. Michael J. Hogan, "European Integration and the Marshall Plan," in *The Marshall Plan: A Retrospective*, ed. Stanley Hoffman and Charles Maier (Boulder: Westview Press, 1984), 2.

5. Acheson, *Present at the Creation*, 228; Hogan, "European Integration," 3; and Truman, *Years of Trial*, 111–112.

6. Acheson, *Present at the Creation*, 229–230.

7. Ibid., 233.

8. Ibid., 232.

9. Fossedal, *Our Finest Hour*, 213.

10. Truman, *Years of Trial*, 109.

11. Fossedal, *Our Finest Hour*, 240; and Hogan, "European Integration," 3–4.

12. Acheson, *Present at the Creation*, 234; and Truman, *Years of Trial*, 115–116. The nations at the Paris meeting were Austria, Belgium, Denmark, France, Greece, Iceland, Ireland, Italy, Luxembourg, the Netherlands, Norway, Portugal, Sweden, Switzerland, Turkey, and the United Kingdom. Czechoslovakia expressed an interest in attending but was dissuaded from doing so by the Soviet Union.

13. Robert A. Pastor, *Congress and the Politics of U.S. Foreign Economic Policy, 1929–1976* (Berkeley: University of California Press, 1980), 211–212.

14. Philip J. Funigiello, *American-Soviet Trade in the Cold War* (Chapel Hill: University of North Carolina Press, 1988), 27–28.

15. Michael Mastanduno, "Trade as a Strategic Weapon: American and Alliance Export Control Policy in the Early Postwar Period," *International Organization* 42 (winter 1988): 125.

16. John Lewis Gaddis, *The United States and the Origins of the Cold War, 1941–1947* (New York: Columbia University Press, 1972), 216.

17. Michael Mastanduno, *Economic Containment: CoCom and the Politics of East-West Trade* (Ithaca: Cornell University Press, 1992), 67.

18. Gaddis, *United States,* 217–220.

19. Ibid., 189–194, 216–217, 222–224, 260–261; and Funigiello, *American-Soviet Trade,* 18–19.

20. Mastanduno, *Economic Containment,* 13; and "Trade as a Strategic Weapon," 125–226.

21. Funigiello, *American-Soviet Trade,* 29.

22. Mastanduno, *Economic Containment,* 13.

23. Funigiello, *American-Soviet Trade,* 33–34.

24. Ibid., 32.

25. Mastanduno, *Economic Containment,* 69–70.

26. Mastanduno, "Trade as a Strategic Weapon," 128.

27. Mastanduno, *Economic Containment,* 76.

28. Ibid., 4.

29. Ibid., 6, 19.

30. Mastanduno, "Trade as a Strategic Weapon," 129.

31. Funigiello, *American-Soviet Trade,* 50–51, 73–74.

32. Ibid., 53.

33. Ibid., 55–59; and Mastanduno, "Trade as a Strategic Weapon," 139.

34. Funigiello, *American-Soviet Trade,* 66–69; and Burton I. Kaufman, *Trade and Aid: Eisenhower's Foreign Economic Policy, 1953–1961* (Baltimore: Johns Hopkins University Press, 1982), 60.

35. Funigiello, *American-Soviet Trade,* 54.

36. Ibid., 59–60, 76–77.

37. Ibid., 80–81; and Kaufman, *Trade and Aid,* 22.

38. Quoted in Mastanduno, "Trade as a Strategic Weapon," 142.

39. Kaufman, *Trade and Aid,* 62.

40. Ibid., 60–61.

41. Ibid., 62.

42. Funigiello, *American-Soviet Trade,* 114.

43. Fossedal, *Our Finest Hour,* 224–225, 237–238.

44. I. M. Destler, *American Trade Politics* (Washington, D.C.: Institute for International Economics, 1995), 17–18.

45. Stephen D. Cohen, Joel R. Paul, and Robert A. Blecker, *Fundamentals of U.S. Foreign Trade Policy: Economics, Politics, Laws, and Issues* (Boulder: Westview Press, 1996), 12.

46. Judith Goldstein, *Ideas, Interests, and American Trade Policy* (Ithaca: Cornell University Press, 1993), 198; Pastor, *Congress,* 172; and Carolyn Rhodes, *Reciprocity, U.S. Trade Policy, and the GATT Regime* (Ithaca: Cornell University Press, 1993), 43–44.

47. Judith Goldstein, "Ideas, Institutions, and American Trade Policy," *International Organization* 42 (winter 1988): 199–200; and Goldstein, *Ideas, Interests,* 198–199.

48. Cohen, Paul, and Blecker, *Fundamentals of U.S. Foreign Trade Policy,* 149; and Anne O. Krueger, *American Trade Policy: A Tragedy in the Making* (Washington, D.C.: AEI Press, 1995), 36.

49. Krueger, *American Trade Policy,* 41; and Pastor, *Congress,* 172.

50. Patrick Low, *Trading Free: The GATT and U.S. Trade Policy* (New York: Twentieth Century Fund Press, 1993), 260.

51. Goldstein, "Ideas, Institutions," 202–203; and Goldstein, *Ideas, Interests,* 203–205.

52. Cohen, Paul, and Blecker, *Fundamentals of U.S. Foreign Trade Policy,* 151; Goldstein, *Ideas, Interests,* 205–206; and Low, *Trading Free,* 261.

53. John H. Jackson, *The World Trading System: Law and Policy of International Economic Relations* (Cambridge: MIT Press, 1997), chap. 7.

54. Goldstein, "Ideas, Institutions," 190–191; and Goldstein, *Ideas, Interests,* 187–189.

55. Goldstein, *Ideas, Interests,* 189.

56. Stefanie Ann Lenway, *The Politics of U.S. International Trade: Protection, Expansion, and Escape* (Boston: Pitman Publishing, 1985), 78.

57. Kaufman, *Trade and Aid,* 3; Lenway, *Politics of U.S. International Trade,* 78; and Pastor, *Congress,* 100–101.

58. Susan A. Aaronson, *Trade and the American Dream: A Social History of Postwar Trade Policy* (Lexington: University Press of Kentucky, 1996), 115–116.

59. Kaufman, *Trade and Aid,* 5.

60. Ibid., 12–13.

61. Dwight D. Eisenhower, *Crusade in Europe* (Garden City, N.Y.: Doubleday, 1949), 477.

62. Dwight D. Eisenhower, *Mandate for Change, 1953–1956* (Garden City, N.Y.: Doubleday, 1963), 208.

63. Raymond A. Bauer, Ithiel de Sola Pool, and Lewis Anthony Dexter, *American Business and Public Policy: The Politics of Foreign Trade* (New York: Atherton Press, 1964), 29.

64. Eisenhower, *Mandate for Change,* 208.

65. Bauer, Pool, and Dexter, *American Business,* 29.

66. Kaufman, *Trade and Aid,* 14–15.

67. Eisenhower, *Mandate for Change,* 209.

68. Quoted in Kaufman, *Trade and Aid,* 15.

69. Bauer, Pool, and Dexter, *American Business,* 31–33; and Eisenhower, *Mandate for Change,* 209, 211.

70. Bauer, Pool, and Dexter, *American Business,* 53; Eisenhower, *Mandate for Change,* 209, 211; Kaufman, *Trade and Aid,* 18–19; and Pastor, *Congress,* 102.

71. Bauer, Pool and Dexter, *American Business,* 42, 45, 48; and Kaufman, *Trade and Aid,* 20–21.

72. Bauer, Pool, and Dexter, *American Business,* 45–46; and Kaufman, *Trade and Aid,* 21.

73. Bauer, Pool, and Dexter, *American Business,* 49; Eisenhower, *Mandate for Change,* 292–293; and Kaufman, *Trade and Aid,* 24.

74. Quoted in Kaufman, *Trade and Aid*, 40. Also see Bauer, Pool, and Dexter, *American Business*, 54.

75. Quoted in Bauer, Pool, and Dexter, *American Business*, 54–55.

76. Ibid., 55.

77. Ibid., 55, 58.

78. I. M. Destler, Haruhiro Fukui, and Hideo Sato, *The Textile Wrangle: Conflict in Japanese-American Relations, 1969–1971* (Ithaca: Cornell University Press, 1979), 29–30; and H. Richard Friman, *Patchwork Protectionism: Textile Trade Policy in the United States, Japan, and West Germany* (Ithaca: Cornell University Press, 1990), 93. Destler, Fukui, and Sato note that Japan saw its U.S. sales of cotton cloth skyrocket from 10 million square yards in 1952 to 140 million square yards in 1955. As for finished goods, in 1952 Japan sold no ladies blouses, but by 1955 it was selling 48 million.

79. Bauer, Pool, and Dexter, *American Business*, 60.

80. Destler, Fukui, and Sato, *Textile Wrangle*, 25; Kaufman, *Trade and Aid*, 40; and Friman, *Patchwork Protectionism*, 91.

81. Lenway, *Politics of U.S. International Trade*, 101.

82. Bauer, Pool, and Dexter, *American Business*, 63–66.

83. Ibid., 71–72; Kaufman, *Trade and Aid*, 42–43; and Pastor, *Congress*, 102–103. Previously the escape clause had applied only to an entire category of production, such as the textile industry. The 1955 change allowed one segment of an industry to seek protection. For example, if towel makers were hurt, they could ask that the escape clause be invoked.

84. Friman, *Patchwork Protectionism*, 96; and Lenway, *Politics of U.S. International Trade*, 42.

85. Destler, Fukui, and Sato, *Textile Wrangle*, 28.

86. Ibid., 30; Friman, *Patchwork Protectionism*, 96–99; and Lenway, *Politics of U.S. International Trade*, 102–103.

87. Kaufman, *Trade and Aid*, 43–44.

88. Ibid., 119–128.

6 The Kennedy and Tokyo Rounds of the GATT

In terms of the popular vote, the 1960 presidential election was among the closest in American history; Sen. John F. Kennedy of Massachusetts defeated Vice President Richard Nixon by about 100,000 votes out of the nearly 70 million cast. Kennedy's victory over the standard bearer for a popular presidential administration stemmed in part from the public's uneasy feeling that the international environment no longer favored the United States. Picking up on this mood, Kennedy stressed throughout the campaign that the United States was stagnant and had nearly lost the momentum that had brought the country unrivaled prosperity and world stature.

Several political, military, and economic trends were responsible for the malaise that Kennedy detected. Strategically, the United States faced dangerous new communist challenges. In 1957, the Soviet Union announced that it had developed the world's first intercontinental ballistic missile, able to deliver nuclear weapons to virtually all parts of the globe. Communism also was on the march in the developing world. In Southeast Asia, communist forces threatened the governments of Laos and South Vietnam, and the chaos in the former Belgian Congolese colony seemed to be a made-to-order opportunity for the extension of Soviet influence into central Africa. There also was the problem of Cuba, where the 1959 revolution produced a communist regime just ninety miles from the Florida Keys. When coupled with aggressive Soviet diplomacy and the impressive performance of the Soviet economy, which boasted a 7 percent overall growth rate and a 10 percent growth rate in industry, these developments left many Americans feeling that the world situation was ominous.[1]

In the commercial realm, by 1960 American businesses and workers were feeling the pressure of competition from their European and Japanese counterparts. The situation in Europe was especially worrisome. In 1957, six countries—Belgium, France, Italy, Luxembourg, the Netherlands, and West Germany—had signed the Treaty of Rome, which created a common market, the European Economic Community (EEC). To Americans, the EEC appeared to be a potential economic powerhouse that might threaten American access to lucrative European markets. After only three years, the EEC was already posting some outstanding results when compared with those of the United States. During the year before the 1960 election, the American economy grew by only 2 percent and posted alarming declines in trade, with imports falling by 0.9 percent and exports by 0.4 percent. The same figures for the EEC were far better, with overall growth increasing by 5.4 percent, imports by 6.7 percent, and exports by 6.4 percent.[2]

When he took office, Kennedy believed that trade could do a lot to solve these problems. Among other things, it could contribute to economic growth in less-fortunate countries, thereby reducing the poverty that made communism attractive. Trade also could strengthen the Western alliance in its effort to contain communism and could promote the economic expansion needed for a better way of life among the democracies. In addition, Kennedy believed that if the United States used the General Agreement on Tariffs and Trade effectively, it could guarantee ever-expanding access to the EEC and other markets around the world.

In treating trade policy as integral to the strategic environment and to the containment of communism, Kennedy was continuing the approach employed by both Truman and Eisenhower. But his use of GATT negotiations to tackle the commercial challenges of the EEC represented a policy departure. The general thrust of GATT negotiations from 1948 until 1961 was built on the item-by-item and country-by-country tariff-cutting procedure found in the American RTAA legislation. As the Kennedy team saw things, future GATT negotiations should include more extensive tariff cuts than those favored previously and should be used to develop new trade rules to handle the other problems bedeviling international commerce. In this way, GATT bargaining could be used to create an evolving trade climate that could solve problems as they arose and forestall demands for protection. Instead of focusing on shielding producers from foreign competition, the GATT-based approach would concentrate on creating new export opportunities for all GATT members. This goal required placing trade barriers on the international bargaining table as they were identified and hammering out rules to eliminate those obstacles.

The Kennedy administration hoped that use of the GATT to expand trade would involve more businesses in trade and entice them to support policies to expand international commerce. In turn, politicians would find it increasingly difficult to follow the protectionist credo, because local businesses and workers would develop an ever-greater reliance on trade for profits and wages. Moreover, old-style protectionism would be undermined by the argument that any problems protectionists might have should be added to the GATT negotiating agenda, where an effort would be made to find a solution without resorting to protectionist legislation.

The emphasis on the GATT had important implications for the institutions conducting American trade policy, including the presidency; in view of the growing complexity of GATT bargaining, the president had to request enhanced negotiating authority. In considering such requests, Congress introduced two important innovations into the policy-making process. First, it stripped the State Department of its authority over trade negotiations and lodged that responsibility in a new agency created specifically for that task. Second, it set up a new set of procedures that would allow Congress to review the GATT deals put together by the executive branch. In each case, Congress designed the change as a means of retaining control over trade policy without undermining the president's ability to work within the GATT framework to get new trade deals.

The GATT negotiating strategy was only part of the solution to the protectionist pressures that multiplied during the 1960s and 1970s as producers in Europe, Japan, and other parts of the world used GATT market-opening deals to expand their exports to the United States. The evolving American approach to trade also called for targeting aid to politically powerful, import-sensitive industries that might have the clout to slow or halt the march toward freer trade. Such grants of assistance were designed to convince members of Congress that efforts were being made to safeguard local producers. Thus American policy was built on a hard-headed sense of political reality, and the judicious application of protection became a vital part of the liberals' pursuit of open trade.

This chapter examines the issues and events surrounding American trade policy during the GATT negotiations of the 1960s and 1970s. It describes the objectives driving the United States during these bargaining sessions, the legislation passed to permit the president to participate in the talks, and the legal innovations Congress created so it could retain a central voice in policy making without too greatly restricting the president's ability to negotiate.

THE KENNEDY ROUND OF THE GATT

After its creation in 1947, the General Agreement on Tariffs and Trade served as a forum for negotiations to lower tariffs and provided rules to regulate trade among its contracting parties. Because tariff negotiations followed the item-by-item and country-by-country approach found in American RTAA laws, GATT bargaining was lengthy, with participants presenting and fielding offers for lowering tariffs on specific products. And because GATT bargaining required reciprocity, all discussions of tariff cuts involved constant calculations and recalculations to ensure that all parties received equal concessions. Further complicating matters were the legal restrictions under which the country with the most trade, the United States, had to negotiate. These restrictions included those on the percentage by which American tariffs could be cut and the "peril points" indicating the lowest tariffs possible on specific items.

All in all, the GATT negotiating process was a trying experience, and its complexity forced negotiators to focus almost exclusively on tariffs. The back and forth nature of the bargaining, with offers constantly circulating among the parties, prompted participants to refer to GATT negotiations as "rounds." By 1962, five rounds of GATT had been held. The first round, held in Geneva in 1947, established the GATT. Later rounds were held in Annecy, France, in 1949; Torquay, United Kingdom, in 1950–1951; Geneva in 1956; and again in Geneva in 1960–1962. The 1960–1962 round was labeled the Dillon Round in honor of the American undersecretary of state for economic affairs, Douglas Dillon, who played a prominent role in the talks.

The Issues

By the time Kennedy became president a host of trade problems was crowding his agenda, many of which were related to the EEC. For one thing, intra-EEC trade was growing faster than American trade, a fact that many Americans resented because they felt the European boom was a product of past trade concessions by the United States. The Europeans also enjoyed a balance-of-payments surplus with the United States; American military spending abroad, foreign aid, and foreign investments were combining with the American appetite for imports to produce an outflow of dollars and gold. Indeed, $4.7 billion in gold was drained from American coffers from 1958 to 1960, while during the same period members of the EEC increased their gold holdings by $6.5 billion. To the new president, it was clear that unless something was done quickly the U.S. dollar would suffer severely and the Bretton Woods fixed exchange rate system would be imperiled because the ready availability of dollars abroad would cause the currency to lose value. As Kennedy observed shortly after taking office, the key to avoiding these problems was increasing American exports to pull some of these excess dollars back into the United States as foreigners paid for their purchases. Higher U.S. exports, however, depended on other countries, especially in Europe, lowering their tariffs.[3]

Although it was easy to see that lower tariffs would help solve many American problems, the actual practice of knocking down tariff barriers was proving difficult in 1961. The Dillon Round of GATT negotiations ran into trouble because of U.S.-EEC technical disputes over the calculation of new EEC tariffs and over the use of the item-by-item approach to tariff reductions. The tariff reduction disagreement was particularly frustrating, because, even though American negotiators sympathized with the EEC view, they were forced by law to use the RTAA item-by-item approach.[4]

Other American concerns in 1961 were Great Britain's application to join the EEC and the negotiations within the EEC to set up a **Common Agricultural Policy (CAP)**. As Kennedy explained to British prime minister Harold Macmillan during an April 1961 meeting, the United States supported the elimination of intra-European trade barriers and the expansion of the EEC, but the growth in intra-European trade appeared to be at the expense of American exports.[5] Administration officials worried that the result would be unemployment and more balance-of-payments problems for the United States. Kennedy expressed these concerns at a press conference when he said, "One third of our trade . . . is in Western Europe, and if the United States should be denied that market we will either find a flight of capital from this country to construct factories within that wall, or we will find ourselves in serious economic trouble."[6] Lowering EEC barriers to American exports was the best way to solve these problems, but, as the Dillon Round negotiations revealed, a new bargaining approach was needed to induce European cooperation.

In the area of agriculture, the United States was apprehensive about the EEC's Common Agricultural Policy and how it might affect American farm exports to Europe. In 1961, the EEC was still in the process of setting up the CAP, but its outline was taking shape. The objectives of the CAP were to guarantee farm income, to raise agricultural productivity and provide food security for the EEC, and to maintain reasonable prices for consumers.[7] To this end, the CAP included farm subsidies and a **variable levy** on imports. The variable levy would tax agricultural imports on a sliding scale to ensure that imports would cost more than comparable goods produced by EEC farmers. When world agricultural prices were low, the tax would be higher to push import prices above EEC prices. When world prices were high, the tax would be lower, because a lower tax would be sufficient to protect EEC producers. Subsidy payments also were included in the CAP to save less-efficient EEC farmers from bankruptcy.

For American trade officials and farm interest groups, the implementation of the CAP promised nothing but trouble. As early as May 1961, Kennedy raised the issue when EEC commission president Walter Hallstein visited Washington. American negotiators also fought to convince their EEC counterparts to modify the CAP, especially the variable levy, during the Dillon Round. But neither effort produced tangible results. When the CAP finally went into effect in mid-1962, it sparked a trade clash known as the Chicken War.

The Chicken War began when the imposition of the variable levy cut American frozen chicken exports to the EEC by two-thirds within a few weeks. This outcome infuriated American agricultural experts and upset several influential members of Congress from Arkansas, a major poultry-producing state. Among the latter were the chairman of the House Ways and Means Committee, Wilbur Mills, and the chairman of the Senate Foreign Relations Committee, J. William Fulbright. Working with the Agriculture Department and a fellow Democrat, President Kennedy, Mills and Fulbright pressed for American retaliation. Threats and counterthreats followed, until the United States and the EEC agreed to allow the GATT to arbitrate a solution in the fall of 1963.[8] In the meantime, the conflict illustrated the need for new GATT negotiations to handle the issues emerging from the formation of the EEC.

The Trade Expansion Act of 1962

By the fall of 1961, Kennedy had decided to press for a new round of GATT negotiations to handle unresolved questions from the Dillon Round. George Ball, undersecretary of state for economic affairs, recommended asking Congress for a bill outlining a more flexible bargaining approach than the one provided under the RTAA. Ball felt the item-by-item method should be discarded in favor of an across-the-board approach allowing tariff cuts of up to 50 percent. In addition, Ball urged Kennedy to ask for the power to eliminate tariffs of 5 percent or less, to do away with tariffs on products for which the United States and the EEC combined controlled 80 percent or more of world trade, and to abolish tariffs on tropical goods. He also proposed that the president seek funds to set up a system of **trade adjustment assistance** that would compensate industries and workers adversely affected by lower trade barriers.[9]

These proposals were meant to allow the president to match any tariff cuts the Europeans might offer. In requesting the across-the-board tariff-cutting authority Congress had refused to give past presidents, the Kennedy administration played on the fear that American exporters would be closed out of the European market. The argument used to justify the request was that only hard bargaining would pull down European tariff walls and therefore it was no time for Congress to skimp on the tools American negotiators needed to tackle the job. Kennedy seized on Britain's application for EEC membership to emphasize the enormity of the challenge posed by the EEC. After all, with Britain's entry the EEC might soon surpass the American market in size and strength. It was essential, then, that the United States begin immediately to secure its trading position in the new Europe.[10]

Another feature of the bill Kennedy and Ball sought from Congress was language encouraging the EEC to look favorably on British membership. This notion was found in the provision to eliminate tariffs if the United States and EEC together controlled 80 percent of world trade in a good. As the administration realized, unless the British joined the EEC few goods would qualify under this standard for abolishing duties. Although many in the administration were worried about the potential clout of an enlarged EEC, many also believed that Britain's entry, if properly managed, could help pull Europe together to resist communism.[11]

When the trade bill was presented to Congress, Kennedy went all out to secure passage. He called on influential public figures to support the bill, including Eisenhower's former secretary of state Christian Herter and Truman's former undersecretary of state for economic affairs Will Clayton. AFL-CIO president George Meany, who was strongly anticommunist, also endorsed the bill when Kennedy stressed the role trade could play in containing communism, and former presidents Truman and Eisenhower were persuaded to support the legislation as a vehicle for expanding U.S.-EEC trade and cooperation.[12]

The trade bill also was featured in Kennedy's State of the Union address on January 11, 1962. Continuing the theme that trade was essential for prosperity, the containment of communism, and harmony within the Western alliance, the president asserted that the proposed legislation "could well affect the unity of the West, the course of the Cold War, and the growth of our nation for a generation or more to come."[13]

Speeches and the support of prominent political figures would not amount to much, however, if Congress did not believe that the authority requested in the new bill would be used to drive hard bargains to benefit the United States. Accordingly, as Congress considered the trade bill in 1962, Kennedy took steps to enhance his credibility as tough on trade. For example, in early 1962 Undersecretary of State Ball was told to negotiate a follow-up to the **Short-Term Arrangement (STA)** that limited cotton textile imports from October 1961 to September 1962. The result was a February agreement known as the **Long-Term Arrangement (LTA)**. The LTA was an **orderly marketing arrangement (OMA)** among thirty nations. In an OMA, importers and exporters of a particular product agree to allocate specific shares of importers' markets to each exporter of the product. The LTA covered sixty types of cotton textiles.

Under the LTA, the quotas set allowed each exporter a specific share of each importing market. Exporters that refused to negotiate a quota were at risk of having them imposed by importers. Provisions were made for a minimum growth rate of 5 percent per year in the size of the quotas. The LTA was to last for five years, through 1967.[14] American cotton manufacturers found the LTA so satisfactory that they endorsed Kennedy's trade bill at a convention in April 1962.[15] Thus the march to secure passage of a bill to promote open trade detoured first down a protectionist path to buy off a politically powerful industry.

Another credibility-building move came in March when Kennedy upheld a Tariff Commission escape clause recommendation calling for increased tariffs on wool carpets and glass products. Members of Congress applauded the move, but the EEC vehemently denounced the decision because it affected Belgium, which exported several of the products covered by Kennedy's action. The EEC's angry response further strengthened Kennedy's stature as a hard bargainer.[16]

The president's public relations and credibility-enhancing moves paid off when Congress considered his trade bill. Although opposition was expressed by protectionist groups, by the conservative magazine *New Republic,* which argued that the EEC would refuse to lower its tariffs, and by the Liberty Lobby, which opposed trade adjustment assistance as socialism, most of the witnesses appearing before Congress supported the bill.[17] The most vocal resistance to the bill emerged from the House Ways and Means Committee, whose members complained about the State Department's handling of trade negotiations. They found the department too secretive, too unresponsive to domestic interests, and too prone to using trade concessions for bargaining chips when pursuing other foreign policy goals. Indeed, generally Congress felt that the authority the administration sought should be granted only if some other agency conducted the negotiations.[18]

Finding an alternative to the State Department was not easy, however, because the Ways and Means Committee objected to other cabinet departments as well. In the end, committee chairman Wilbur Mills proposed the creation of a new position in the Executive Office of the President—a **special trade representative (STR),** who would have the rank of ambassador and would be appointed by the president with the consent of the Senate. This official would run American trade negotiations, head an interagency committee to advise the president, and look after the needs of American producers.[19]

The idea for a special trade representative quickly caught on in Congress, but it was coolly received in the executive branch. The State Department protested the loss of its authority to conduct trade negotiations; meanwhile, the Commerce Department argued that control should be transferred there. When the Ways and Means Committee stood firm, Kennedy acquiesced, selecting Christian Herter for the STR job. As a moderate Republican and former secretary of state and member of Congress, Herter was popular with Congress and acceptable to the State Department. Herter also strongly supported open trade and believed that the United States should take a tough stance toward the EEC.[20]

With an agreement on the special trade representative in hand, the House approved Kennedy's trade bill in June by a 298–125 vote. The Senate also passed the bill in September, 78–8.[21]

The **Trade Expansion Act of 1962** was the first American legislation to authorize U.S. participation in GATT negotiations. The law also created an important new actor in the policy-making process, the special trade representative; set up the trade adjustment assistance program for those harmed by imports; and permitted negotiations to cut tariffs on an across-the-board basis. Armed with this legal authority, Kennedy called for new GATT negotiations.

The Negotiations

The move toward new GATT negotiations came in November 1962 when the United States and Canada proposed holding exploratory talks for a new round. Because other parties to the GATT were amenable, a meeting was scheduled for May 1963.[22]

Meanwhile, Western Europe, the United States, and many other parties to GATT reacted with shock when on January 14, 1963, President Charles DeGaulle of France vetoed Great Britain's entry into the EEC. DeGaulle explained that he felt the British were not committed to a united Europe. Many in the United States and Britain suspected that DeGaulle also was jealous of the special relationship between the United States and Britain and that he believed Britain's entry into the EEC would lead to American meddling in European affairs.

Whatever the reason for DeGaulle's veto, many in the Kennedy administration and in Congress worried about the effect it might have on the new GATT round, or the Kennedy Round as it was called. For one thing, the provision of the 1962 law allowing for the elimination of tariffs when the United States and the EEC controlled 80 percent of world trade was now moot because without Britain as an EEC member few goods would qualify. Another problem centered on agriculture; the United States had hoped Britain might help move the talks along. The United States also was concerned about the trade preferences the EEC had accorded over a dozen former colonies in Africa. This EEC preference system reminded American trade specialists of the British Imperial Preference System they had tried to dismantle years earlier, and they had hoped Britain's entry into the EEC would facilitate negotiations to do away with both systems. Thus DeGaulle's veto of British membership complicated several issues the United States hoped to handle in the new GATT round.[23]

When the GATT parties convened in May 1963, two problems emerged immediately. The first involved the technical rules that would guide the negotiations. One of the most hotly contested of these disputes pertained to tariff cuts. Although an across-the-board system was in order, the United States and EEC differed over how to calculate the reductions. The Europeans favored a system that would focus on lowering extremely high duties. Prompted by Congress, American delegates rejected this notion and called instead for all parties to lower rates

Provisions of the Trade Expansion Act of 1962

Tariffs

- The president may negotiate for five years to lower tariffs by up to 50 percent on an across-the-board basis.
- The president may eliminate tariffs of 5 percent or less if the European Economic Community does the same.
- The president may abolish tariffs if the United States and the EEC control 80 percent of world trade for a good.
- The president may increase tariffs on fish from countries refusing to practice conservation.

Trade Adjustment Assistance

- A program of trade adjustment assistance is to be created to aid those injured by trade.

Special Trade Representative

- The president is to create by executive order the new position of special trade representative.

Escape Clause

- The test for invoking the escape clause is to be changed so that trade is the major cause (that is, more important than any other cause) of injury to an industry applying for protection. (The old standard was that trade had to be at least equal to any other cause of injury to the petitioner.) Congress is to have the authority to override by a majority vote presidential escape clause decisions. (Previously, a two-thirds vote was required.)

Most-Favored-Nation Status

- The president may not grant most-favored-nation status to communist countries.

Unfair Trade and National Security Concerns

- The president may retaliate against unfair trade in the agricultural sector and restrict imports for national security reasons.

Sources: I. M. Destler, *American Trade Politics* (Washington, D.C.: Institute for International Politics, 1995), 12; Edward S. Kaplan, *American Trade Policy, 1923–1995* (Westport, Conn.: Greenwood Press, 1996), 65–75; Stefanie Ann Lenway, *Politics of U.S. International Trade: Protection, Expansion, and Escape* (Boston: Pitman Publishing, 1985), 79–82; and Patrick Low, *Trading Free: The GATT and U.S. Trade Policy* (New York: Twentieth Century Fund Press, 1993), 54–55.

by the same amounts. Additional technical conflicts arose over the rules for conducting the discussions on agriculture, the procedures for participation by developing countries, and the negotiations over quotas. These technical disputes delayed the start of substantive discussions by nearly two years.[24]

The second problem had to do with decision-making procedures in the EEC, which participated in the negotiations as a single unit. Internal bickering plagued the EEC as member countries fought over negotiating priorities. And just as the impasses over technical rules were ironed out, an argument over EEC funding for farm supports prompted the French to walk out of the EEC's main decision-making body, the Council of Ministers. This dispute was not resolved until early 1966, when President DeGaulle again stunned countries on both sides of the Atlantic and slowed the GATT negotiations by withdrawing French military forces from the NATO unified command structure.[25]

In the substantive GATT discussions, which continued even in the face of all these distractions, several issues stood out. The first was agriculture; the United States joined Australia, Canada, and New Zealand in seeking elimination of the variable levy and the subsidies that were the heart of the EEC's Common Agricultural Policy. The American position on farm trade had changed substantially in the years since the GATT was created in 1947–1948. Then, the farm crisis of the interwar years was still fresh in Americans' minds, and the New Deal agricultural support programs made American negotiators reluctant to push for open trade in that sector. But by the early 1960s, American farm exports were growing rapidly, and farmers were anxious to use the GATT to eliminate trade barriers such as those associated with the CAP.

From the European point of view, the CAP guaranteed a vocal group of constituents, farmers, a chance to compete in world trade. Without the CAP, many European farmers would be hard-pressed to compete with more efficient producers in other parts of the world. Because few EEC leaders wished to face the political troubles posed by farm bankruptcies, the CAP was not negotiable, and the agricultural talks foundered. The U.S. special trade representative, Christian Herter, offered to discuss American agricultural support programs if other delegations would do the same. The EEC, joined by Britain and Japan, both of whom had noncompetitive agricultural sectors, demurred.[26]

By the fall of 1964, Herter and his deputy, William Roth, were arguing for a tougher stance toward the EEC. The Agriculture Department agreed with this position, but the State Department dissented, saying that a get-tough approach would produce no concessions and might damage Western unity. Taking these views into account, McGeorge Bundy, President Lyndon B. Johnson's special assistant for national security affairs, convinced Herter to put agricultural negotiations on the back burner.[27] Thus selected agricultural duties were cut by an average of 20 percent, but items covered by the variable levy, such as grain, flour, rice, poultry, and eggs, were left untouched.[28] The first of what became a multi-round event between the United States and the EEC over the CAP clearly was won by the EEC.

Another issue on the Kennedy Round agenda was the **nontariff barriers (NTBs)** to trade. Nontariff barriers are the administrative, safety, health, and other regulations that are used to obstruct trade in the absence of tariffs. For example, American negotiators complained about European road taxes that discriminated against the larger cars produced in the United States. These taxes often were so high that they hurt American auto exports even though the auto tariffs of the countries in question were relatively low.

Although it was easy to point to the evils of nontariff barriers, American negotiators found it tough to do anything about them. For one thing, they were difficult to define. For another, the Europeans, Japanese, and others pointed to a host of American NTBs that they wished to eliminate before they would respond to American grievances. Because American delegates did not have the legal authority to do away with American NTBs, the GATT parties contented themselves with noting that NTBs should be the subject of future negotiations.[29]

Two other prominent issues during the negotiations were textile tariffs and the American Selling Price. The United States offered to cut textile tariffs by 50 percent, the full amount allowed under the 1962 law, but only if the Long-Term Arrangement was extended beyond its 1967 expiration date. This position eventually prevailed, but the reductions in duties averaged less than 50 percent because the EEC preferred a smaller mutual cut.[30]

The controversy over the American Selling Price posed a special problem for the United States. The ASP was first introduced in the Fordney-McCumber Tariff of 1922 (see Chapter 3). It called for calculating the duties on certain imports, primarily chemicals, based on what it would cost American producers to make the product. Because most such products cost less to make abroad, the ASP provided extra protection for American firms. Foreigners, especially the EEC, found the ASP outrageous and demanded that the United States terminate it. American negotiators, however, did not have the legal authority to touch the ASP. In the end, a two-track approach was devised—along the first track ran the tariff cuts for chemicals if the ASP stayed in place; along the second ran the steeper reductions that would go into effect if the ASP was eliminated. Doing away with the ASP required an act of Congress, which was unlikely given the mood in that legislative body.[31]

After a flurry of last-minute negotiations, the Kennedy Round ended in June 1967. Overall, it reduced tariffs on approximately $40 billion in trade by an average of 35 percent. This result helped to ensure that the United States would have the continuing access to European markets that it had sought from the negotiations. The talks had little effect, however, on two key issues the United States had hoped to address, agricultural trade and nontariff barriers. These issues would have to await another GATT round.[32]

The Reaction

The response in the United States to the Kennedy Round was less than enthusiastic. It had been promoted as a means of safeguarding the prominent American position in international commerce. For many critics, if this was the purpose of the GATT talks, then they were a failure. In the year after the negotiations ended, both the EEC and Japan enjoyed economic and export growth rates that exceeded those of the United States. In the EEC, economic growth moved forward at a 5.6 percent clip, and exports surged ahead by 12.4 percent. Japan had even more impressive figures, with economic growth increasing by 13.4 percent and exports by 22.3 percent. Although the American figures of 5 percent for economic growth and 8.5 percent for exports were respectable, they left many with the feeling that the United States had concluded a trade deal that benefited foreigners more than Americans.[33] And making matters even worse, in 1968 the U.S. balance of trade (exports minus imports) fell to its lowest post–World War II level, totaling only $1.4 billion, compared with $4.7 billion in 1967 and figures that had routinely surpassed $5 billion in the years before that.[34]

For Republicans, these economic results were evidence of the wrong-headed Democratic approach that treated trade as an adjunct to other aspects of foreign policy and sacrificed American workers and corporations to keep America's allies happy. In the 1964 election, held in the midst of the Kennedy Round, the Republican presidential candidate, Sen. Barry Goldwater of Arizona, had argued that the GATT negotiations were a giveaway to America's trading partners that did little to contain communism. Goldwater urged that the United States threaten to close American markets unless others opened their markets to American exports.[35]

Even though Goldwater was routed in the 1964 election by incumbent president Lyndon Johnson, Republicans continued their attacks on the Kennedy Round. In late 1966, as the GATT talks approached their climax, Sen. Everett Dirksen, the Republican minority leader from Illinois, repeated Goldwater's themes and added some of his own in a speech in New York, stating that "the United States appears intent upon concluding an agreement which will not repair the damage to our farmers [done by the EEC's CAP], while inflicting new damage upon our manufacturing. . . . It looks very much as though we are offering to give them [other GATT parties] our shirt in exchange for a handkerchief."[36]

In Congress, concern focused on agriculture, the American Selling Price, and nontariff barriers. The outcome in agriculture angered members because the EEC had held firmly to the CAP, and the two-track deal for the ASP and the reduction in tariff rates for chemicals was attacked vigorously by the American chemical industry.[37] In addition, the failure of GATT negotiators to do anything about nontariff barriers left many observers with the feeling that America's trading partners were outfoxing it by replacing tariffs with imaginative new trade restrictions. Rep. Thomas Curtis, R-Mo., expressed this sentiment when he observed that "as tariffs have been dismantled . . . quotas, licenses, embargoes, and other . . . trade barriers have been created."[38]

The anger over the supposedly inequitable results from the Kennedy Round led many in Congress to propose various bills restricting trade. Even though none of these bills passed, they did prompt Sen. Russell Long, D-La., chairman of the Senate Finance Committee, to hold hearings in the fall of 1967 to investigate foreign and American trade practices.[39]

In the spring of 1968, President Johnson sent a bill to Congress that eliminated the ASP and requested additional tariff-cutting authority. When the House Ways and Means Committee chairman, Wilbur Mills, held hearings on the bill, things went poorly. Witness after witness complained that American trade concessions had gone too far, and spokespersons for the steel, oil, shoe, and textile industries called for quotas on imports. Organized labor, which had been supporting open trade, was now lukewarm and worried about foreign challenges to U.S. producers.[40] In the end, the bill did not pass, the ASP remained law, and the Kennedy Round deals that depended on the repeal of the ASP fell through.[41]

As the 1968 election approached, trade was a sore point for many in the United States. Some interest groups and members of Congress felt it was time to reconsider the market-opening approach that had dominated trade policy since the RTAA first passed in 1934. Among those favoring freer trade there was concern that three decades of accomplishments might be reversed.

THE TOKYO ROUND

During the 1968 campaign, the Republican presidential candidate, Richard Nixon, picked up on several of the trade themes that had become commonplace in American politics. In campaign swings through the Carolinas, which were home to numerous textile firms, he argued it was time to expand the Long-Term Arrangement to add woolens and synthetics to the cotton goods already covered by the agreement. When visiting Ohio and Pennsylvania, states with large steel industries, Nixon emphasized the need for trade deals to help steel, and in farm states he advocated promoting agricultural exports. In other words, Nixon tailored his trade message to his audience.[42] Nixon eventually won the election, defeating Vice President Hubert Humphrey, the Democratic candidate.

Nixon's Trade Decisions

President Nixon's early trade decisions were inconsistent. First, he appointed an advocate of open trade, Carl Gilbert, former chairman of the board of Gillette, as his special trade representative. When appearing before the House Ways and Means Committee, Gilbert maintained that freer trade benefited American firms because "the lively influence of . . . foreign competition on the U.S. marketplace is an essential source of discipline on . . . [the] practices of U.S. industry and labor."[43] The nod to **liberalism** represented by the selection of Gilbert, however, was counteracted by Nixon's reliance on his secretary of commerce, Maurice Stans, for trade advice and by his decision to consider incorporating the Office of the Special Trade Representative into the Commerce Department. But opposition from the State Department, the Treasury Department, several interest groups, and Ways and Means chairman Wilbur Mills finally convinced Nixon to shelve this notion.[44]

Nixon also moved to secure his political flanks from the demands of protectionists. In November 1969, he sent Congress a bill that he said would fulfill American Kennedy Round promises and would update U.S. trade law to assist American producers in handling the challenges of the 1970s. Accordingly, the bill sought repeal of the American Selling Price and presidential authority to negotiate over tariffs and nontariff barriers. In addition, Nixon requested the authority to raise tariffs when countries refused to open their markets to American exports, called for relaxing the rules for the escape clause and trade adjustment assistance, and offered to defer taxes on exports.[45] The requested changes in the escape clause and trade adjustment assistance were in response to complaints that the standards in the Trade Expansion Act of 1962 were impossible to meet (during the 1960s no petition for either form of assistance received a favorable response from the Tariff Commission).[46]

Congress was not receptive to Nixon's bill. The provisions relating to the escape clause and trade adjustment assistance did find support, but there was no interest in doing away with the ASP or negotiating new tariff cuts. Instead of Nixon's bill, Congress passed the Trade Act of 1970 to set quotas on textiles and footwear and to ease escape clause rules. Nixon considered the bill protectionist, but was spared the need for a veto when Congress adjourned before a conference committee reconciled the House and Senate versions of the bill.[47]

But these events hardly ended the demands for protection because the trade picture seemed to worsen every month. In the spring of 1969, the Commerce

Department predicted that the United States was heading for its first trade deficit since 1936. On top of this, the EEC's CAP was a major irritant for American farmers. Japan also was beginning to run up a considerable trade surplus with the United States, a development that made many in Congress question Japanese import quotas that limited American sales.[48]

Congress responded to these trade irritants with a flurry of protectionist bills to help specific industries. Most of these bills had no chance of passage, but they allowed members of Congress to appear supportive to constituents hurt by imports. One of the most radical of these bills was proposed in September 1971 by Rep. James Burke, D-Mass., and Sen. Vance Hartke, D-Ind. The Burke-Hartke bill called for quotas on imports, increased tariffs, relaxed standards for the escape clause and trade adjustment assistance, limits on American corporate foreign investments in the belief that such investments cost the United States jobs, and the creation of a Foreign Trade and Investment Commission to regulate America's international commerce.[49] This bill never passed, but it was a sign of how serious the trade situation had become. Particularly troubling was the strong support Burke-Hartke received from the labor movement, which was beginning to worry that imports might cost union members their jobs.

In response to these protectionist pressures, Nixon decided to negotiate selected import restraints. As usual, textiles were slated for help. The industry's political clout was stronger than ever, in part because it hired disproportionately large numbers of minorities and women. In a country wracked by racial tensions and the scene of a women's movement that was emerging as a political force, the representation of women and minorities in the textile workforce made it doubly important to attend to the industry's needs.[50]

To help textile producers, Nixon sent Commerce Secretary Stans and Special Trade Representative Gilbert to Europe to work out a system for controlling the textile trade. But they had no success. The same was true of a similar effort in Asia a few months later. But these failures did not deter Nixon; in the fall of 1969 he enlisted his special assistant for national security affairs, Henry Kissinger, to seek a deal with Japan to limit woolens and synthetics. Yet try as he might, Kissinger could not reach a bargain with the Japanese. As the months passed, American impatience grew until Nixon finally announced in August 1971 that mandatory quotas would be imposed if the Japanese and other Asian producers did not limit their exports. At that announcement, Japan, Korea, Hong Kong, and Taiwan accepted American demands.[51]

The Nixon administration was not finished with textiles, however. Its ultimate goal was a comprehensive agreement that would cover the textile trade among virtually all countries that bought or sold such products. It finally reached this goal when the **Multi-Fiber Arrangement (MFA)** was set up under GATT auspices in 1973, taking effect in 1974. The MFA set quotas for nearly all countries, most of them developing, that exported textiles. The quotas, which were set on a product-by-product basis, were allowed to increase by 6 percent a year. A Textile Surveillance Board made up of representatives of both importing and exporting nations was created to oversee the MFA. In the years after its creation, the MFA was renewed five times and new types of textile products were continually brought under its umbrella.[52]

The protectionist measures for textiles were only part of the Nixon administration's "get tough" policy for trade. Nixon played another card in August 1971 when he effectively suspended U.S. participation in the Bretton Woods fixed exchange rate system. This move, which surprised people at home and abroad, stemmed from America's balance-of-payments problems. As noted earlier, the Kennedy Round was undertaken in part to knock down trade barriers and therefore increase U.S. exports to ease American balance-of-payments problems. By 1969, instead of easing, these problems were worse. Expenditures for U.S. military bases in Europe and Asia and for the Vietnam War combined with American foreign investment, spending abroad by private citizens, and a balance of trade that turned negative in 1971 to make it ever more difficult to maintain the dollar at the Bretton Woods value of $35 per ounce of gold.

Almost from the moment they took office, Nixon's economic advisers grappled to control the flow of dollars abroad. They considered the possibility of suspending the convertibility of the dollar into gold, but they set it aside in favor of negotiations with the leading participants in the Bretton Woods System. As time passed, it became clear that negotiations were not panning out. By early 1971, several of Nixon's advisers, foremost among them Treasury Secretary John Connally, were urging a tougher approach, arguing that European and Japanese currencies should be revalued upward against the dollar, that American allies should pay more of the cost of foreign military bases, and that trade barriers should be eliminated to increase American exports. Some in Congress concurred with Connally and called for revaluing the dollar.[53]

On August 15, 1971, after meeting with his advisers at the Maryland presidential retreat, Camp David, Nixon announced his **New Economic Policy (NEP).** The new policy included a wage and price freeze to reduce inflation, a suspension of the convertibility of the dollar into gold, and a 10 percent surcharge on imports. The package was designed in part to force other countries to revalue their currencies.[54]

Once they digested the announcement, several countries responded. Denmark imposed an import tax, and the French government said it was considering a similar move. In Geneva, American GATT representatives had to confront the charge that American moves undermined the GATT and the Western alliance.[55]

Finally, cooler heads prevailed, and a December 1971 conference at the Smithsonian Institution in Washington patched together a deal to devalue the dollar by 10 percent. The NEP's import surcharge was then lifted. The **Smithsonian Agreement** proved ephemeral, however, because in early 1973 speculative pressures forced another 10 percent devaluation of the dollar and finally led to a decision to allow the world's major currencies to float, which meant that market forces would set their exchange rate values.[56]

Thus Nixon's tougher stance toward international trade and finance led to two major developments that greatly changed the commercial structure of the world. The first was the system of textile quotas in the Multi-Fiber Arrangement. The second was a revamping of the Bretton Woods System, moving it from fixed exchange rates to the floating system that prevails even today. Nixon's moves also paved the way for a new GATT round.

The Trade Act of 1974

Movement toward a new GATT round began almost as soon as the Kennedy Round ended. Several forces pushed in this direction. One was unresolved issues such as nontariff barriers and agricultural trade. Another was the need to defuse protectionist pressures from Congress. There also was concern among many trade specialists that orderly marketing arrangements, such as the Multi-Fiber Arrangement, would become so commonplace that they would disrupt international trade. To deflect these forces, liberals hoped to use a new GATT round to open foreign markets and to eliminate the undesirable foreign trade practices that so angered American special interests and Congress.

As a prelude to a trade campaign, Nixon appointed a Commission on International Trade and Investment Policy in 1970. The commission was given the task of examining the challenges confronting the United States in international commerce and drawing up recommendations for the president. Eventually, the commission reported that the United States faced new international competition, that this competition would lead to new calls for protection, and that many of the difficulties confronting the United States were due to the reluctance of Europe and Japan to open their markets to American products. The commission then argued for a new round of GATT negotiations to cut tariffs and address nontariff barriers.[57]

By early 1973, most parties to the GATT were amenable to a new round of negotiations, and the Nixon administration confronted the task of securing congressional authorization to participate. To this end, Nixon sent a bill to Congress in April. The bill was designed both to please key members of Congress and to provide the president with greater flexibility in handling international political

Provisions of the Trade Act of 1974

Tariff Negotiations

- The president may engage in a new round of GATT talks under fast-track procedures.
- The president may cut post–Kennedy Round tariffs by 60 percent.
- The president may offer special tariff concessions to developing countries.

Escape Clause, Unfair Trade Practices

- The escape clause may be invoked for any trade-related problem, instead of merely for problems stemming from trade agreements. The standard for relief: trade must be equal to any other cause of an industry's distress. (Section 201)
- American producers may seek relief from: discriminatory rules of origin, discriminatory licensing, discriminatory currency exchange controls, restrictive business practices, inappropriate border tax adjustments, and discriminatory product standards. (Section 301)
- Rules pertaining to dumping are eased to facilitate findings favoring American firms.
- The president may negotiate to eliminate nontariff barriers to trade.

Trade Adjustment Assistance

- Rules for trade adjustment assistance are eased, communities are permitted to apply, and Labor and Commerce Departments are authorized to handle future investigations.

International Trade Commission

- Tariff Commission is renamed International Trade Commission.

Special Trade Representative

- The special trade representative will have cabinet rank. The office is to be established by law, instead of by executive order, as it was previously.

Communist Countries

- The president is permitted to confer most-favored-nation status on communist countries if they allow their citizens to emigrate. (Jackson-Vanik Amendment)
- Act outlines rules for relief from imports from nonmarket (communist) countries. (Section 406)

Sources: See Steve Dryden, *Trade Warriors: USTR and the American Crusade for Free Trade* (New York: Oxford University Press, 1995), 181; Edward S. Kaplan, *American Trade Policy, 1923–1995* (Westport, Conn.: Greenwood Press, 1996), 97–98; Stefanie Ann Lenway, *The Politics of U.S. International Trade: Protection, Expansion, and Escape* (Boston: Pitman Publishing, 1985), 82–85; Patrick Low, *Trading Free: The GATT and U.S. Trade Policy* (New York: Twentieth Century Fund Press, 1993), 55–58; and Carolyn Rhodes, *Reciprocity, U.S. Trade Policy, and the GATT Regime* (Ithaca: Cornell University Press, 1993), 122–123.

and commercial policy. Among other things, the bill gave the president the authority to reduce tariffs and eliminate nontariff barriers, to restrict imports from countries that engaged in unfair trade, to set special low tariff rates on imports from developing countries, and to grant most-favored-nation status to communist countries.[58] It also changed the standards for the escape clause and trade adjustment assistance.

Several of Nixon's requests were controversial. One debate centered on the elimination of nontariff barriers. Presidents had been permitted to negotiate tariff reductions since 1934, but bargaining over nontariff barriers was another matter altogether. Most NTBs were written into laws Congress had passed over the course of several decades. Allowing the president to negotiate NTBs in effect granted him the power to change laws by proclamation if American negotiators received comparable benefits from other countries. Even though Nixon proposed a congressional review of any deal on NTBs, members of the Senate Finance Committee led by Herman Talmadge, D-Ga., were not comfortable with the president's suggestions.

After negotiations between the Office of the Special Trade Representative and the Senate Finance Committee, an alternative emerged. Although the arrangement was called a **fast-track** procedure, it was anything but fast.[59] Under fast-track, the president would conduct negotiations without a prior congressional guarantee that the results would be put into effect, as had been the case under the RTAA program and in the Kennedy Round. Meanwhile, the special trade representative would keep the House Ways and Means and Senate Finance Committees fully informed of progress in the negotiations. When the special trade representative felt the negotiations were nearing completion, he would give Congress ninety days' notice. Once the final trade deal was presented to Congress, it would vote within sixty days under rules that prohibited amendments. By forbidding amendments, designers of the fast-track procedure sought to prevent special interests from trying to alter the trade deal so it would no longer conform to the promises made to the other parties in the negotiations. This process would give Congress a voice and America's negotiating partners could still be sure they would get a relatively quick answer about congressional approval.[60] Fast-track became so convenient that it is now the standard procedure used by the United States in trade negotiations.

Somewhat less controversial than the new powers proposed for the presidency were the proposed changes in the escape clause and trade adjustment assistance. Nixon called for relaxing the standard in the Trade Expansion Act of 1962, under which trade had to be the most important cause for an industry's woes before relief could be granted. Nixon proposed that relief be provided if trade was equal in importance to any of the other economic problems (that is, a recession, changes in consumer preferences, natural disasters, and so on) that an industry might face. This proposal was greeted warmly in Congress, although several of Nixon's advisers, most notably Treasury Secretary George Shultz, argued that trade adjustment assistance should be incorporated into the many other forms of aid already available to distressed workers and industries. Shultz felt it inappropriate to single out those hurt by trade for special assistance. Nixon rejected Shultz's position because of the popularity of trade adjustment assistance among members of Congress.[61]

A controversy did arise, however, over Nixon's call for lower American tariffs on goods from developing countries. Within the GATT system, the most-favored-nation principle required that all parties be granted the same tariff rates—in other words, it was forbidden to grant some GATT parties lower tariffs than others. During the Kennedy Round, advanced countries agreed to make an exception to MFN for developing countries so they would have greater access to the advanced country markets. At that time, President Johnson pledged the United States would cooperate in this effort, as did Nixon when he became president. In 1972, the EEC began implementing tariff preferences for poorer countries, and the Nixon administration incorporated the idea into its trade bill. Certain limitations, however, were placed on the preferences. These included the suspension of preferences when imports from a country reached 50 percent of total American imports for a particular product or exceeded $25 million in value. In addition, preferences were denied to developing countries that discriminated against American exports or American corporations.[62]

In Congress, the discussion of preferences for developing countries, known as the **generalized system of preferences (GSP),** focused on whether low tariffs would harm American producers and induce some American corporations to close shop in the United States and move production to lower-wage developing countries, where goods would be made and sent back to the United States for sale. If this happened, the result would be lost jobs for American workers.

Probably the bitterest controversy surrounding Nixon's trade bill was the request for authority to grant most-favored-nation status to communist countries. Nixon regarded expanded trade with eastern bloc countries as a cornerstone of his new foreign policy of détente, designed to ease Cold War tensions. Nixon believed that a reduction in U.S.-Soviet hostilities would pave the way for negotiations that would allow him to extract American troops from Vietnam and to get a handle on a defense budget that was nearly out of control.

To achieve détente, however, Nixon needed to offer the Soviet Union some incentives for cooperation. One such incentive was trade. By 1970, it was clear that the Soviet economy was performing poorly and that many basic consumer goods were scarce. Trade with the United States was one way the Soviets could make up these shortages. Nixon believed that economic ties would benefit both east and west, the communists would receive the goods they badly needed, and the Western democracies would find new outlets for their merchandise. In addition, through more trade the West might be able to introduce liberal values into the communist world, which might eventually bring a degree of democratic reform. And trade also could be used as a stick; if the Soviets engaged in unacceptable foreign policy actions, they could be threatened with loss of the trade, and therefore the goods, they needed.

Nixon's interest in granting most-favored-nation status to communist countries ran counter to two previous acts of Congress denying the president the power to take such action. These were the Trade Agreements Extension Act of 1951 and the Trade Expansion Act of 1962. Although by 1973 many members of Congress wished to relax Cold War tensions, many still believed that MFN was a privilege the Soviets should pay for with political concessions. Those concessions were proposed by Sen. Henry Jackson, D-Wash., and Rep. Charles Vanik, D-Ohio, in an amendment to the trade bill. The amendment tied most-favored-nation trade status to the Soviets' willingness to allow Jews and others who wished to emigrate from the Soviet Union to do so.

The **Jackson-Vanik Amendment** gained widespread support in both houses of Congress. Nixon realized that offering MFN under such conditions would offend the Soviets and attempted to have the provision dropped from the bill altogether, but to no avail.[63] What followed was a year-long tug-of-war between the White House and Congress. In the end, the Jackson-Vanik Amendment was part of the trade bill Congress finally passed in December 1974. As Nixon had predicted, with Jackson-Vanik in place the Soviets refused to negotiate over MFN.[64]

In its final form, the **Trade Act of 1974** reflected Congress's tendency to use trade bills to take care of as many trade issues as possible. The law's most prominent features included the fast-track approach to trade negotiations, the easing of escape clause procedures (**Section 201**), the generalized system of preferences for developing countries, the conferral of cabinet rank on the special trade representative, new standards for handling unfair trade (**Section 301**), and a new name for the Tariff Commission, which became the **International Trade Commission** (**ITC**). These provisions updated American trade law and provided the legal foundation for participation in new GATT negotiations.

The Tokyo Round

On September 12, 1973, a new round of GATT trade negotiations began in Tokyo, a site chosen because several parties to the GATT wished to emphasize the importance of Japan in international commerce. Even though most of the negotiations for this round were eventually held in Geneva, they were known as the Tokyo Round.

Because the Toyko Round began before Congress passed the Trade Act of 1974, U.S. delegates sat in on the talks for over a year before they had the legal authority to make deals. In the end, the absence of legal authority for the American team had little effect on the negotiations, which bogged down over technical disputes for months at a time. In fact, the nearly six-year Tokyo Round, which spanned three presidential administrations (Nixon, Ford, and Carter), was far longer than any previous GATT round.

The Tokyo Round revolved around four key issues: (1) reducing tariffs, (2) developing rules for trade in agriculture, (3) putting together a generalized system of preferences for developing countries, and (4) eliminating nontariff barriers. Another issue (and conflict) that emerged early was whether the EEC owed the United States trade concessions as a result of Britain's entry into the EEC in early 1973. After considerable posturing by American and European negotiators, the EEC put the issue to rest by reducing its duties on citrus products, tobacco, and construction equipment to balance the trade the United States claimed it was losing because of Britain's new EEC membership.[65]

Like in the Kennedy Round, the discussion of tariff cuts succumbed to arguments over the formulas to use when calculating reductions. The Europeans pushed for a system that would cut higher tariffs more than lower tariffs, and the United States called for lowering all tariffs by approximately the same amount. After months of haggling, a weighted procedure was adopted that cut some duties more than others, but less than the Europeans wanted.[66]

Also like in the Kennedy Round, the primary contestants in the agricultural arena were the United States and the EEC. The American position called for converting to tariffs the many measures employed by GATT parties to protect agriculture. The United States hoped such a step would facilitate negotiations to do away with agricultural trade barriers. It also argued against the EEC export subsidies that allowed the EEC to sell farm products to markets once dominated by American producers. In response, the EEC defended the Common Agricultural Policy and, under pressure from the French, refused to discuss any rules that would alter EEC practices.[67]

As time went by, American representatives found themselves in a losing battle. For one thing, American agricultural interests were divided over the American position. In general, wheat and grain farmers, citrus growers, the poultry industry, and tobacco interests favored going all out to eliminate agricultural trade barriers, because they expected to gain from such a move. Other interests, such as the dairy industry, sugar producers, cotton farmers, and cattle and sheep ranchers, opposed an overly strident U.S. position in the negotiations out of fear they might suffer retaliatory damage.[68] These divisions in the agricultural sector left both the Ford and Carter administrations unwilling to fight too vigorously to change the CAP and eventually led Carter's special trade representative, Robert Strauss, to compromise. The CAP remained untouched, and the EEC lowered tariffs on meat and dairy products to give American producers better access to EEC markets.[69] In addition, the United States and EEC agreed that agricultural export subsidies would not be used to gain a disproportionate share of world markets.

Three issues were involved in setting up the generalized system of preferences: (1) amending the most-favored-nation principle to permit discrimination in behalf of developing countries, (2) eliminating discriminatory rules by which some developing countries gave preferential treatment to imports from some advanced countries, and (3) establishing the principle of **graduation.** The first issue was handled by allowing, but not requiring, advanced countries to set lower tariff rates for goods from developing countries. To resolve the second issue, the EEC set aside agreements that gave EEC products special treatment in some developing countries. Finally, negotiators agreed on the principle of graduation, which would allow the GATT to determine when a developing country had reached a level of development sufficient to render that country no longer eligible to participate in the generalized system of preferences. With these issues ironed out, the GSP was included in the Tokyo Round agreement.[70]

The discussion of the final major issue, nontariff barriers, focused on six areas: (1) subsidies and countervailing duties, (2) dumping, (3) technical barriers to trade, (4) customs valuations, (5) import licensing, and (6) government procurement. The examination of subsidies and dumping concentrated on existing GATT rules and on ensuring that penalties were applied only after injury to a domestic producer had been demonstrated.[71] The talks on technical barriers, customs valuations, and import licensing centered on how governments tested and certified imports, on how the value of imports was calculated, and on how permission to import was granted. Many American corporations had complained for years that foreign governments used such procedures as informal trade barriers. For foreigners, a major issue in this area was the still-unresolved American Selling Price. Procedures were worked out to address these problems, and again some countries called for the elimination of the ASP.[72]

The final nontariff barrier, government procurement, was considered at length. Government procurement is the purchase of supplies by government agencies. All governments purchase a variety of items, ranging from paper clips to automobiles, often resulting in big profits for the companies receiving the government contracts. At the time the Tokyo Round began, most such contracts went only to domestic firms in order to assist local workers and companies and to satisfy national security concerns (that is, to avoid an undue dependence on foreign firms for vital goods). In fact, in the United States the use of local suppliers was written into law; the Buy American Act of 1933 required the U.S. government to give preference to American companies when making purchases. A 1954 revision of this law established a 6 percent differential to favor American firms, which rose to 12 percent for small businesses and businesses in depressed areas, and to 50 percent when the goods pertained to national defense. Many other countries had similar laws.[73]

By the early 1970s, governments' attitudes toward procurement had shifted as their purchases had expanded rapidly. American firms saw an opportunity to increase sales if they could obtain contracts to supply foreign governments. Many governments also hoped open bidding would reduce costs and improve the quality of their purchases. As a result, government procurement was placed on the Tokyo Round agenda, and the parties agreed to allow for open bidding procedures, to release to the public the rules for bidding on contracts, to give foreigners adequate time to submit bids, to publicize the winning and losing bids, and to exempt from the agreements only purchases for national defense and those involving small quantities of goods.[74]

In January 1979, Special Trade Representative Strauss informed Congress under the fast-track procedures that the Tokyo Round would end within ninety days. The parties had agreed on tariff cuts averaging 30 percent on industrial goods, reductions in selected agricultural tariffs, a generalized system of preferences for developing countries, and **GATT codes** to regulate nontariff barriers to trade. The GATT codes, which were not mandatory, set standards to guide the behavior of the parties to the GATT. In practice, most GATT contractors based their adherence to the codes on reciprocity, observing them when others observed them and ignoring them when others refused to accept them. The Tokyo agreement also improved GATT dispute settlement procedures, set new rules for protecting infant industries in developing countries, and contained an agreement on trade in aircraft.[75]

The Trade Agreements Act of 1979

The end of the Tokyo Round in April 1979 was the first time Congress was faced with passing legislation according to the fast-track procedures established in the Trade Act of 1974, which called for voting on the agreement, up or down with no amendments, within sixty days. The Office of the Special Trade Representative cooperated with the staffs of the Senate Finance Committee and the House Ways and Means Committee to write the bill.[76] In general, the process went smoothly because Congress had been kept informed throughout the Tokyo

Round and because President Jimmy Carter pleased Congress by taking a tough protectionist position on several issues in the months before Congress voted.

Among Carter's protectionist moves were those helping the specialty steel industry, television producers, shoe manufacturers, and the textile industry. Specialty steel received help in late 1977 when Carter decided to continue quotas initiated by his predecessor, Gerald Ford. The aid for the television industry took the form of a voluntary export restraint agreement that Strauss negotiated in 1977 with Japan. The VER cut Japanese exports from 3 million to 1.75 million sets per year. The industry wanted an even lower quota, but members of Congress accepted the result as reasonable. As for shoes, an orderly marketing arrangement set up in 1977 with Taiwan and South Korea rolled imports back to their 1974 levels. Carter also announced trade adjustment assistance to help the industry modernize. Again, industry spokespersons indicated they wanted more help, but Congress found the outcome satisfactory.[77]

During the Tokyo Round, the textile industry once again was given special attention to avoid having opposition from that quarter undermine the negotiations. As noted earlier, the Multi-Fiber Arrangement put together in 1973 helped to secure passage of the legislation needed to begin the Tokyo Round. As the round proceeded, industry representatives pressured Congress to pass a bill to exempt textiles from any tariff concessions that might be made. President Carter vetoed this bill in November 1978, but he ordered the special trade representative to review measures that might be needed to help the industry.[78]

After considerable give and take between industry representatives, the Office of the Special Trade Representative, the Treasury and Commerce Departments, and Carter's Council of Economic Advisers, a policy was worked out in 1979 calling for the U.S. government to carefully monitor world textile production, paying special attention to countries such as South Korea, Hong Kong, and Taiwan to guard against sudden surges in exports. The deal also called for tariffs on textiles to return to their pre-Tokyo Round levels if the Multi-Fiber Arrangement was not extended when it came up for renewal in 1982. The administration pledged further that it would work to secure extension of the MFA. Even though the industry was not fully pleased with this result, it went far enough to suit most members of Congress.[79]

The **Trade Agreements Act of 1979,** which passed the House on July 7 by a vote of 395–7 and the Senate on July 23 by a 90–4 vote, wrote into law the results of the Tokyo Round. This law did, however, make two small changes. The first amended American participation in the government procurement code to allow for legal preferences for minority-owned businesses in the United States. The second denied GSP privileges to communist countries, members of international resource cartels that disrupted supplies and manipulated prices, and countries that did not cooperate in the war against illegal drugs. The new law also changed American dumping and countervailing duty legislation by allowing foreign exporters to avoid legal action by voluntarily raising their prices, by setting a three-month time limit for dumping and subsidy investigations, by transferring those investigations from the Customs Bureau to the Commerce Department to facilitate findings favoring American producers, and by setting an injury test, as the GATT agreement required.[80]

CHAPTER SUMMARY

In the Kennedy and Tokyo Rounds of the GATT, the United States sought to use multilateral trade negotiations to handle some of the fundamental international commercial challenges that emerged in the 1960s and 1970s. The Kennedy Round was designed to guarantee continued American access to European markets; the U.S. government feared such access might become less available as the EEC consolidated itself and intra-European trade supplanted transatlantic commerce. In addition, the United States attempted to use the Kennedy Round to put agricultural trade on the GATT agenda and to begin eliminating barriers to trade in this sector. Of particular interest to the United States was the newly emerging Common Agricultural Policy and its variable levy which threatened to close EEC markets to American farm exports.

As it turned out, the United States achieved only some of its goals in the Kennedy Round. Tariffs were lowered (but not as much as Americans wanted), and American trade in manufactured goods with the EEC continued to grow. The United States failed, however, to change the CAP because Europeans essentially took agricultural products off the international bargaining table in the 1960s.

These results, together with the growing competition posed by European and Japanese producers for American corporations, helped to foster a resurgence of protectionist demands in the late 1960s and early 1970s. The basic strategy employed by the Nixon, Ford, and Carter administrations in handling cries for protection involved a dose of tough rhetoric, accompanied by limited arrangements to help key industries and an easing of the legal requirements American firms had to meet to qualify for escape clause relief and to receive favorable subsidy and dumping rulings. In addition, these presidents pushed for more GATT negotiations to create new international rules that would limit the trading practices the United States found objectionable.

During the Tokyo Round of GATT, the most important items on the agenda from the American point of view were acceptable rules for agricultural trade and nontariff barriers. Like earlier, in the Kennedy Round, American negotiators found Europeans unwilling to bargain over the EEC's Common Agricultural Policy, and the result was frustration for the United States. The nontariff barrier talks led to better results, however; codes were set up to regulate these trade barriers. Because the codes were optional, the United States practiced reciprocity when observing the new rules.

All things considered, the Kennedy and Tokyo Rounds maintained the momentum toward the expansion of international trade and defused some demands for protection. Despite the limited success of these GATT rounds, world trade in general and American trade in particular were buffeted by powerful forces in the 1970s that for a time appeared likely to destroy the system of international commerce that had been so carefully built during the previous four decades. These disruptive forces are the subject of the next chapter.

NOTES

1. The growth figures for the Soviet economy are from United Nations, *Yearbook of National Accounts Statistics*, Vol. 3, 1975.

2. Ibid.

3. Steve Dryden, *Trade Warriors: USTR and the American Crusade for Free Trade* (New York: Oxford University Press, 1995), 45; John W. Evans, *The Kennedy Round in American Trade Policy: The Twilight of the GATT?* (Cambridge: Harvard University Press, 1971), 134–135; and Joan Edelman Spero and Jeffrey A. Hart, *The Politics of International Economic Relations* (New York: St. Martin's Press, 1997), 14.

4. Evans, *Kennedy Round*, 136, 163.

5. Stephen D. Cohen, Joel R. Paul, and Robert A. Blecker, *Fundamentals of U.S. Foreign Trade Policy: Economics, Politics, Laws, and Issues* (Boulder: Westview Press, 1996), 261; and Evans, *Kennedy Round*, 137.

6. Quoted in Evans, *Kennedy Round*, 140.

7. Cohen, Paul, and Blecker, *Fundamentals of U.S. Foreign Trade Policy*, 203.

8. Dryden, *Trade Warriors*, 73–77; and Evans, *Kennedy Round*, 173–180.

9. Dryden, *Trade Warriors*, 34; and Robert A. Pastor, *Congress and the Politics of U.S. Foreign Economic Policy, 1929–1976* (Berkeley: University of California Press, 1980), 107–108.

10. Evans, *Kennedy Round*, 138–139.

11. Dryden, *Trade Warriors*, 33–34, 42.

12. Ibid., 34, 47.

13. Quoted in ibid., 49.

14. Judith Goldstein, *Ideas, Interests, and American Trade Policy* (Ithaca: Cornell University Press, 1993), 228–229; Stefanie Ann Lenway, *The Politics of U.S. International Trade: Protection, Expansion, and Escape* (Boston: Pitman Publishing, 1985), 104–105; and Patrick Low, *Trading Free: The GATT and U.S. Trade Policy* (New York: Twentieth Century Fund Press, 1993), 107–108.

15. Dryden, *Trade Warriors*, 54; and Pastor, *Congress*, 109.

16. Dryden, *Trade Warriors*, 54; and Evans, *Kennedy Round*, 167–170.

17. Dryden, *Trade Warriors*, 49; and Pastor, *Congress*, 110–112.

18. I. M. Destler, *American Trade Politics* (Washington, D.C.: Institute for International Economics, 1995), 18.

19. Dryden, *Trade Warriors*, 51–53; Evans, *Kennedy Round*, 156; and Pastor, *Congress*, 112.

20. Dryden, *Trade Warriors*, 56–57, 65.

21. Pastor, *Congress*, 113–114.

22. Evans, *Kennedy Round*, 164.

23. Dryden, *Trade Warriors*, 62; Evans, *Kennedy Round*, 171–173; and Pastor, *Congress*, 111.

24. Evans, *Kennedy Round*, 183–200.

25. Although the French withdrew from the NATO military command structure, they remained a member of the NATO alliance. See Dryden, *Trade Warriors*, 90–91; and Evans, *Kennedy Round*, 235–237.

26. Evans, *Kennedy Round*, 207.

27. Dryden, *Trade Warriors*, 86–87.

28. Evans, *Kennedy Round*, 292; and Pastor, *Congress*, 118–119.

29. Evans, *Kennedy Round*, 256–259.

30. Ibid., 230–232, 269.

31. Dryden, *Trade Warriors*, 91–92; and Evans, *Kennedy Round*, 90–91, 227–228, 268.

32. Edward S. Kaplan, *American Trade Policy, 1923–1995* (Westport, Conn.: Greenwood Press, 1996), 84–85; and Pastor, *Congress*, 118–119.

33. The data are from United Nations, *Yearbook of National Accounts Statistics*, Vol. 3, 1975.

34. These trade figures are computed from data found in United Nations, *Yearbook of International Trade Statistics*, various years. Most political analysts regard a positive balance of trade as desirable.

35. Dryden, *Trade Warriors*, 83.

36. Ibid., 94.

37. Low, *Trading Free*, 174.

38. Evans, *Kennedy Round*, 305.

39. Dryden, *Trade Warriors*, 119.

40. Evans, *Kennedy Round*, 302–304.

41. Pastor, *Congress*, 121.

42. Evans, *Kennedy Round*, 321.

43. Quoted in Dryden, *Trade Warriors*, 133.

44. Dryden, *Trade Warriors*, 130–132, 140.

45. Ibid., 124–125.

46. Pastor, *Congress*, 118.

47. Cohen, Paul, and Blecker, *Fundamentals of U.S. Foreign Trade Policy*, 38–39.

48. Kaplan, *American Trade Policy,* 91–92. The data supporting the comment about American trade deficits are from United Nations, *Yearbook of International Trade Statistics,* various years.

49. Cohen, Paul, and Blecker, *Fundamentals of U.S. Foreign Trade Policy,* 39; and Kaplan, *American Trade Policy,* 90.

50. Lenway, *Politics of U.S. International Trade,* 98.

51. Dryden, *Trade Warriors,* 141–142, 156; and Pastor, *Congress,* 131.

52. Cohen, Paul, and Blecker, *Fundamentals of U.S. Foreign Trade Policy,* 224; Lenway, *Politics of U.S. International Trade,* 105–107; Goldstein, *Ideas, Interests,* 230; and Low, *Trading Free,* 108.

53. Joanne S. Gowa, *Closing the Gold Window: Domestic Politics and the End of Bretton Woods* (Ithaca: Cornell University Press, 1983), 127–130, 149–160.

54. Cohen, Paul, and Blecker, *Fundamentals of U.S. Foreign Trade Policy,* 39; and Pastor, *Congress,* 30–31.

55. Dryden, *Trade Warriors,* 155–158.

56. Spero and Hart, *Politics of International Economic Relations,* 21–22.

57. Low, *Trading Free,* 175–176; and Pastor, *Congress,* 130.

58. Kaplan, *American Trade Policy,* 89–99.

59. Among other reasons, the "fast-track" procedure is not fast because the GATT negotiations it applies to can stretch out for years. For example, the Kennedy Round lasted four years, from 1963 to 1967, and the Tokyo Round spanned six years, from 1973 to 1979.

60. Destler, *American Trade Politics,* 72–73.

61. Goldstein, *Ideas, Interests,* 191; and Pastor, *Congress,* 142–143.

62. Pastor, *Congress,* 144–145.

63. Nixon's fear that the Soviets would be offended by the Jackson-Vanik Amendment was well founded. See Anatoly Dobrynin, *In Confidence: Moscow's Ambassador to Cold War Presidents* (New York: Random House, 1995), 269–270.

64. Discussion of the Jackson-Vanik Amendment can be found in Stephen E. Ambrose, *Rise to Globalism: American Foreign Policy since 1938* (New York: Penguin Books, 1993), 268; Philip J. Funigiello, *American-Soviet Trade in the Cold War* (Chapel Hill: University of North Carolina Press, 1988), 185–187; John Lewis Gaddis, *Strategies of Containment* (New York: Oxford University Press, 1982), 314–315; Henry Kissinger, *Years of Upheaval* (Boston: Little, Brown, 1982), 985–998; and Michael Mastanduno, *Economic Containment: CoCom and the Politics of East-West Trade* (Ithaca: Cornell University Press, 1992), 149–153.

65. Dryden, *Trade Warriors,* 175–178.

66. Lenway, *Politics of U.S. International Trade,* 85.

67. Kaplan, *American Trade Policy,* 100; and Low, *Trading Free,* 180.

68. Low, *Trading Free,* 180.

69. Dryden, *Trade Warriors,* 194–195, 222; and Kaplan, *American Trade Policy,* 106.

70. Dryden, *Trade Warriors,* 178; and Low, *Trading Free,* 184–185.

71. Goldstein, *Ideas, Interests,* 204; and Low, *Trading Free,* 183–184.

72. Low, *Trading Free,* 183–184.

73. Lenway, *Politics of U.S. International Trade,* 172.

74. Ibid., 85–86, 173–175.

75. Cohen, Paul, and Blecker, *Fundamentals of U.S. Foreign Trade Policy,* 262–263; Dryden, *Trade Warriors,* 247; and Low, *Trading Free,* 185–186.

76. Destler, *American Trade Politics,* 73.

77. Dryden, *Trade Warriors,* 210–215, 235.

78. Ibid., 235; and Lenway, *Politics of U.S. International Trade,* 108.

79. Lenway, *Politics of U.S. International Trade,* 116–119.

80. Dryden, *Trade Warriors,* 253; Goldstein, *Ideas, Interests,* 170, 201, 204; Low, *Trading Free,* 59; and Pastor, *Congress,* 177.

7 Oil and Turmoil

In August 1859 near Titusville, Pennsylvania, "Colonel" Edwin Drake founded the modern oil industry by using a salt well drill to tap subterranean oil.[1] Drake's operation was such a surprising success that he had no storage facilities for the petroleum. As a stopgap measure, he relied on 52-gallon whiskey barrels to hold the oil. Not only, then, did Drake create an industry, he also came up with the standard measure for oil, the **barrel.**

Drake's petroleum found a ready market in a rapidly industrializing America. When refined, oil became a lubricant that was used widely in manufacturing, and kerosene was the best illuminant money could buy. In no time, the oil industry became one of the fastest growing of the enterprises dotting the American landscape after the Civil War. Giant corporations formed to explore, transport, refine, and market oil throughout the country and around the world. Petroleum products became one of America's largest exports, and entire industries came to rely on the availability of cheap oil.

By 1900, the importance of oil had increased dramatically, because another petroleum-based product, gasoline, had become the fuel for the newly invented internal combustion engine. This engine, and the modes of transportation built around it, quickly became vital to strategic affairs as navies the world over realized that oil-powered ships moved faster and traveled farther than those driven by steam. The newly forming air forces of the world's great powers also used internal combustion engines; trucks became a key means of transportation for soldiers and supplies; and tanks and other fighting vehicles increasingly dominated battlefields. Indeed, one of the most important assets of the Western allies in both world wars was oil from American wells, which produced over 60 percent of the world's petroleum during those conflicts.[2]

As oil attained ever-greater strategic significance, a stable supply became a key national security interest for most countries. With the discovery of oil in the 1920s and 1930s in out-of-the-way desert regions, those areas became vital almost overnight. Britain and the Soviet Union competed for control of Iranian oil fields, while American, British, and French oil companies scrambled for pieces of the action in Saudi Arabia, Iraq, and Kuwait. In fact, during the Second World War some of the most important battles in the European theater were fought to prevent the oil-thirsty Germans from breaking through to Soviet oil fields at Baku and from controlling the oil of the Middle East. In Asia, the Japanese assault on Pearl Harbor was part of a plan to seize oil fields in the Dutch East Indies, and their inability to obtain the oil they needed eventually crippled the Japanese war effort.

The strategic significance of oil was matched by its importance in economic affairs, for industrialized societies everywhere developed an ever-greater reliance on oil for their prosperity. This reliance was especially evident in the United States, where oil was essential to the production of everything from electric power to plastics and motor vehicles were a way of life. Auto manufacturers capitalized on the American affection for cars to build a mammoth industry that became an essential ingredient in determining the health of the American economy. Politicians therefore had to exercise caution in passing legislation affecting these industries lest they upset the American economic apple cart. Moreover, the political campaign contributions produced by these corporations and the labor unions working for them were immense and could mean the difference between victory and defeat in elections.

By the middle of the twentieth century, American automobile and oil companies were enjoying nearly unchallenged domination of their respective areas of production. In the auto industry, the vast majority of the vehicles sold in the United States were made by American firms, and American consumers had such loyalty to the companies from which they bought their cars that they spoke of "Chevy families" and "Ford families." A similar situation existed in the oil industry, where American firms dominated the domestic market and took the lead in exploring for oil at home and abroad.

And yet oil was a nonrenewable resource, as had been demonstrated time and again as wells ran dry from Pennsylvania to Texas. Dry wells, however, were always replaced by ample new discoveries. Yet by the 1950s, the oil companies were having difficulty locating new fields in the United States, which meant the country was edging ever closer to dependence on foreign sources for the oil it needed. Such dependence in turn meant that the American way of life, American national security, and American industries, especially the auto industry, all could be at the mercy of the newest oil-producing countries, many of which were in the volatile Middle East.

The upshot was that in the years after World War II, the United States faced controversial trade decisions affecting two important parts of the American economy, the oil industry and automobile manufacturers. Early on, the issue was framed in classic protectionist terms—that is, some American oil producers called for limits on low-cost oil imports. These calls found ready support in Congress, and trade barriers went up.

As time passed, however, the problem changed as the reliance on oil imports increased and the rising price of foreign oil wreaked havoc on the American economy. As a result, the president and Congress were faced with the challenge of finding politically palatable solutions to the problems of reducing America's dependence on foreign oil and preventing high oil prices from damaging American industries that traditionally had relied on cheap oil. One factor complicating the search for solutions was the certainty that an end to America's dependence on oil imports would mean higher energy costs, a development that could undermine the health of many American manufacturers, most notably those who made automobiles.

The result of this conundrum was a nearly paralyzing political fight as Congress and the president sought to provide for American security and to assist the special interests most affected by changing conditions in the oil market. These political contests were particularly troublesome because so many Americans believed that the United States had an abundance of oil and that problems revolving around the supply and cost of oil represented an attempt by the oil industry to pad profits. Further complicating the situation was the clash between those who believed that a government-sponsored solution was the only way to guarantee equity and those who felt that getting the government out of the business of regulating the oil industry was the proper approach. Beyond this, interest groups fought vigorously to promote solutions favoring their special needs and displayed little willingness to compromise over policies that in some cases had profound implications for their survival. Bureaucratic squabbles also hindered policy making; the government agencies that controlled different aspects of the energy puzzle struggled with one another and often worked at cross purposes.

This chapter outlines the oil controversies that bedeviled the United States in the 1970s. The picture that emerges is one of political confrontation, policy confusion, and conflicts over fundamental beliefs and commercial survival. The discussion in the sections that follow devotes special attention to two aspects of the energy problem: the search to reduce the dependence on foreign oil and the attempt to protect the auto industry from foreign competition. These issues touch on questions that are strategically significant and commercially important and that go to the heart of beliefs about the American way of life and the role of government in the United States.

TRADE IN OIL

In the years after World War II, oil became the fuel of choice throughout the industrialized world because it was cheap and plentiful. Production in Iran, Iraq, Kuwait, Libya, Saudi Arabia, and Venezuela climbed steadily as new discoveries were made and previously tapped fields reached their full potential. Indeed, during the 1950s the world's largest oil companies were constantly pressured to find markets for petroleum to placate governments in developing countries that wished to use oil revenues to finance economic growth. As a result, low-cost oil from North Africa, the Middle East, and Venezuela flooded markets, including those in the United States, where the share of imports in the American market nearly doubled during the 1950s, reaching 19 percent of total sales by 1957.[3]

Quotas and National Security

Low-cost imported oil may have been good news for American consumers, but it spelled trouble for domestic producers; foreign oil displaced locally mined coal and oil as energy sources. In the face of this competition from imports, local producers followed the longtime tradition of going to Congress with pleas for protection. And, as usual, members of Congress responded with attempts to restrict imports. Senators and representatives from the coal-producing states—such as Kentucky, Pennsylvania, and West Virginia—teamed with those from the oil states—such as Oklahoma, Louisiana, and Texas—to pressure the president to block imports of oil.

Congress first attempted to limit oil imports in the late 1940s through higher tariffs on petroleum. When the Truman administration resisted new tariffs, protectionists shifted their arguments during the Eisenhower years to stress questions of national security. The security argument was built on the claim that the inflow of inexpensive foreign oil was a threat to the higher-cost output from America's wells. If foreign oil continued to enter the United States, these wells would be forced to close, and the United States might find itself with a dearth of operating wells in the event of a national security emergency. Hearing the cry, some members of Congress representing the oil states, such as Sen. Lyndon Johnson and Speaker of the House Sam Rayburn, both Texas Democrats, maintained that quotas should be used to limit imports so American wells could remain operational.

Eisenhower and his advisers regarded the arguments for quotas as spurious, noting that because oil was a nonrenewable natural resource, any American oil consumed during periods of international tranquility would be unavailable for emergencies. Therefore, if national security was the concern, shutting down domestic wells to save their oil for the future and importing foreign oil for immediate consumption made more sense than quotas. After all, reopening oil wells was a relatively simple task.[4]

This was not the message that domestic oil producers, known as "independents," wanted to hear. Their focus was on staying in business, and that meant preventing imports. In response, and despite Eisenhower's objections, Congress gave the president the authority to set oil import quotas when it renewed the Reciprocal Trade Agreements Act program in 1955.[5] Oil interests then pushed for the president to set quotas, arguing that the domestic exploration for new oil and energy research and development depended on limiting imports so that the independents could obtain the profits they needed to invest in such projects.

Eisenhower obliged the oil interests in 1957 by establishing a voluntary quota system that became mandatory in March 1959. Under the program, imports were restricted to 9 percent of the American market. The result was higher oil prices for American consumers and a more rapid depletion of domestic supplies, something that would return to haunt policy makers in the coming years.[6]

The American quota system had international implications as well. By restricting access to the American market, the quotas contributed to a worldwide glut in oil. And because the supply of oil outstripped demand, prices began sliding downward. As prices fell, the world's largest oil companies, know as the "majors," cut their payments to oil-exporting countries, including those in the Middle East.[7]

In the face of the price cuts by the majors, five of the world's largest petroleum-exporting countries—Iran, Iraq, Kuwait, Saudi Arabia, and Venezuela—met in Baghdad, Iraq, in September 1960 to set up an organization that would coordinate their bargaining efforts with the oil companies. Together, the five countries controlled nearly 80 percent of the oil sold on global markets. The organization they created was christened the **Organization of Petroleum Exporting Countries**, or OPEC.[8]

The Tables Turn

During the 1960s, OPEC expanded its membership to include Algeria, Indonesia, Libya, Nigeria, Qatar, and the United Arab Emirates, but it was unable to obtain higher prices for its petroleum exports. Powerful forces at work in the oil markets, however, soon changed things completely. From 1960 to 1970, the demand for oil among Western countries increased by 21 million barrels a day. During the same period, oil production in the Middle East went up by only 13 million barrels a day. As a result, the oil glut of the early 1960s was gone by 1970. At the same time, in the United States the demand for foreign oil climbed steadily. From 1967 to 1973, net oil imports nearly tripled, from 2.2 million to 6 million barrels a day, while American production of oil peaked in 1970 at 11.3 million barrels a day and then began to decline. As a result of these trends, the United States found itself increasingly vulnerable to any foreign suppliers that decided to take advantage of the situation.[9]

These changes in oil markets were accompanied by political changes in Iraq and Libya, where radical regimes seized power. Moreover, many Arab leaders had developed an intense resentment of the support Western nations, and especially the United States, was extending to Israel. Arab leaders were particularly angered by the pro-Israeli stance many Western countries took during a June 1967 war in which Israel routed several neighboring Arab countries. These political developments set the stage for changes in the nature of the relationships between Western countries and oil-producing nations and between major oil corporations and OPEC.

One important step down the road toward these new relationships occurred in 1970 when the new leader of Libya, Col. Muammar Qaddafi, forced the oil companies to accept a 20 percent increase in the price of Libya's crude oil. When they learned of the Libyan deal, other OPEC members also wanted more money, and in 1971 Iran, Iraq, and Saudi Arabia signed agreements matching the new Libyan prices. As a sign of things to come, Libya then demanded still higher prices that the majors felt they had no choice but to meet given the tightening world supply of crude.[10]

The U.S. response to these changes in the price of a vital import was strangely quiescent. After all, it had done nothing to prepare for a world of higher-cost petroleum. Indeed, just four months after the second Libyan price increase, President Richard Nixon announced wage and price controls that froze domestic American prices, thereby preventing the rapidly accumulating international price increases from affecting the American consumer. Far from helping, these controls encouraged Americans to continue consuming oil in ever-larger amounts and eventually led to shortages as supplies of lower-cost oil dwindled.

In response to the tightening oil market, State Department energy specialist James Akins wrote a report in 1972 suggesting changes in American oil import policy, increased domestic oil exploration, and conservation. The report received little attention, however, because of the sacrifices it implied for consumers. The only action taken by the Nixon administration was termination of the oil import quota program in April 1973 and the announcement of a voluntary allocation system to guarantee an equitable distribution of oil throughout the country.

The Oil Weapon

By late 1972, Arab countries were insisting more than ever that the United States reconsider its support for Israel. In September, Ahmed Zaki Yamani, the Saudi Arabian oil minister, told Middle Eastern specialists in Washington that a trade alliance between the United States and Saudi Arabia was natural and that the only hindrance was the American policy favoring Israel. Yamani's comments were politely ignored. Saudi warnings were more urgent eight months later, when King Faisal warned visiting American oil company executives that Arabs were extremely disturbed by American support for Israel. The king even suggested that Arab oil exporters might use an oil embargo to pressure the United States.[11]

Fearing the implications of an embargo, the executives reported the king's comments to the State Department. The Mobil Corporation also began running advertisements in American newspapers calling for a reexamination of Middle Eastern policy. The furor surrounding these developments led to questions during a presidential news conference in September 1973. Dismissing the concerns as unfounded, Nixon remarked that "oil without a market . . . doesn't do a country much good."[12]

Within a month, Nixon would learn a startling lesson in oil economics. The lesson began on October 6, 1973, when Egypt and Syria attacked Israel. The Israelis rallied and counterattacked, but soon found themselves low on supplies. On October 8, 10, and 11, Israeli planes picked up armaments in the United States, but the amounts provided did not meet Israeli needs. On October 12, the Israelis requested that American planes be used for additional deliveries. Nixon agreed, and a resupply effort soon was under way in unmarked American aircraft. When the growing size of the operation made it impossible to disguise the American role, the Saudis were informed of the resupply effort. They responded with a warning that the airlift might harm U.S.-Saudi relations.[13]

While these developments unfolded, another drama was playing out in a Vienna meeting between OPEC oil ministers and several major oil companies. The purpose of the meeting was to negotiate an increase in the price of crude oil. When the majors refused to bargain, the oil ministers adjourned the meeting and later announced a unilateral decision to nearly double the price of crude. Members of OPEC had realized that the worldwide shortage of petroleum put them in the driver's seat in determining prices.[14]

But even more drama was yet to come. Beginning on October 7, one Arab country after another announced an embargo of oil against the United States and other nations that supported Israel. They also announced that on November 5 they would cut production by 25 percent and would cut another 5 percent each month thereafter until Israel returned the territory it had captured from the Arab countries during the 1967 war.[15]

These events sent international petroleum markets into near hysteria. Corporations around the globe purchased oil to guarantee they would not be caught short. In the meantime, bidding for the available oil became fierce, and by December 1973 prices on the spot market, where oil is sold on a short-term basis, reached $17 a barrel, nearly six times higher than the $3.01 charged in October.

Arab governments gave the major oil companies the responsibility for enforcing the embargo, because the majors owned the transportation, distribution, and marketing systems that moved Arab oil to consumers around the globe. Thus, even though the Arabs could decree a production cut and forbid shipments to certain destinations, it was the majors that had to put the system into operation. The oil companies were harshly warned that if they did not abide by the embargo, they would be penalized. As a result, the majors did as they were told, but, because some of the embargoed countries had valuable markets, the majors directed Arab oil to acceptable customers and non-Arab oil to embargoed customers. In addition, the majors attempted to spread any shortages evenly among their customers so they would not be accused of favoring one over another.[16]

In the United States, the Arab embargo produced higher fuel prices, shortages, and anger. And along the way, it jeopardized a suburban lifestyle built around the automobile. The response to all these inconveniences was a rush to buy as much fuel as possible, which only exacerbated the problem. Soon, long lines were forming at gasoline stations as drivers filled their tanks to the brim. These lines and the maddening waits that came with them produced frustration that boiled over into rage at oil companies, the Arabs, and the Nixon administration.

In Congress, the Senate Permanent Subcommittee on Investigations, chaired by Henry Jackson, began hearings on the energy crisis in early 1974. The purpose of the hearings was to determine why the energy crisis had occurred and whether the major oil companies were reaping excessive profits. As it turned out, the hearings were long on publicity and short on results—they produced no meaningful legislation.[17]

The American Response

The Arab oil embargo and the production cuts that accompanied it were among the most serious trade-related problems the United States has ever faced. In response to the embargo, the Nixon administration put together a three-tiered policy that was expected to have immediate, medium-term, and long-term benefits for the United States. The immediate goal was to have the embargo lifted and to reverse the reductions in production. The medium-term goal was to coordinate consumer responses to future oil-related trade problems through a new international organization. And, finally, Nixon proposed that United States set a longer-range goal of reducing its dependence on unreliable foreign sources for its petroleum.

The goal of lifting the embargo was pursued through diplomatic initiatives to bring the Arab-Israeli war to an end and to secure cease-fire terms that would satisfy all parties to the conflict. These goals were accomplished through the "shuttle diplomacy" of Secretary of State Henry Kissinger, who jetted from one Middle Eastern capital to another in late 1973 and early 1974. The Egyptian view that the United States was the only intermediary that could manage the negotiations facilitated Kissinger's effort, as did the Saudi leaders' fear of communism.

In November, Kissinger and Egyptian president Anwar Sadat met in Cairo and agreed that the United States would arrange a cease-fire that would save the Egyptian Third Army from its encirclement by the Israelis. At the same time, Kissinger let Egyptian officials know that domestic political pressures resulting from the oil embargo would limit his ability to broker a deal and that true progress would require an end to the embargo. The same message was repeated to the Saudis when Kissinger visited Riyadh a few days later.[18]

In December, Kissinger convinced the Israelis to allow the Third Army to be resupplied, and Egyptian and Israeli forces around the Suez Canal disengaged. Although this development did not meet the initial Arab demands for the return of Israel to its 1967 borders, it did represent a more even-handed policy on the part of the United States. In response, the Saudis indicated that the embargo would be relaxed and might soon be lifted.[19]

January 1974 brought a complete Egyptian-Israeli disengagement and the creation of a United Nations–patrolled buffer zone to prevent renewed fighting. Sadat then called for an end to the embargo. The Saudis waited, however, until mid-February, when an Algiers summit of Arab leaders agreed to end the embargo if the United States pledged to use shuttle diplomacy to work out a disengagement between Israeli and Syrian forces. When Nixon and Kissinger agreed, the embargo was terminated on March 18, 1974.[20]

The second part of Nixon's strategy for handling American energy needs called for creating a new international organization through which consuming countries could deal together with energy problems. To this end, the White House convened a Washington Energy Conference to begin planning for the new entity. To their consternation, U.S. officials found that "none of [America's] allies was eager for a consumer conference, and attitudes ranged from resignation to reluctance." Most countries feared such a conference would antagonize producing nations and might lead to additional supply problems. This attitude was especially predominant among Europeans, who preferred to work out bilateral agreements to obtain oil.[21]

Nevertheless, in deference to the strong American interest in a conference foreign ministers from virtually all advanced democracies assembled in Washington in mid-February. During a series of meetings, the American negotiators convinced a skeptical audience that planning to share energy supplies during emergencies, instituting energy conservation programs, and developing alternative energy sources were reasonable actions that need not antagonize members of OPEC. By the end of the conference, French foreign minister Michel Jobert was the lone holdout in approving a proposal for a "comprehensive . . . program to deal with

Table 7-1 U.S. Imports of Crude Petroleum by Weight and Value, 1967–1981

	Weight (thousand metric tons)	Value (million U.S. dollars)
1967	65,717	$1,079
1968	74,266	$1,208
1969	79,806	$1,320
1970	74,955	$1,448
1971	92,672	$1,879
1972	123,035	$2,607
1973	177,087	$4,593
1974	186,726	$16,479
1975	215,461	$19,250
1976	277,263	$25,446
1977	340,661	$33,546
1978	336,344	$34,256
1979	323,731	$49,014
1980	259,707	$64,633
1981	229,526	$64,318

Source: United Nations, *Yearbook of International Trade Statistics,* various years.

all facets of the world energy situation." At another meeting held later in the year in Paris, the **International Energy Agency (IEA)** was created to handle the tasks the United States outlined at the Washington conference.[22]

Although ending the embargo and setting up the IEA were useful steps, in themselves they did little to reverse America's mounting dependence on foreign oil. Unless something could be done to reduce that dependence, the United States would remain vulnerable to future interruptions in supply. Yet by 1974, U.S. dependence was growing by leaps and bounds (see Table 7.1). In 1967, the United States had imported approximately 66 million metric tons of crude oil valued at just over $1 billion, but by 1974 that weight had nearly tripled, to 186 million metric tons, and had skyrocketed in value to $16 billion. If these rates of consumption continued, American leaders realized, the United States was headed toward a potential economic disaster that could have profound effects on its national security and its way of life. Nixon, however, believed his long-term Project Independence could make a contribution toward preventing such a disaster.

The president was seeking through Project Independence to make the United States self-sufficient in energy production by 1980. In announcing his proposal in a speech in March 1974, Nixon noted the importance of energy, and of oil in particular, to American national security and called on Americans to tackle energy independence with the same spirit they displayed when responding to President

John Kennedy's call in the 1960s to put a man on the moon. Nixon was vague, however, about the means of attaining self-sufficiency and glossed over the implications of ending America's dependence on foreign oil.[23]

The initial public reaction to Project Independence was favorable; after all, the nation was fed up with the dislocations associated with its reliance on imported oil. But this enthusiasm died quickly when it became clear that independence would have costs. For one thing, energy analysts calculated that independence would create pressures toward higher, not lower, prices for certain forms of energy such as gasoline. The Commerce Department floated a plan for a government-backed synthetic fuels (or synfuels) enterprise that would cost nearly $100 billion. Nixon's Council of Economic Advisers also pointed out that because any new synfuels would be expensive, they have to be protected by means of tariffs on lower-cost foreign oil. Environmentalists chimed in as well, noting that any switching to coal to conserve oil would lead to air pollution and more strip mining, both of which would be unacceptable. And finally, trade specialists warned that the trade barriers associated with Project Independence would set a precedent other countries could use to close their markets to American products.[24]

As the limitations of Project Independence became apparent, the public's interest in the project faded. The lifting of the embargo in mid-March only contributed to the project's demise by making the need for action seem less pressing. In the end, then, Nixon's notions about a long-term solution to America's energy needs fell flat and were lost amid the clatter surrounding the energy debate.

Confusion on the Home Front

After Gerald Ford became president on August 9, 1974, in the wake of Richard Nixon's resignation, one of the most pressing problems he confronted was America's dependence on oil imports. But in view of the public's reaction to the oil embargo and to Project Independence, he knew he would have a tough time convincing anyone to take decisive action. Moreover, enormous financial stakes were associated with any decisions about energy, such as promoting conservation, nuclear power, solar options, and exploration for oil and natural gas within the United States. Further complicating the situation, segments of the public had different attitudes toward handling energy matters: conservatives favored raising prices to reduce consumption, and liberals called for a rationing system to allocate supplies on an equitable basis.

Compounding these problems was the helter-skelter collection of sometimes overly intrusive energy policies found in Washington and the obstructive bureaucratic in-fighting. For example, on August 17, 1973, the Federal Cost of Living Council initiated a multitier oil price policy. The most important tiers distinguished between "old" oil and "new" oil. Old oil was defined as that flowing from domestic wells operating in 1972. To prevent producers of this oil from acquiring excessive profits, its price was set at the March 1973 level plus $.35 a barrel. New oil was anything produced beyond 1972 levels. Producers of this oil were free to sell it at market prices, which were higher than the prices fixed for old oil. Imported oil was priced at world market levels. Because the various types of oil were not uniformly available throughout the United States, an allocation system was set up to control the flow of each type of oil to different parts of the country to ensure that fuel prices would be the same everywhere.[25]

These pricing and distribution mechanisms quickly became a source of irritation for everyone. Domestic producers had no incentive to produce old oil, because they could not sell it at market prices. As a result, the demand for imported oil continued to rise, which put upward pressure on world prices and angered America's allies. Finally, the low prices stemming from regulation in the United States meant that less money was available for exploring for oil there.

Other problems emerged from attempts to convert from oil to alternative energy sources, such as nuclear power and coal, and to explore for new oil. Nuclear power, which could replace oil to generate electricity, was laden with technical problems and opposed by environmental groups as dangerous. Coal was another possible fuel for generating electricity that also could be used to heat homes and businesses. Although coal was abundant, it was a controversial alternative for generating electricity; its use also generated pollution, and coal mining techniques were dangerous and harmful to the environment.

Of the many environmental concerns surrounding exploration for oil, one was the fear that offshore drilling would lead to oil spills. Another concern was that projects in remote locations, such as Alaska's North Slope, would harm areas famed for their pristine beauty. Indeed, legal action by environmental groups postponed for four years the construction of a pipeline to bring North Slope oil to market.[26]

Bureaucratic confusion and conflicts also affected the policy-making process itself. When Ford took office in 1974, no one agency was in charge of the entire energy situation. At the height of the embargo in December 1973, Congress had created the Federal Energy Office to engage in emergency energy planning, but this office was eventually abolished and in 1974 Congress established the Federal Energy Administration to coordinate a national energy policy. Neither of these agencies, however, had any authority over other parts of the federal bureaucracy. As a result, the Treasury Department still claimed authority over the effect of oil imports on the American balance of payments; the Defense Department sought to ensure the supply of fuel for the military, no matter where it came from; the State Department handled energy problems with other countries; the Environmental Protection Agency worried about how converting to coal and nuclear energy would affect the environment; and the Justice Department examined whether cooperation among the oil companies to distribute scarce oil was a violation of American antitrust laws. In such a situation, attempts by one part of the bureaucracy to promote conservation or to reduce oil imports ran into resistance from other parts of the bureaucracy.[27]

Faced with these problems, Ford attempted to construct an energy program that would, through incentives, increase domestic energy supplies, encourage conservation, and establish emergency procedures for handling crises. Ford's proposal, which he sent to Congress in January 1975, set a goal of reducing growth in energy consumption from 4 percent to 2.5 percent a year, called for tax incentives to double the use of coal for generating electricity, sought to eliminate federal regulations governing the price of domestically produced oil, advocated stockpiling oil for future emergencies, and requested funds to develop synfuels. Ford also announced on February 1 that he would use his authority under the 1974 Emergency Petroleum Allocation Act to increase the import fee on oil by $1 a barrel. Moreover, on March 1 he would raise the fee to $2 and to $3 on April 1.[28] The new fees were designed to discourage the consumption of foreign oil by raising the price.

The congressional reaction to Ford's plans ranged from tepid to hostile. The Democratic majority in both houses opposed deregulating domestic oil and raising import fees and passed a law to delay the fee increases by ninety days. Ford vetoed this legislation, but he decided to bargain with Congress over the issue. These negotiations dragged on for months until Congress passed the Energy Policy and Conservation Act in December 1975. This law, which Ford signed, stipulated that price controls could be phased out over a forty-month period if the president agreed to the price increases.

The bill also allowed the federal government to stockpile oil and provided incentives to encourage electric utilities to convert from oil to coal. Another law, passed earlier in the year even though vigorously opposed by the auto industry, required auto manufacturers to more than double the corporate average fuel economy (CAFE) for their vehicles by 1985, from 13 to 27 miles per gallon.[29]

These laws, however, were a far cry from the sweeping proposals many observers felt were needed to eliminate America's dependence on foreign oil. Over the short run, the volume of oil imports continued to increase, rising from 215 million metric tons in 1975 to 277 million in 1976 and 340 million in 1977. Only in 1978, after domestic price controls were eliminated, did imports fall for the first time, to 336 million metric tons.[30] Clearly, the political turmoil associated with energy policy was so intense that the United States remained vulnerable to future interruptions in trade.

The Moral Equivalent of War

In his 1976 run for the presidency, Georgia governor Jimmy Carter made energy policy a major issue, promising to reduce the still-growing American dependence on foreign oil. As Carter noted later in his memoirs, many Americans "deeply resented that the greatest nation on earth was being jerked around by a few desert states."[31]

As president, Carter's approach to energy was three-pronged: (1) promoting conservation, (2) setting up a single Department of Energy to manage the many aspects of the energy puzzle, and (3) decontrolling the price of domestic oil in a way that would funnel at least some of the billions of dollars in income generated by decontrol toward solving the energy problem. Soon after his inauguration, Carter announced that he would present a comprehensive energy plan to Congress in ninety days. In taking his first step toward fulfilling this pledge, he requested on March 1 that Congress create an Energy Department. He asked James Schlesinger, who had served as secretary of defense under Ford, to head the new department.

When the rest of Carter's plan was submitted to Congress in April, it included provisions for phasing out price controls, promoting the use of coal, instituting tax breaks for the efficient use of energy, reforming utility rates, and undertaking conservation. In the speech outlining his energy plans, Carter sought to convince his audience of the need for action by saying, "The energy crisis has not yet overwhelmed us, but it will if we do not act quickly. . . . This difficult effort will be the moral equivalent of war."[32]

Many of Carter's proposals were ideas recycled from previous administrations. One unique feature of the Carter program was a crude oil equalization tax (COET), designed to bring the price of domestic oil up to world market levels and force conservation, while giving the government the authority to determine how the tax revenues generated by the higher prices would be used. Carter proposed funneling some of the COET tax money back to the poor and middle-class consumers who would be most affected by the price increases. The tax also could be used to promote mass transit and energy research and development. More fundamentally, though, Carter did not want decontrol to result in massive profits for the politically unpopular oil companies.

Despite the Democrats' control of both houses of Congress, Carter's proposals ran into flak on Capitol Hill from the beginning. One problem was the public's lack of enthusiasm. One pundit caught the mood of many by noting that the acronym for "moral equivalent of war" was MEOW, hardly a battle cry that would inspire people to action. Another problem was the hostile reception COET received in the Senate, where Russell Long, chairman of the Finance Committee, felt it allocated too little for new exploration by oil companies. Squabbles over which committees should have jurisdiction over other parts of the proposal also stalled action. Further difficulties emerged when the House and Senate argued over whether gas-guzzling cars should be banned or simply taxed to discourage their purchase, over the role utility companies would play in promoting conservation, and over the question of using tax credits or tax penalties to encourage the switch from fuel oil to coal for generating electricity. In the end, Congress failed to take action before it adjourned in 1977.[33]

Progress also was slow in 1978. To Carter's consternation, no energy legislation was in sight when he met with the leaders of the other major industrial democracies in Bonn, Germany. At the summit meeting, Carter came under strong pressure from the other leaders because of the failure of the United States to curb its appetite for fuel. They urged the president to push appropriate energy legislation through Congress at the earliest possible date, a sentiment expressed with particular force by Chancellor Helmut Schmidt of West Germany.[34]

When Carter returned from Europe, Congress finally passed a toned-down version of his energy plan on October 15, 1978. The key features of the legislative package were: (1) tax penalties to discourage the purchase of gas-guzzling cars, (2) revamped utility rates to encourage conservation, (3) tax incentives to promote the use of energy-efficient appliances, (4) tax incentives to push for the use of coal and solar power, and (6) the phased decontrol of natural gas prices. Congress dropped Carter's COET proposal from the final legislation. Altogether, this package was a modest step toward reducing America's need for foreign oil. It was not, however, the independence that had been so boldly, if unrealistically, proclaimed earlier in the decade.

Revolution in Iran

Even as Congress was putting the finishing touches on Carter's energy package in October 1978 trouble was brewing on the other side of the world that would soon send world oil markets into a frenzy. The source of the trouble was Iran, where the shah's once-firm grip on power was unraveling at an alarming rate that caught officials in Washington and around the world by surprise.

In retrospect, most analysts trace the shah's problems to his attempt to modernize Iran too rapidly and to his unwillingness to share political power. The drive toward modernization, which began in the 1950s and accelerated in the 1960s and 1970s, was financed with revenues from the sale of Iran's greatest asset, oil. Modernization brought new ideas and ways of doing things, but many of them were foreign and antithetical to the traditional Islamic teachings that guided the lives of most Iranians. In the end, then, even though many people benefited immensely from economic development, others believed they were losing things they cherished greatly.

As time went on, both those who profited from the shah's reforms and those who felt alienated began opposing him. For example, Iran's new middle class, upset by the shah's refusal to share political power, had by the early 1970s begun to demand a role in governing Iran. On the other side of the social divide, conservatives felt the shah was undermining the religious doctrine they regarded as fundamental to their lives. For these people, the shah appeared bent on eliminating Islam from its place at the heart of Iranian society.

Tehran was the focal point for much of the early opposition to the shah. But by the fall of 1978, the protests had spread to other parts of the country and, most alarmingly, to the oil fields of southern Iran. The foreign technicians who managed many of the petroleum facilities were forced to leave, and Iranian workers at one well after another went on strike. Amid this disorder, Iranian production plummeted, and the world soon confronted a shortfall of 3.5 million barrels of oil a day.[35] After attempts to quell the turmoil failed, the shah left the country in January 1979. The upheaval took on a revolutionary tone when the Ayatollah Khomeini, a conservative Islamic cleric and a staunch opponent of the shah, returned to Iran from his shah-imposed exile on February 1. For the rest of the world, it was now clear that the shah was finished and that Iran would be ruled by an anti-Western government that held a special hatred of the United States.

These events immediately destabilized world oil markets, eliciting the same kind of panic that had plagued markets during and after the Middle East war of October 1973. And again, the spot market was hardest hit. Long-term contracts for most grades of oil increased by a dollar a barrel between October 1978 and January 1979 and by another dollar a barrel by April, but spot prices soared— from $16 a barrel in January 1979, to $22.50 in February, to $35 in June.[36]

Like in 1973 and 1974, the price increases were driven mainly by the businesses, such as transportation companies, that made abnormally large purchases to guarantee a sufficient supply of fuel. Many oil companies and consumers also purchased and stored oil as a precaution against future disruptions.[37] Even though by mid-1979 almost all of the lost production had been made up by increased output from other oil producers, the crisis persisted as demand continued to exceed normal levels. Under these conditions, the disruptions to the American economy surpassed those experienced during the crisis of 1973–1974. Motorists again found long lines at gas stations, inflation and interest rates rose to record levels, and truckers around the country went on strike to express their displeasure over the shortages and price increases.

The Windfall Profits Tax

In response to the new energy crisis, President Carter announced on April 5, 1979, that he would accelerate the decontrol of domestic oil prices and ask Congress to levy a **windfall profits tax** whose proceeds would be used to limit the impact of the price increases on low-income families. In addition, money from the tax would finance mass transit projects and energy research and development. Once again, Carter hoped to use his tax plan to convince the public to accept decontrol.

The congressional reaction to the windfall profits tax was far from warm. The administration's presumption that only the government could decide wisely how to use the tax money generated by price increases drew heavy fire from Republicans. Representatives of the oil-producing states also felt there was too much emphasis on the promotion of synfuels. Taking the opposite tack, liberals and those with ties to consumer groups and to industries that were heavy fuel users, such as trucking firms and the airlines, claimed decontrol would injure their lifestyles and businesses and was nothing more than a give way to the oil industry.

When he attended a summit meeting in Tokyo in June, Carter once again drew the fire of other countries. Several leaders, most especially Chancellor Schmidt of Germany, strongly criticized the slow American response to the energy crisis. When Carter proposed that countries develop specific energy goals, "Schmidt became personally abusive. . . . He alleged that American interference in the Middle East trying to work for a peace treaty was what caused the problems with oil all over the world."[38] Eventually, Japanese prime minister Masayoshi Ohira and French president Valèry Giscard d'Estaing were able to work out a compromise, but the tensions in Tokyo added to Carter's frustrations as he tried to work his way through the energy political minefield.

Upon returning to the United States, Carter concluded that his administration needed a fresh approach to dealing with the problems confronting the nation. After an extraordinary series of meetings at Camp David, Maryland, he removed several members of his cabinet; Treasury Secretary Michael Blumenthal, Secretary of Health, Education, and Welfare Joseph Califano, and Energy Secretary James Schlesinger were replaced.[39] Far from creating the spirit of cooperation that he hoped for, Carter's moves simply brought confusion and uncertainty about his leadership.

By the fall of 1979, it was clear that the windfall profits tax would not pass Congress in the form Carter wanted. The tax bill that cleared a House-Senate conference committee in February 1980 had been reworked to reflect congressional priorities. Instead of earmarking the tax proceeds for the synfuel and mass transit programs Carter wanted, the conference committee decided on a three-way split that would target 25 percent of the funds for energy aid to the poor, 15 percent for energy research and development, and 60 percent for an income tax cut. The new bill also phased out the tax after 1988.[40]

With these alterations, the tax became little more than a means of replacing one kind of revenue with another. Carter did sign the bill, but he was disappointed with the outcome. He felt that another chance to take a long-range approach to America's energy problems had been squandered.[41]

Rolling Back Energy Prices

Although many energy analysts felt that America's reaction to its oil imports problem was tepid and that the U.S. government was refusing to come to grips with an extremely serious trade problem, by 1980 forces were at work that soon transformed energy markets. One such force was the growing stockpiles of oil. As noted earlier, the interruption in production that had accompanied the revolution in Iran spurred many oil companies and industrial consumers to purchase and store oil so they could ride out future crises.

Thus when war broke out in September 1980 between two giant oil producers, Iraq and Iran, storage facilities around the world were brimming over with oil that could be used to replace the lost production. In addition, the International Energy Agency machinery for handling emergencies was running by 1980, and many of those who might have panicked were persuaded to remain calm.[42]

Another factor that changed oil markets was demand. Throughout the post–World War II period, oil consumption had increased persistently. In the 1950s and 1960s, this growing demand did not lead to higher prices because the availability of oil outstripped demand. By 1970, however, supplies were tight, demand continued to rise, and prices began to move upward. Moreover, the political turmoil in the Middle East and the feverish reactions of some consumers introduced additional pressures that pushed prices even higher. Consumers reacted to the higher prices and the fear that the future might bring even more instability to oil supplies by changing their fuel consumption habits. Among other things, they sought alternatives to oil for heating homes and businesses and for generating electricity. As a result, natural gas, coal, and solar energy became increasingly popular and even fashionable options for businesses and for those building new homes. People also began to turn to more fuel-efficient automobiles and to using more insulation in their homes to conserve fuel.

The result of these measures was that, even though worldwide fuel consumption grew at an average annual rate of 3.9 percent from 1976 to 1979, it began to decline after that, falling by 0.7 percent in 1980, by 0.6 percent in 1981, and by 0.2 percent in 1982.[43] The consumption of imported oil in the United States fell even more rapidly during the same years—from a peak of over 340 million metric tons in 1977 to just under 230 million metric tons by 1981, a decline of nearly one-third over a four-year period (see Table 7.1, page 152). Even at that, the increasing price of oil meant that the bill for these reduced imports almost doubled over the same period.

This drop in demand was accompanied by new oil discoveries in the 1970s that began influencing oil markets by 1980. Among the most important finds were fields in Alaska (actually discovered in the late 1960s but brought to market in the mid-1970s), the North Sea, Mexico, and on the west coast of Africa. In addition, financial problems in the Soviet Union prompted that country to begin selling more oil on world markets. The result was an increase in the availability of oil, much of it from non-OPEC sources. The average annual increase in world oil production was 4.2 percent from 1976 to 1979, 4.9 percent in 1980, and 6.9 percent in 1981.[44]

When these increases in production were coupled with the declining demand for oil, the inevitable result was an oil glut that led producers to discount their prices to retain their share of the market. As the price of oil fell, the many petroleum-exporting governments that had been lured in the 1970s into new economic development projects paid for with high-flying oil revenues found themselves pressed to sell more oil to bring in the revenue needed to finance these projects. As a result, prices dropped from a peak of over $30 a barrel to $20 and lower.[45]

As oil prices continued to fall in 1981 and in early 1982, the energy crisis that had hounded the United States throughout the 1970s, and that most analysts believed would haunt the country for years to come, suddenly and quite unexpectedly came to an end. As it turned out, the crisis was ended by the many small policy steps that so many had decried as insufficient, such as promoting conservation and changing lifestyles to favor smaller and more fuel-efficient cars and better-insulated homes. In addition, the higher prices of the 1970s provided incentives to search for and produce new oil supplies.

One fallout of the sudden end to the crisis was that almost overnight the massive and expensive synfuels projects, which had been promoted as the only true long-term solution to America's energy needs, fell prey to the trends the Commerce Department foresaw in its initial analysis of Project Independence. As the price of oil imports fell after 1981, the huge investments required to fund synfuels research began to make less sense commercially. By 1982, the largest of the synfuel enterprises, the Colony Project in Colorado, was closed. For many in the oil industry, this signaled the end of the abnormal market pressures associated with the topsy-turvy world of OPEC.

THE AUTOMOBILE INDUSTRY

The tumult stemming from the oil crises of the 1970s severely affected several American industries, but no one suffered more than the auto makers. In retrospect, the devastating consequences of sharp increases in oil prices for American auto manufacturers should have been easy to predict, because American firms and consumers had become addicted to big gas-guzzling cars. But industry analysts simply failed to recognize that the demand for these vehicles would fall quickly if fuel costs began climbing rapidly. After all, in the years before 1970 American auto makers so dominated their home markets that the prospect of trouble seemed fantastic.

America's Love Affair with Big Cars

Like the oil industry, the mass production of automobiles was largely an American invention. Under the influence of industrial pioneers such as Henry Ford, American car manufacturing grew rapidly in the early part of the twentieth century. By the 1920s, the United States was making nine out of every ten vehicles produced throughout the world.[46] Such domination continued during the interwar period and led auto makers to press for a reduction in American trade barriers as a means of encouraging international trade.

For a time in the post–World War II period, American auto firms faced almost no foreign competition in the United States, because the European and Japanese auto industries were still recovering from the war. The U.S. consumer's preference for large cars, however, made it difficult to export American vehicles to foreign markets, where customers preferred smaller, fuel-efficient designs. Ford and General Motors made up for this inability to export by building plants in Europe to produce cars more in tune with European tastes. At the same time, during the 1950s foreigners found it difficult to penetrate the American market because of their limited experience with American consumers and because most Americans regarded their products as substandard. American producers therefore occupied an enviable position; they almost totally controlled their home market, which was the world's largest for motor vehicles, while their foreign operations gave them strong footholds in European markets.

By 1960, however, American auto manufacturers saw their supremacy begin to fray as first European and then Japanese cars appeared in the U.S. market. The first attempts were spearheaded by European companies, with Volkswagen leading the way. Between 1957 and 1959, European exports to the United States grew from a 3.5 percent market share to a 10.2 percent share.[47] Although these numbers indicated a significant increase in foreign sales, American corporations were not alarmed. After all, most imported cars were small, had a limited profit potential, and appealed to a tiny segment of the American market. Moreover, American firms felt they could meet the foreign challenge by producing small cars of their own, such as the Ford Falcon and the Chevrolet Corvair. Thus they remained confident they would continue to dominate an American market in which consumers preferred powerful cars and in which the unveiling of the manufacturers' new models each September was a much-anticipated event. The auto makers were then gratified to see that the share of the American market represented by imports grew slowly during the 1960s, reaching only 15.3 percent in 1970.[48] Content with the status quo, American firms were slow to accept change and either refused to introduce innovative products such as the minivan or else did so only reluctantly, which was the case with the Ford Mustang.[49]

The ability of American companies to retain a tight grip on their home turf, however, rested on fragile conditions. The love affair between consumers and big cars was built on a foundation of cheap fuel. As long as gasoline cost approximately $.30 a gallon or less, the American public found the vehicles produced in Detroit irresistible. An increase in the price of fuel, however, might move auto producers and consumers rapidly into uncharted territory where the consumer preferences of the past would be a very unreliable guide to their purchases of the future. And that, as we have seen, was exactly what happened; by 1970 the days of cheap gasoline were nearly over.

The Foreign Challenge

As described earlier in this chapter, between October 1973 and February 1974 the price of crude oil increased fourfold and gasoline prices in the United States more than doubled. Confronted by these problems, many Americans developed a sudden preference for more fuel-efficient automobiles. Because American firms produced few of these vehicles, foreign producers sensed an opportunity to seize a larger share of the American market.

As it happened, Japanese firms were best positioned to take advantage of these sudden changes. The Japanese had been seeking to enter the American market for over a decade, but during much of that time Japanese cars had lacked the quality American buyers expected. Although they at first hesitated to change their designs, the Japanese learned from their mistakes, and by the early 1970s and the onset of the oil embargo Japanese auto firms had found just the car American consumers interested in fuel economy were looking for.[50]

Sales of Japanese cars were brisk, and soon Toyota Corollas and Datsun B-210s were crowding American highways and parking lots. Confronted by these challenges, American companies seemed unable to develop a well-thought-out response. Ford and General Motors introduced the Pinto and the Vega, but neither vehicle could match what the Japanese were offering. The Vega was a colossal failure when its engine performed poorly, and the Pinto was sluggish and had a nasty habit of bursting into flames when hit at the wrong angle. American firms also were reluctant to introduce front-wheel-drive cars, even when these vehicles were becoming wildly popular abroad.[51]

American firms therefore found themselves in the uncomfortable position of being on the defensive as they tackled the newly emerging world of auto marketing. Instead of adapting as quickly as possible, executives in Detroit insisted that Americans would never lose their preference for large cars, that the love affair with small cars and fuel efficiency would be short-lived, and that the market for big cars would revive as soon as oil prices stabilized.

And, to a degree, that is what happened. By mid-1974, energy prices had leveled off, gasoline shortages had abated, and consumers were once again purchasing the larger vehicles they had shunned just months earlier. Sales of foreign vehicles remained high in comparison to pre-embargo days, but the renewed interest in larger cars convinced American auto executives they had made the right choice in sticking with their traditional products. The "big three" American car companies—General Motors, Ford, and Chrysler—soon returned to business as usual and took their time designing and producing smaller and more fuel-efficient vehicles. These companies also opposed congressional proposals that would have required them to meet fuel efficiency standards. As far as most American auto executives were concerned, their companies had weathered the storm, and it was their job to sell as many large cars as possible to make up for the sales lost in 1973 and 1974.[52]

In 1979 and 1980, however, this rather smug approach to auto production was derailed when the Iranian revolution forced dramatic increases in oil prices. In the ensuing panic, American consumers again abandoned large vehicles and raced to purchase more fuel-efficient cars. This time, the shift to smaller cars was more devastating for American firms, because between 1974 and 1979 foreign companies had steadily captured a larger share of the American market. Thus the switch to imports in 1979 and 1980 allowed foreign firms to capture an alarmingly high 26.7 percent share of the market, up from just over 15 percent in 1970.[53]

Worse news followed. Sales of Japanese cars in the American market went up by nearly 500 percent from 1973 to 1980, and American car sales plunged, with production falling from 14.7 million cars in 1978 to only 9 million in 1980. Between January and June 1980, the big three car makers reported collective losses of nearly $3 billion. Ford and General Motors were able to rely on profits from their foreign operations to stem this tide of red ink, but only a government-sponsored loan saved Chrysler. Yet, even though the companies were saved, many of the jobs within those companies were lost. Approximately 300,000 auto workers and almost 500,000 workers in related industries were laid off. By mid-1980, the unemployment rate in the automobile industry and in related industries was at

30 percent. A true depression had descended on an industry that accounted for 4 percent of the total gross national product of the United States.[54]

Seeking Relief

The economic turmoil among auto makers prompted industry representatives to approach the Carter administration and Congress in late 1979 and early 1980 with requests for protection. The United Auto Workers (UAW) union took the lead in seeking action from the Carter administration. As the UAW saw it, two courses of action were needed to save the industry: the negotiation of a voluntary export restraint agreement to limit the sale of imported cars and talks to encourage the Japanese to build production facilities in the United States. Limiting imports was expected to push consumers toward the purchase of American-made vehicles, and enticing the Japanese to produce cars in the United States would generate jobs for American workers.

The Carter administration had a mixed reaction to the UAW's appeals. Many Carter advisers felt that energy conservation and fighting inflation were the most important of the administration's economic objectives and that limiting imports of low-cost, fuel-efficient Japanese cars would undermine these goals. When Rubin Askew, the U.S. trade representative (USTR), argued that the Japanese should be encouraged to build factories in America, the Treasury Department disagreed, fearing that such demands might become standard practice whenever an industry faced foreign competition, raising in turn the already high stakes in trade negotiations.[55]

UAW president Douglas Fraser continued to press the case for the construction of Japanese factories in America when he visited Japan in February 1980. In an attempt to gain bargaining leverage, Fraser told his Japanese hosts that an agreement to construct auto plants in the United States might head off possible congressional restrictions on imports. The Japanese **Ministry of International Trade and Industry (MITI)** was concerned, especially because it had received the same message from USTR negotiators, but the leading Japanese auto firms were reluctant either to invest in the United States (they cited high American labor costs and too many labor strikes) or to limit their exports.[56]

In March, Fraser took his campaign for assistance to Congress, where he appeared before the House Subcommittee on Trade to call for a VER and to push for Japanese production facilities in the United States. A Ford Motor Company representative also went before the subcommittee to make the case for a VER. These appeals, however, were partially counteracted by testimony from George Eads, a member of Carter's Council of Economic Advisers, who argued that following Fraser's recommendations would lead to price increases for cars and would do little to help American manufacturers. Eads also predicted that restrictions on imports would lead to higher fuel consumption, would undermine efforts to cut oil imports, and would result in the rehiring of only a very small number of workers. In their report, subcommittee staff came to the same basic conclusions, leaving the subcommittee wavering on the appropriate course of action.

Apparently stymied on Capitol Hill, the UAW decided in June to file a petition for import relief under Section 201 of the 1974 Trade Act. In August, the Ford Motor Company joined the UAW in its petition. The question of protection was now in the hands of the International Trade Commission.

The Escape Clause Case

Section 201 of the 1974 Trade Act serves as the American legal counterpart to Article XIX of the GATT, which allows a country to invoke the escape clause to provide protection to an industry harmed by imports. The escape clause, which is temporary, must be employed in accordance with the most-favored-nation principle—that is, it must be applied to all imports of the product from whatever source, and it cannot be used against imports from a single country. In addition, countries that utilize the escape clause must recognize, under the principle of reciprocity, that they must compensate their trading partners for the business the partners lose as a result of escape clause action. This stipulation usually leads trading partners to restrict exports from the country availing itself of the escape clause. These counterrestrictions can be, and usually are, applied to goods that have little to do with the product protected under the escape clause action, thereby placing pressure on the country employing the escape clause to end its use as soon as possible.[57]

In the United States, requests for escape clause relief under Section 201 of the 1974 Trade Act are heard by the International Trade Commission. The ITC accepts testimony in public hearings from both the parties seeking protection and those opposing such action. The parties seeking protection must show that they have suffered an injury, that imports are a "substantial cause" of the industry's injury, and that the imported goods constitute a product that is of the same type as the good they produce. A "substantial cause" is defined by law as one that is at least as important as any other cause of the industry's troubles. For its part, the ITC must define the industry in question, determine whether the industry has suffered an injury, and decide whether imports constitute a substantial cause of that injury. In deciding the question of substantial cause, the ITC considers whether import restrictions will allow the industry to recover and become competitive with imports.[58]

The ITC's auto industry hearings were held in the early fall of 1980. Both the UAW and Ford demonstrated that imports of cars had surged and that American corporations and workers had suffered serious injury. They also argued that the small, fuel-efficient foreign cars were the same basic product as the larger cars built by Detroit. The remedies requested by the UAW included a 20 percent tariff on imported cars, quotas based on the 1975 or 1976 level of imports, and new production requirements that would encourage foreign companies to manufacture in the United States. Ford's petition requested a more modest quota based on the 1976 level of imports.[59]

The five members of the ITC carefully scrutinized the petitions for protection and asked the petitioners extensive questions. The importers also were given an opportunity to state their case. One difficulty arose when UAW attorneys hinted that a key industry problem was the shift in consumer preferences from larger cars to smaller and more fuel-efficient vehicles. If this shift was the case, the ITC noted, then imports were not the cause of the industry's woes; rather, American producers were not making the products consumers wanted to purchase.[60]

Another problem for the petitioners cropped up when Ford representatives implied under questioning that American firms had a prior right to control of the American market and that import relief did not necessarily mean Ford would speed up the conversion of its manufacturing process to implement a shift to smaller-car production. These comments made it appear the domestic industry simply wanted to avoid foreign competition and to create an environment that would force American consumers to buy American-made autos whether or not they felt such cars met their needs.[61]

Additional hurdles for the petitioners appeared when those opposing protection presented a convincing case that the primary problems faced by the American auto industry were the onset of a recession in 1979 that hurt the demand for high-cost automobiles, the sky-high interest rates that affected consumer financing, and the decisions by American executives to go with a product mix that emphasized larger cars at a time when consumers increasingly were demanding smaller ones. These arguments were reinforced by the analysis in an ITC staff report.[62]

After considering the evidence, the ITC released its decision in October 1980. By a 5–0 vote, the commission stated that the auto industry had suffered injury and that imports were a cause of that injury. But, by a 3–2 vote, the commission decided that imports were not a substantial cause of the industry's injury; the U.S. recession, the resulting credit crunch, and the shift in consumer preferences from large to small cars were all regarded as more important causes. Because the law required that imports be a substantial cause of injury, the commission ruled that the auto industry would receive no relief from imports under the provisions of the escape clause as set out in Section 201.

Back to Congress

The ITC rejection of the UAW/Ford Section 201 petition created an outcry not only from union and corporate officials but also from Congress. For many observers, the outcome indicated that the legal system of protection was flawed and unable to handle even the most flagrant cases of damage to American industry by imports. During the time he had left in office after losing the 1980 election, Carter authorized trade adjustment assistance for the auto industry. It did little, however, to assuage the anger of those who felt something more was needed to save automobile manufacturing in the United States.[63]

For some members of Congress, the message was clear: if current legislation could not help a producer as large and important as the auto industry, then new legislation was needed. On December 2, the House of Representatives passed a resolution giving the president the authority to negotiate auto import restraints with Japan. When Congress convened in January 1981, Senators John Danforth, R-Mo., and Lloyd Bentsen, D-Texas, cosponsored a bill to set a quota that would limit auto imports from Japan to 1.6 million cars a year. Japan had sold 1.9 million cars in the United States in 1980 and expected to sell 2.1 million in 1981. Danforth, who chaired the Trade Subcommittee, also opened hearings to inquire into the problems confronting the auto industry.[64]

In the new Reagan administration, proposals for import quotas were treated as ideological heresy. Ronald Reagan was a committed free trader who believed firmly that markets should be allowed to work their magic and that when they were permitted to do so the end result would be superior to any contrivance that might be devised by those who tried to manipulate the market. Reagan was supported in these beliefs by almost all of his closest advisers. And yet the auto industry was vitally important. Not only was there the possibility of losing approximately a million jobs, but there also was the political matter of retaining the support of voters in Michigan, a key state in presidential elections. In addition, the auto industry produced items required for the nation's defense. And last, but not least, Reagan had indicated during the 1980 election campaign that he would lend a sympathetic ear to those who wanted to protect the auto industry. He felt, then, duty-bound to do something about the industry's plight, even though some members of the executive branch continued to strongly resist anything that smacked of blatant protectionism.

As the demands for action grew in Congress, the Senate majority leader, Bob Dole, a Republican from Kansas, reported that two-thirds of the Senate supported the Danforth-Bentsen bill. In an effort to achieve consensus, Reagan put together a task force, under the direction of Transportation Secretary Drew Lewis, to develop appropriate recommendations.

When the task force reported to a March 19 cabinet meeting, it favored a quota system. Treasury Secretary Donald Regan and the director of the Office of Management and Budget, David Stockman, vehemently opposed such a course. Vice President George Bush offered a compromise by suggesting that it might be possible to induce Japan to voluntarily accept export restrictions as a means of heading off congressional legislation. Reagan seized on the idea, apparently believing that the negotiation of a VER truly would be voluntary.[65]

One complicating factor, however, was a Justice Department ruling that a quota system worked out entirely by Japanese auto firms would violate American antitrust laws. The only way a VER could be set up without legal complications was to base the arrangement on an explicit order from the Japanese government requiring Japanese companies to scale back their shipments to the United States. In response, Reagan instructed Secretary of State Alexander Haig to have the American ambassador to Japan, Mike Mansfield, raise the issue quietly in Tokyo to see if a deal could be arranged.[66]

When it received Washington's message, the Japanese government realized that a VER was the best means for handling an explosive political situation that could damage relations with Japan's most important export market. More than cars were at stake, because a wide variety of other products, ranging from electronics to steel, might be affected if the auto dispute was not resolved quickly. Japanese auto executives had a different attitude, however, believing that they were being asked to sacrifice to save American auto executives from their own incompetence. But after a round of intense debate, Japanese firms agreed to accept MITI's proposed voluntary export restraint agreement, and the Japanese announced on May 1, 1981, that the export of automobiles to the United States would be limited to 1.68 million units for the coming year.[67] Having secured most of what he had aimed for when he introduced his quota bill, Senator Danforth withdrew his proposal from further consideration.

Renewals and Domestic Content

The Japanese VER did not end the controversy over automobiles. American companies recovered slowly, and many workers remained jobless for months after the agreement was reached. Moreover, the VER was good for only one year; unless it was extended, there would be renewed pressures from imports at the end of that year. In view of that situation, the auto companies and the UAW continued pressuring Congress for assistance.

In response to this lobbying, Rep. Richard Ottinger, D-N.Y., introduced a domestic content bill in February 1982. The bill, intended to force Japanese auto manufacturers to locate production facilities in the United States, required companies selling cars in the American market to produce a specified proportion of each vehicle in the United States, with the proportion increasing according to the number of vehicles sold. For larger Japanese firms, such as Nissan and Toyota, passage of the law would mean that nearly 90 percent of each vehicle they sold would have to be U.S.-produced. In effect, then, these companies no longer would be able to make cars in Japan to export to America.[68]

Not only did the Japanese resent the domestic content bill, but the free-market Reagan administration found it objectionable as well. The proposal did, however, convince the Japanese Ministry of International Trade and Industry that tempers were still hot in Washington when it came to the auto issue. Therefore, the Japanese announced in March that the automobile VER would be renewed for another year at 1.68 million export units. In 1983, pretty much the same scenario played out again; a nearly identical domestic content bill was introduced in the House in February, and the Japanese agreed in March to extend the VER for another year. On both occasions, the domestic content bill passed the House but was not considered by the Senate.[69]

While this game over renewing the VER was played out in Washington, American and Japanese auto producers were adapting to the new world of regulated trade. American companies began purchasing shares in selected Japanese firms and signing co-production agreements so that more Japanese components could be used to make American vehicles. Arrangements also were made to sell some Japanese cars under American brand names.

Japanese changes in tactics included exporting more expensive models that brought higher profits. Accordingly, the upscale Honda Accord and Toyota Camry soon made their way into America's showrooms. Moreover, Nissan, Honda, and Toyota built plants in the United States to produce cars for the American market that would not count against the VER. As a result of these moves, the average prices American consumers paid for automobiles went up substantially, American car manufacturers were by 1985 once again profitable, and Japanese companies were making more money than ever.

In the fall of 1983, U.S. Trade Representative Bill Brock and MITI officials handled the VER renewal. MITI suggested a 2.2 million quota, but backed off to 1.85 million when Brock balked. By this time, the auto industry was split over whether a VER was desirable. Ford, Chrysler, and the UAW favored renewal, but General Motors and the American International Automobile Dealers Association opposed it. GM hesitated because it wanted to move aggressively into the Japanese market, and extending the VER might allow the Japanese to stonewall over questions about market access for American vehicles.[70]

When the auto VER was due for renewal in late 1984, the Reagan administration opted to forgo an extension, believing that American producers were fully recovered from the problems they had faced in 1981. In addition, Washington wanted to shift the focus of American-Japanese discussions from autos to other products and believed the Japanese would use negotiations over autos to divert attention from those other issues. Because the regulated trade of the previous four years had been so profitable for Japanese companies, and because they wished to avoid trouble in Congress, the Japanese renewed the VER on their own at 2.3 million units a year.[71]

This ended the U.S.-Japanese conflict over automobiles, which had its origins in the oil crises of the 1970s and early 1980s. Although this battle was over, the chapters that follow will reveal that the war over autos and auto parts was not finished.

CHAPTER SUMMARY

With the advent of the oil-related problems of the 1980s, American consumers had to confront for the first time the potentially costly effects of interdependence. These problems also spelled trouble for the powerful American auto industry. American consumers responded to their troubles by panicking, becoming resentful toward those they blamed for their inconveniences, and demanding that the American dependence on foreign oil be eliminated. The public's panic merely exacerbated what might have been a manageable situation, which in turn heightened the rage felt by consumers. As the situation worsened, jobs evaporated, inflation grew, and even more anger was directed at oil-exporting countries, major oil firms, and a government in Washington that seemed unable to act.

Government action, however, was hampered by battles among interest groups, for there were many clashing views over what the appropriate policy should be. Heavy consumers of petroleum, such as airlines and the trucking industry, wanted ample fuel at low and stable prices. Petroleum producers split according to whether they acquired their oil at home or abroad and, if at home, whether they pumped new oil or old oil. Environmentalists were concerned about policies that called for using more coal, drilling oil wells in wilderness areas, and building pipelines that might threaten nature preserves. Taxpayers and some members of Congress worried about programs calling for massive spending on synfuels, and farmers pushed for new spending on corn-based alcohol that could be added to gasoline. Domestic liberals wanted cost controls and rationing to help the poor, but conservatives believed that only by decontrolling prices could the country solve its supply problems. In other words, every group favored a policy that was in that group's interest. And every group opposed solutions that would entail costs the group did not wish to bear.

Within this swirl of controversy, the Ford and Carter administrations found it difficult to convince Congress to pass legislation to deal with the nation's energy needs. Further complicating the legislative process were the populist reactions against proposals, such as decontrolling the price of domestic oil, that were perceived as favoring the very oil companies the public held accountable for fuel shortages. Matters were muddied even more by the public's expectation that sweeping and rapid solutions could be devised for America's energy needs. President Nixon's Project Independence only worsened the latter problem.

By their very nature, grand and sweeping solutions encouraged the public to believe that energy problems could be solved overnight and undermined the consideration of more realistic, if boring, proposals that might handle parts of the energy problem over a period of many months. Thus the conservation plans advanced by Presidents Ford and Carter were greeted with little public enthusiasm, even though they were valuable steps toward reducing America's energy needs.

In the end, the nation's energy problems were handled by a combination of conservation, exploration for new oil at home and abroad, and rising prices. As prices increased, exploration and conservation became more popular. The result was more oil and falling demand, leading eventually to lower oil prices and a loosening of OPEC's apparent stranglehold over the world economy.

But it was just as OPEC's power was about to give way that the auto industry's woes began. Although it was battered by the 1973–1974 oil crisis, the American auto industry chose to ignore the warning that the day of the big car might be over. When the second crisis came in 1979, the industry found itself in deep trouble. Like so many others before them in American history, the auto makers turned first to Congress for help. When a quick legislative solution was not available, the industry turned to the legal system and filed an escape clause petition.

The escape clause of the 1974 Trade Act requires the complainant to show injury and demonstrate that imports are a substantial cause of the injury—that is, that imports are just as important as any other cause of the industry's injury. As it turned out, the auto industry failed to make its case, and the International Trade Commission rejected the industry's petition.

The ITC rejection put the matter back into the hands of Congress, where vigorous trade-restricting legislation was immediately introduced. Realizing that such legislation would pose a threat to the overall health of the liberal trading system, the Reagan administration set aside its commitment to open trade and found a way to negotiate a voluntary export restraint agreement with Japan, the principle source of competition for American producers.

The auto case illustrates several things about the American trading system. First, it shows that trouble in one trade sector, such as oil, can have profound effects on other sectors. Indeed, as the level and scope of American trade have increased, such effects have become the general rule. Second, it reveals how specific the legal rules governing protection have become. Those seeking assistance must be able to prove that they qualify under the guidelines established by law. If complainants cannot do so, they are not likely to receive a favorable ruling, even when they are as large and important as the auto industry. Finally, the auto case demonstrates that the failure to qualify for aid under the law does not end the protectionist game, especially for powerful industries; Congress can always write new laws or threaten to do so. If enough pressure is exerted in the political arena, then some form of special assistance may be forthcoming.

NOTES

1. The title for this chapter is borrowed from Dankwart A. Rustow, *Oil and Turmoil: America Faces OPEC and the Middle East* (New York: Norton, 1982).

2. These figures are from *Statistical Yearbook of the League of Nations, 1931/32*, 138; and *Statistical Yearbook of the League of Nations, 1941/42*, 135.

3. Daniel Yergin, *The Prize: The Epic Quest for Oil, Money, and Power* (New York: Simon and Schuster, 1992), 537.

4. Rustow, *Oil and Turmoil*, 119–120; and Yergin, *Prize*, 537–538.

5. Raymond A. Bauer, Ithiel de Sola Pool, and Lewis Anthony Dexter, *American Business and Public Policy: The Politics of Foreign Trade* (New York: Atherton Press, 1964), 71; and Robert A. Pastor, *Congress and the Politics of U.S. Foreign Economic Policy, 1929–1976* (Berkeley: University of California Press, 1980), 103.

6. Burton I. Kaufman, *Trade and Aid: Eisenhower's Foreign Economic Policy, 1953–1961* (Baltimore: Johns Hopkins University Press, 1982), 89–90; Rustow, *Oil and Turmoil*, 120–121; and Yergin, *Prize*, 538–539.

7. The majors were (and still are) large corporations that explore for oil around the world, run the operations that pump oil from wells, transport that oil to refineries, and market petroleum products to consumers. In the late 1950s, the largest of these corporations were sometimes labeled the "seven sisters." They were Exxon, Mobil, Gulf, Texaco, Chevron, British Petroleum, and Shell.

8. Anthony Sampson, *The Seven Sisters: The Great Oil Companies and the World They Shaped* (New York: Bantam Books, 1991), 190–194.

9. Yergin, *Prize*, 567–568.

10. Rustow, *Oil and Turmoil*, 136–137; Sampson, *Seven Sisters*, 266–269; and Yergin, *Prize*, 577–582.

11. Rustow, *Oil and Turmoil*, 153–154.

12. James W. McKie, "The United States," in *The Oil Crisis*, ed. Raymond Vernon (New York: Norton, 1976), 81; the quote is from Rustow, *Oil and Turmoil*, 155.

13. Henry Kissinger, *Years of Upheaval* (Boston: Little, Brown, 1982), 513–515, 518–529; Richard Nixon, *RN: The Memoirs of Richard Nixon* (New York: Simon and Schuster, 1978), 926–927; and Yergin, *Prize*, 604–605.

14. Rustow, *Oil and Turmoil*, 145–146; and Sampson, *Seven Sisters*, 292–298.

15. Nixon, *RN*, 931; and Rustow, *Oil and Turmoil*, 145–146.

16. Rustow, *Oil and Turmoil*, 112; Sampson, *Seven Sisters*, 297–298; and Yergin, *Prize*, 621, 624. Yergin notes that the embargo-induced oil shortages were 17 percent for Japan, 18 percent for the United States, and 16 percent for the European Community.

17. Yergin, *Prize*, 656–657.

18. Kissinger, *Years of Upheaval*, 619, 640–641, 664.

19. Ibid., 776–777.

20. Ibid., 829–846, 891–895.

21. Ibid., 896–905. The quote is from p. 901.

22. Ibid., 908–925. The quote is on p. 920. See also Robert Keohane, "The International Energy Agency: State Influence and Transgovernmental Politics," *International Organization* 32 (autumn 1978): 929–951; and Ulf Lantzke, "The OECD and Its International Energy Agency," in *The Oil Crisis*, ed. Raymond Vernon (New York: Norton, 1976), 217–227.

23. *Wall Street Journal*, March 6, 1974, 1, 33.

24. *Wall Street Journal*, March 7, 1974, 1, 22, 33.

25. G. John Ikenberry, "Market Solutions for State Problems: The International and Domestic Politics of American Oil Decontrol," *International Organization* 42 (winter 1988): 155–157; James W. McKie, "United States," 77; and Rustow, *Oil and Turmoil*, 219.

26. McKie, "United States," 75–76; and Yergin, *Prize*, 571–574, 665–666.

27. McKie, "United States," 83; and Rustow, *Oil and Turmoil*, 171.

28. Gerald R. Ford, *A Time to Heal* (New York: Harper and Row, 1979), 228, 241–242, 339; Ikenberry, "Market Solutions," 165; and Yergin, *Prize*, 660.

29. Ford, *Time to Heal*, 243, 340–341; Ikenberry, "Market Solutions," 165; and Yergin, *Prize*, 660.

30. These data are from United Nations, *Yearbook of International Trade Statistics*, various years.

31. Jimmy Carter, *Keeping Faith* (New York: Bantam Books, 1982), 92.

32. Ibid., 91.

33. Ibid., 91–101; and *New York Times*, October 7, 1977, 1, D5; October 18, 1977, 1, 24; October 15, 1977, 1, 35; October 21, 1977, D1, D5; October 26, 1977, 5; November 1, 1977, 1, 63.

34. Carter, *Keeping Faith*, 104.

35. Rustow, *Oil and Turmoil*, 183; and Yergin, *Prize*, 678.

36. Rustow, *Oil and Turmoil*, 184.

37. Yergin, *Prize*, 686.

38. Ibid., 112.

39. Ibid., 121.

40. *New York Times,* February 10, 1980, 29; February 21, 1980, A1, D5.

41. Carter, *Keeping Faith,* 122.

42. Yergin, *Prize,* 711–712.

43. Bijan Mossavar-Rahmani, "The OPEC Multiplier,"*Foreign Policy* (fall 1983): 136–140.

44. Ibid., 136–140.

45. Yergin, *Prize,* 717–718.

46. *Statistical Yearbook of the League of Nations, 1931/32,* 224.

47. Stefanie Ann Lenway, *The Politics of U.S. International Trade: Protection, Expansion, and Escape* (Boston: Pitman Publishing, 1985), 129.

48. Carolyn Rhodes, *Reciprocity, U.S. Trade Policy, and the GATT Regime* (Ithaca: Cornell University Press, 1993), 158.

49. David Halberstam, *The Reckoning* (New York: Avon Books, 1986), 366–368, 572–576.

50. Ibid., chaps. 16 and 24.

51. Ibid., chap. 32, 543–544.

52. Ibid., 33; and Lenway, *Politics of U.S. International Trade,* 131–132.

53. Judith Goldstein, *Ideas, Interests, and American Trade Policy* (Ithaca: Cornell University Press, 1993), 230–231; Lenway, *Politics of U.S. International Trade,* 133; and Rhodes, *Reciprocity,* 158.

54. Goldstein, *Ideas, Interests,* 230–231; Halberstam, *Reckoning,* 566–567; and Lenway, *Politics of U.S. International Trade,* 133.

55. Steve Dryden, *Trade Warriors: USTR and the American Crusade for Free Trade* (New York: Oxford University Press, 1995), 257; Anne O. Krueger, *American Trade Policy: A Tragedy in the Making* (Washington, D.C.: AEI Press, 1995); and Lenway, *Politics of U.S. International Trade,* 134–135.

56. Lenway, *Politics of U.S. International Trade,* 136.

57. John H. Jackson, *The World Trading System: Law and Policy of International Economic Relations* (Cambridge: MIT Press, 1997), 181–199.

58. Ibid., 184–189; and Lenway, *Politics of U.S. International Trade,* 140.

59. Lenway, *Politics of U.S. International Trade,* 141.

60. Ibid., 148–150.

61. Ibid., 146–151.

62. Ibid., 148–149.

63. Goldstein, *Ideas, Interests,* 231.

64. Ibid., 231; Lenway, *Politics of U.S. International Trade,* 157; and Rhodes, *Reciprocity,* 160.

65. Goldstein, *Ideas, Interests,* 232; and Ronald Reagan, *An American Life* (New York: Simon and Schuster, 1990), 242, 253–254.

66. Dryden, *Trade Warriors,* 271; and Rhodes, *Reciprocity,* 161.

67. Dryden, *Trade Warriors*, 273–274; and Lenway, *Politics of U.S. International Trade*, 158.
68. Goldstein, *Ideas, Interests*, 232; and Patrick Low, *Trading Free: The GATT and U.S. Trade Policy* (New York: Twentieth Century Fund Press, 1993), 116.
69. Goldstein, *Ideas, Interests*, 232; and Low, *Trading Free*, 116.
70. Goldstein, *Ideas, Interests*, 233; and Rhodes, *Reciprocity*, 167–168.
71. Goldstein, *Ideas, Interests*, 233; and Rhodes, *Reciprocity*, 172–173.

8 From the Cold War to the WTO and NAFTA

When he assumed the presidency in 1981, Ronald Reagan believed that American trade policy had two important roles to play in strategic affairs. The first involved using trade to bind the Western alliance into a collection of commercial juggernauts that would provide higher standards of living for their people, that would serve as models for the rest of the world, and that would have the wherewithal to finance the spending needed to counter the military might of communist countries. Second, by restricting trade with eastern bloc countries, the United States could guarantee that they would not be able to use commercial exchanges with the West to make up for their own economic incompetence. As Reagan saw it, strategic imperatives demanded that the United States continually seek to lower trade barriers among noncommunist countries while strictly controlling exports to the Soviet Union and its allies.

Both of the roles Reagan envisioned for trade policy were controversial from the start and plagued by lack of cooperation from other countries and by protests from American special interests. America's allies complained that restrictions on east-west trade would result in lost business opportunities and in lost essential imports from the Soviet Union. American companies also resisted restrictions because they did not want to lose the profits such trade represented. Moreover, many believed that Reagan's demand to control trade was contradicted by his decision to cancel trade sanctions imposed by the Carter administration on the Soviet Union a year earlier. This cancellation seemed designed to appease American farm interests and implied that Reagan only favored limiting trade when American interests were not hurt.

Reagan's desire to push for freer trade also ran into trouble from Americans' growing perception in the 1980s that the United States was facing an unfair international competitive environment. One American producer after another bombarded the president and Congress with protests that foreign markets were not as open as American markets. Beyond this, many corporations, some of them important to American national security, alleged that they were the victims of questionable foreign tactics designed to drive them into bankruptcy.

These concerns about international competitive practices fell on receptive ears in Congress, which immediately began to search for legislative remedies. Dominated as it was under Reagan by ardent free traders who believed in leaving international markets alone, the executive branch at first used the same hands-off approach it had favored early in the auto dispute described in Chapter 7. As time passed and the complaints about unfair behavior persisted, the White House realized that unless it took action the president's goal of more open trade would be imperiled by congressional moves to help beleaguered American producers. Thus the Reagan administration put together a two-pronged strategy. The first part, employing the approach used during the Kennedy and Tokyo Rounds, called for new GATT negotiations to set up international rules that would ban the practices confounding American businesses. The second part initiated bilateral talks with countries thought to be engaging in unfair trade, such as Japan. The talks would aim to open foreign markets and to halt anticompetitive behavior.

Each of these approaches, however, proved difficult. The GATT talks nearly foundered because the United States insisted on bargaining about issues that other countries felt reflected their cultural preferences and affected vitally important local producers. The talks with Japan ran into trouble not only because of cultural problems, but also because the Japanese believed the negotiations were intended to shift the blame for America's economic failures from American to Japanese shoulders. Both sets of negotiations ultimately yielded agreements that only included a portion of what the United States sought.

Also in the 1980s, important trade negotiations began on the establishment of the **North American Free Trade Agreement (NAFTA).** For Reagan, these talks represented a chance to realize his dream for a single North American market. The NAFTA talks also created a firestorm of political controversy in the United States when the original bargain with Canada was extended to include Mexico, which was perceived as playing by very different political and commercial rules from those that prevailed north of the Rio Grande. As the NAFTA drama unfolded, interest group confrontations and conflicts between the White House and Congress sprang up over issues related to workers' rights and the environment.

This chapter examines the debates over restricting trade with the Soviet Union, pressuring Japan to conform to American ideas about market opening, initiating and completing the Uruguay Round of the GATT, and creating and ratifying the North American Free Trade Agreement. The examination of these issues focuses on the degree to which most American leaders had developed a strong attachment to liberal trade by the 1980s. Indeed, by that time this attachment had become so ingrained that, when frustrated by trade problems, politicians increasingly responded not by seeking to close American markets, but by demanding that other countries open their markets to American goods and services—a far cry from the high tariff walls Congress constructed in the early twentieth century.

EAST-WEST TRADE

Throughout the 1970s, the American interest in easing Cold War tensions brought a relaxation in east-west trade restrictions. This policy ended abruptly when the Soviet Union invaded Afghanistan in December 1979. In President Jimmy Carter's view, this move imperiled the oil fields of Iran and the Persian Gulf and represented "the gravest threat to peace since World War II."[1] As a result, Carter felt he had "to lead the . . . world in making [the invasion] as costly as possible."[2]

The Grain Embargo

In considering responses to the aggression, Carter rejected a diplomatic protest as an insufficient display of American concern and a military operation as too risky. An analysis of U.S.-Soviet trade, however, revealed that reductions in the sales of grain and high-technology goods would have the greatest effect on the Soviet economy. Without grain imports, the Russians would not have sufficient stocks to feed livestock and to export to the Eastern European economies they subsidized. Limitations on high-technology exports would rob the Soviets of the computers, machine tools, and other equipment they needed to produce innovative weapons. The administration believed that trade sanctions would demonstrate U.S. resolve and warn the Soviets against taking additional moves. As Carter's national security adviser Zbigniew Brzezinski observed, "We had no illusions that [trade] sanctions in themselves would force the Soviets out [of Afghanistan], but we felt that the Soviet Union had to pay some tangible price for its misconduct."[3]

Each of the contemplated trade sanctions brought with it domestic and international political problems. On the domestic side, the special interests might rise in protest, citing the business lost from the interruption in trade. On the international front, neither type of trade restriction would prove effective unless other countries joined in the effort. Difficulties soon emerged in both areas.

On January 4, 1980, President Carter announced the U.S. sanctions against the Soviet Union. At first, most Americans supported his policy. Among other things, Carter said he was: (1) requesting increased American defense spending, (2) introducing legislation to restore registration for the draft, (3) recalling the U.S. ambassador from Moscow, (4) pledging American protection to the Persian Gulf region (known as the Carter Doctrine), (5) calling for a boycott of the summer Olympic Games scheduled for Moscow, (6) announcing a partial grain embargo, and (7) tightening U.S. exports of high-technology goods to the Soviet Union.[4]

The grain embargo cancelled a recently negotiated sale of 17 million metric tons. An 8 million-ton sale that was part of a five-year plan Carter had promised not to embargo was allowed to go forward. To ensure that American farmers would not suffer from the embargo, Carter ordered Agriculture Secretary Bob Bergland to seek markets in Mexico and China. As Carter later noted, even though grain prices fell after the embargo was announced, they recovered within a week. Indeed, the search for new markets was so successful that by the end of 1980 an all-time export record had been set.[5]

Yet despite such efforts, support for the sanctions soon soured. For one thing, farmers became alarmed when foreign producers began to replace the embargoed American grain. From the beginning, Argentina had refused to endorse the embargo, and Australia and Canada had promised not to increase their grain sales. Soon, however, both countries greatly expanded their exports.[6] Even though U.S. farmers' 1980 sales figures were good, the future seemed questionable and they feared the permanent loss of the Soviet market. Republican contenders for the presidency, including Ronald Reagan, capitalized on the situation and called for an end to the embargo. As Reagan later wrote, the grain embargo "was hurting our farmers more than it was hurting the Russians."[7]

A similar fate befell Carter's limitations on high-technology exports. American companies quickly protested to Congress that they were losing business. Export controls would not harm the Soviet Union unless other countries also cut their sales, they noted. Members of the Coordinating Committee for Multilateral Export Controls said they would study the situation, but they were reluctant to take action that might destroy normal east-west relations and undermine the health of European and Japanese firms that were selling goods to the Soviet bloc. In the end, then, because of Carter's decision to restrict American high-technology exports, the American firms Armco and Alcoa lost some $300 million in contracts to build steel and aluminum factories in the Soviet Union, and French and German companies picked up the deals.[8]

This was the politically charged situation that awaited Reagan when he became president in 1981. During the campaign, the former governor had promised he would lift the grain embargo when he took office, and, after some initial hesitation, he did so on April 24, 1981.

The Pipeline Sanctions

At the same time he was moving to terminate the grain embargo, Reagan ordered a review of American exports to the Soviet Union and of the Western credit sources that financed Soviet purchases. Of special concern were the high-technology sales that the Carter administration had already moved to limit, technology that could be used for both civilian and military purposes, projects that allowed the Soviets to earn the income needed to purchase Western goods, and the subsidized financing that many nations offered to attract Russian business. Reagan believed these practices should be eliminated because they helped the Soviets maintain a powerful military. He was joined in this belief by Secretary of Defense Caspar Weinberger, who observed that east-west trade "helped preserve the Soviet Union as a totalitarian dictatorship."[9]

Reagan was particularly worried about a Soviet proposal to build a 3,500-mile pipeline that would bring Soviet natural gas to European markets. He feared Europeans would become so dependent on Soviet-supplied natural gas that they would be unable to conduct an independent foreign policy. The White House also believed that Moscow would use the billions of dollars produced by the pipeline to prop up the faltering Soviet economy and to buy technology for the Red Army. Beyond this, it was suspected that some of the technology purchased by the Soviets to build the pipeline could be used for military purposes.

In an attempt to halt the pipeline and to tighten east-west trade restrictions, Reagan urged that the Coordinating Committee for Multilateral Export Controls, or CoCom, review the pipeline project. With this request, however, Reagan opened himself up to accusations of inconsistent behavior, given that he was lifting the grain embargo. Administration officials responded to the accusations by pointing out that the pipeline deal would provide the Soviets with income to spend on high-technology imports, whereas grain was a nonstrategic good that absorbed Soviet money and reduced the Soviet Union's ability to purchase items for the military.[10] European leaders, however, were not convinced. As they saw it, the United States was allowing trade that helped Americans while trying to block commerce that benefited others.

As Reagan persisted in his arguments, he found his West German, French, British, and Italian colleagues unmoved. Negotiations with the Soviet Union continued, and in September and October the Soviets signed contracts with West German, French, and Italian firms to deliver equipment for the pipeline. At this point, in December, the Soviet Union sponsored a crackdown on the pro-democracy Solidarity movement in Poland. Like the Carter administration two years earlier, Reagan's team felt that the Soviet move required a tough American response and that economic sanctions were the best course of action. Under the circumstances, the natural gas pipeline was a good target for those sanctions, and so Reagan announced on December 29, 1981 that American firms would be prohibited from participating in its construction. The move caught America's European allies by surprise. It also led to the loss of contracts worth $90 million to the Caterpillar Corporation and $175 million to General Electric.[11]

Despite the American move, Europeans went ahead with the pipeline. At a June 1982 summit meeting in France, Reagan attempted to convince other Western leaders to abandon the project, but he made no headway. As a result, when he returned home Reagan extended the American trade sanctions to include sales by the foreign subsidiaries of American firms and by foreign companies operating under license from American corporations.

Extension of the sanctions sparked an immediate controversy. It angered Western European governments because it represented an attempt at extraterritoriality, or the application of American law to other countries. Europeans also were enraged that at the very moment the United States tightened the sanctions it was negotiating new grain agreements with the Soviet Union.[12] At home, the extension led to the resignation of Secretary of State Alexander Haig, who was upset that the decision was made while he was away from Washington.

Tensions increased in August when French and British companies operating under licenses from American firms shipped equipment to the Soviet Union. In response, the Reagan administration ordered the American corporations to terminate their relationships with the European firms. At the same time, officials in Washington began realizing that the sanctions were having an adverse effect on the North Atlantic Treaty Organization. Reagan therefore accepted the advice of his new secretary of state, George Shultz, to negotiate an agreement with the Europeans to limit credit to the Soviet Union and to work out more stringent CoCom controls on high-technology exports—all in exchange for terminating the sanctions.[13]

The negotiations on credit limits, export controls, and the pipeline took place at a NATO foreign ministers meeting in Canada in October. Although the French insisted that any new trade or credit limitations should be treated as a separate issue from the pipeline question, enough progress was made at the meeting to satisfy President Reagan. He therefore announced during a radio broadcast on November 13 that the pipeline sanctions would be lifted. In return, but without explicit linkage to the sanctions, Europeans agreed to conduct a study of their dependence on Soviet natural gas, to examine the issue of extending credit to the Soviets, and to consider enlarging CoCom export controls as the United States wished.[14]

With that, the pipeline controversy ended, but, as it turned out, few changes were made in European credit practices or in the CoCom list of export controls. Indeed, Reagan had had to confront the same problem Carter had faced earlier: America's allies were hesitant to agree with trade restrictions against the Soviet Union. Without such cooperation, any sanctions imposed by the United States were merely symbolic expressions of outrage that harmed American exporters more than they hurt the Soviet Union. The one bright spot for the United States was that its estimates of Russian economic weakness were accurate, and the revenues from the sale of natural gas were not sufficient to put off the day of economic reckoning that was just over the horizon for the Soviet Union.

THE JAPANESE CHALLENGE

The pipeline controversy was not the only trade problem confronting the United States in the early 1980s; another was the Japanese imports flooding the United States. In the years immediately after the Second World War, the United States enjoyed economic superiority over Japan (see Chapter 7), but that superiority began to fade in the 1960s and 1970s as several American producers felt the pressure of Japanese competition. By 1980, the Japanese appeared to be threatening the existence of several industries, including those making automobiles, steel, and televisions. Indeed, one of Reagan's first jobs as president was setting up a voluntary export restraint agreement to limit Japanese auto exports.

The Japanese Difference

As many analysts saw things, the challenge from Japan transcended any single industry and raised the possibility that the United States might lose its position as the world's largest economic power. During the decade ending in 1980, Japan's total economic output grew by 4.6 percent and its manufacturing production by 6.5 percent, compared with American growth rates of 3.0 percent and 3.1 percent, respectively. These superior rates of growth allowed the Japanese economy to nearly double its size in relation to that of the United States—that is, in 1970 Japan produced only 20 percent as much as the United States, but by 1980 that figure had reached nearly 40 percent.[15]

American explanations for the Japanese surge frequently pointed to trade and growing Japanese exports. For example, during the 1970s Japan's total exports grew at an average annual rate of 10.5 percent, while American exports increased by a more modest 6.7 percent.[16] Japan's exports to the United States increased even more rapidly, rising from $5.9 billion in 1970 to $30.9 billion in 1980, an increase of over 500 percent. As a result, the U.S. balance of trade with Japan, which habitually was in the black until the mid-1960s, began bleeding ever more red ink throughout the 1970s, swelling from a deficit of $1.2 billion in 1970 to one of $10.1 billion by 1980.[17]

In themselves, the growth in the Japanese economy and the increase in exports to the United States were not nearly as troubling as the growing suspicion that Japan played by unusual economic rules. Awareness of the differences between the United States and Japan first surfaced in the 1970s when the Japanese dismantled many of their formal trade barriers as required by the Kennedy and Tokyo Round GATT agreements. For example, 59 percent of all Japanese imports were subject to quotas in 1960, but by the mid-1970s such restrictions affected only a handful of products.[18] Tariffs also fell substantially, so that by 1980 Japanese rates were comparable with those in the United States and the European Community (EC),[19] averaging 4.6 percent on semi-manufactures and 6.0 percent on finished manufactured goods, compared with average rates of 3.0 percent and 5.7 percent on the same goods in the United States and 4.2 percent and 6.9 percent in Europe.[20]

The Japanese also displayed a willingness to negotiate in the 1970s as their trade surpluses soared and American complaints became frequent. One of the most notable bargains between the two countries was a January 1978 agreement that called for Japan to eliminate quotas on twelve types of imports, to increase its beef imports from 3,000 to 10,000 tons a year, to set a target of 7 percent annual growth in Japanese imports, and to balance its imports and exports.[21] At first, this agreement was hailed as a step in the right direction, but then American special interests and members of Congress began to doubt the value of the accord when the U.S. trade deficit with Japan climbed to $10.1 billion in 1980 and $15.8 billion in 1981.[22] Instead of calming troubled trade waters, the 1978 agreement simply confirmed for many that Japan was engaging in commercial chicanery.

Doubts about the sincerity of Japanese market-opening moves prompted many American trade analysts to look at how Japanese imports and exports compared with the patterns for other advanced countries. The results often were disturbing. Research revealed that Japan imported large quantities of raw materials but few manufactured goods. Indeed, for the size of their manufacturing output the Japanese imported a much smaller volume of manufactured goods than did any other major industrialized country. For example, in 1980 the ratio of manufactured imports to manufacturing output for Japan was less than half that of the United States, less than a third the figures for Italy and Germany, only a fourth of the French amount, a fifth of the British level, and a ninth that of Canada.[23]

Another feature of Japanese trade that caught the attention of many Americans was the aggressive Japanese practice of targeting specific industries for rapid growth and heavy exporting. By the early 1980s, some American trade specialists were asserting that Japan was deliberately selecting key industries for special government assistance. They went on to allege that Japanese export decisions were not market driven as they were in the United States, but instead were carefully calculated to move into certain industrial arenas and to dominate specific markets at home and abroad. Japanese exports to the United States represented more than just an attempt to reap profits, analysts believed; they also were part of an assault on American industry that was aimed at allowing Japan to dominate world markets. To these observers, Japan's hostility to imports, especially of manufactured goods, and the energetic approach the Japanese took toward exports were a dangerous combination that required a vigorous American response.[24]

Market Opening: Round One

The free trade orientation of the early Reagan administration meant that it was ill-suited to confront the Japanese over trade. Early on, members of the White House staff and representatives of the State and Treasury Departments maintained that the continuing trade problems with Japan stemmed from a lack of effort by American firms. Instead of pressing the Japanese to discontinue questionable behavior and to open their markets to foreign goods, American producers should develop better products and become more effective in appealing to foreign consumers.[25] In short, many members of the administration argued that the problem was not Japan; it was the sloppy practices of many American businesses.

Finding these arguments infuriating, many American corporate executives and labor union leaders turned to Congress, where the growing Japanese trade surplus already had several members on edge. As described in Chapter 7, the troubles in the auto industry brought calls for quotas on Japanese-made cars and for domestic content requirements. Legislation also was introduced to limit steel imports.

In early 1982, things went even further; Republican senator John Danforth introduced a measure to require a new form of reciprocity. The Danforth bill aimed to restrict imports from countries that did not provide American producers the same degree of access to their markets as was available in the United States to foreign producers.[26] This proposal reflected the growing belief that American markets were more open than other markets and that foreigners should be forced to match the openness found in the United States.

In the Reagan administration, Commerce Secretary Malcolm Baldrige, a former chairman of the Scovill Corporation, shared the sentiments of many of those who criticized Japan. Having led the Scovill drive to enter the Japanese market, Baldrige knew first-hand the problems foreigners faced when they dealt with the Japanese.[27] Baldrige was joined in his concerns by his senior adviser on Japan, Clyde Prestowitz, a former business executive who spoke fluent Japanese and had worked in Japan for several years. Despite their knowledge of Japanese business practices, both men repeatedly confronted strong opposition from doctrinaire free traders in the administration who agreed with Secretary of State George Shultz when he said that any government attempts to help American companies might make them "too fond of the protection." [28]

As a result, most of Reagan's advisers looked for ways to sidetrack Danforth's bill. In 1983, the president appointed a special task force, headed by Vice President George Bush, to look into the Japanese "problem." Prestowitz, who represented the Commerce Department on the task force, found the job frustrating. Officials from the National Security Council and from the Defense, Treasury, and State Departments repeatedly argued against negotiating with the Japanese over trade issues. One especially troubling incident concerned Japan's attempt to pass new laws restricting foreign access to the Japanese telecommunications market. For task force members from the Commerce Department, these laws illustrated the degree to which the Japanese were manipulating trade to favor domestic producers. And yet most members of the task force refused to agree to pressure Japan to drop the legislation, saying that doing so might offend the Japanese government.[29] The upshot was that while the task force talked a lot, it actually did little.

The pressure from Congress, however, was unrelenting. In 1984, the trade deficit with Japan jumped to $33.6 billion, up from $19.3 billion, which was itself a record.[30] In response, Congress asserted itself by attaching a modified version of the Danforth bill to White House-sponsored legislation to extend American participation in the GATT generalized system of preferences program and to set up a free trade agreement with Israel. The Senate passed the altered bill by a vote of 96–0 in July 1984. A few weeks later, the House passed similar legislation. When Reagan threatened to veto the bill, a House-Senate Conference Committee deleted the Danforth amendment, but retained the GSP and Israeli measures in what was known as the **Trade and Tariff Act of 1984.**[31]

Other signs of congressional distress came in 1985. First, the House and Senate passed nonbinding resolutions criticizing Japan.[32] Second, Rep. Richard Gephardt, D-Mo., introduced a measure in the House to require countries having excessive trade surpluses with the United States to lower their surpluses by 10 percent a year or face stiff trade barriers. Over three hundred other trade-restricting bills also were placed in the congressional hopper by mid-1985.[33]

Amid this climate of growing concern about Japan, Reagan changed course and opened negotiations to secure greater access to the Japanese market for American firms producing world-class quality goods. The discussions, which began in January 1985, were labeled the **Market-Oriented Sector-Selective (MOSS)** talks.[34] The administration hoped the negotiations would deflect congressional anger about Japan by securing an agreement to open Japanese markets to a range of American goods. To guarantee that the Japanese would not complain they were being forced to accept inferior American products, the talks focused only on top-notch American goods, including certain electronics items, medical equipment and pharmaceuticals, telecommunications equipment and services, and forest products.

During the negotiations, the American team concentrated on securing better protection for the technology and intellectual property of American firms, eliminating heavy-handed Japanese government procurement practices, simplifying Japanese government testing and certification procedures, eliminating practices that allowed Japanese businesses to participate in setting standards for imports, and changing Japanese building codes to allow greater use of foreign-made materials. The United States eventually obtained agreements meeting most of these goals. But as time passed, American firms began complaining that their access to the Japanese market was no greater than before MOSS. For example, Motorola noted that it continued to face problems in selling cellular telephones in Japan even though under MOSS the Japanese had agreed to allow Motorola to do business. This situation led to accusations that the Japanese either were ignoring the agreement or were finding new ways to hamper other countries from entering their market.[35]

Market Opening: Semiconductors

The difficulties associated with doing business in Japan led to increasing levels of frustration, and many observers began to voice the possibility that Japan was attempting to dominate the United States commercially. Writing in the summer of 1985, Theodore White, one of America's most respected journalists, noted that forty years after the end of World War II "the Japanese are on the move again in one of history's most brilliant commercial offensives, as they go about dismantling American industry." Picking up on the theme, Sen. Bob Dole warned that while no one wanted a trade war, "a point may soon be reached where economic arguments are replaced by political imperatives."[36]

Responding to these sentiments and to the growing trade deficit, the Reagan administration decided in September 1985 to seek the cooperation of France, Great Britain, Japan, and West Germany in lowering the value of the dollar against the world's major currencies. At that time, the exchange rate of the dollar was high in part because foreigners, in response to an American budget deficit and high interest rates, were demanding dollars so they could take advantage of investment opportunities in the United States. These high exchange rates pushed the American trade deficit upward by making foreign-produced goods cheaper for Americans to buy and goods from America more expensive for foreigners. Earlier, many administration officials, with their laissez-faire beliefs, had been reluctant to intervene in currency markets. But these attitudes changed as the trade picture darkened.

The move to drive down the value of the dollar began at a meeting on September 22 at the Plaza Hotel in New York. At about the same time, Reagan unveiled in Washington an "action plan" on trade to address many of the problems worrying congressional critics. Declaring that "I will not stand by and watch

American workers lose their jobs because other nations do not play by the rules," Reagan made it clear that he intended to take a get-tough approach to trade.[37] Included in the action plan were: (1) a promise to act more aggressively on unfair trade, (2) a pledge to eliminate foreign violations of American copyrights and patents, (3) a special $300 million "war chest" for the Export-Import Bank to use in countering foreign subsidies, and (4) a call for new GATT talks to develop rules to forbid the trade practices bedeviling Americans.[38]

The devaluation of the dollar, the action plan, and the MOSS talks were not the only items on Reagan's trade agenda by September 1985; the administration also was negotiating on behalf of the semiconductor industry.[39] Through the 1970s, the world regarded U.S. achievements in semiconductor development and production a hallmark of industrial success. The industry was born in the United States in 1947 when Bell Laboratories created the transistor. As time passed, the industry made revolutionary improvements in the design of the "chips" that served as the electronic hearts of products such as radios, televisions, computers, household appliances, airplanes, and automobiles. Chips also played a vital role in the defense industry, where they were important for aircraft guidance systems, navigation, radar, surveillance, and a host of other functions.

Because Bell Laboratories was a part of the AT&T empire, at the time a government-controlled monopoly, other companies were able to obtain semiconductor technology merely for a licensing fee. As production spread, foreign companies soon entered the game, including firms in Japan. From the beginning, the Japanese market was virtually closed to foreign chips because the Ministry of International Trade and Industry was targeting the Japanese semiconductor industry for rapid expansion. Although formal trade barriers were eliminated in 1976, foreign companies still found it nearly impossible to sell chips in Japan.

With help from their government, Japanese chip makers made rapid strides as they drove to overtake American firms. And, as was the case in so many other industries, exporting was a vital part of the Japanese development strategy. To Americans, Japan's progress was breathtaking. In 1978, U.S. semiconductor companies had a 55 percent share of industry revenues worldwide, and Japanese firms had only a 28 percent share. By 1986, however, the share held by U.S. companies had fallen to 40 percent, while the Japanese saw their share rise to 46 percent. Indeed, the Japanese assault was so intense that by 1986 seven of the nine U.S. companies producing DRAMs, one of the most basic types of chips, had abandoned the field because they could no longer match Japanese prices. This development had particularly ominous implications for an industry that was vital to American national security because the start-up costs for chip production were so enormous that once a company closed it would be nearly impossible for it to reopen.

In 1985, faced with its rapid reversal of fortunes, the continuing informal closure of the Japanese market to its chips, and the exceptionally low prices of the Japanese chips sold in the American market, the American semiconductor industry took action. In June 1985, the Semiconductor Industry Association (SIA) filed a complaint under Section 301 of the 1974 Trade Act. Section 301 gives the president the authority to investigate unfair trade and to negotiate its elimination. If the negotiations fail, the president has the power to retaliate. The SIA complaint alleged that Japanese government regulations and Japanese business practices had led to informal closure of the Japanese market to foreign chips. Micron Technology, Intel, Advanced Micro Devices (AMD), and National Semiconductor also filed dumping cases against Japanese producers.

Under the threat of the dumping cases and the Section 301 action, the Japanese government expressed a willingness to negotiate over semiconductors. In conducting the negotiations, the United States pushed for specific numerical indicators that could be used to assess Japanese compliance. After all, previously the Japanese appeared to break their promises, such as in the MOSS outcome. After a year of talks, the United States and Japan reached an agreement in July 1986. The accord, which had a limit of five years, obligated Japanese firms to stop dumping chips in the United States and in third markets, and MITI pledged to monitor Japanese sales to guard against dumping. The Japanese also promised to improve foreign access to the Japanese market, and a side letter set a target of 20 percent for the foreign share. For its part, the United States suspended the dumping and Section 301 cases.

The agreement met with divergent responses in the United States. Free traders in the Reagan administration denounced the understanding and directed special venom at the 20 percent market share clause, which was regarded as micromanaging free markets. U.S. Trade Representative Clayton Yeutter and officials in the Commerce Department considered the accord a major achievement. On Capitol Hill, most members of Congress were delighted that the United States had forced Japan to set a specific market-opening target.

The semiconductor story did not end here, however. In 1987, the Semiconductor Industry Association complained that Japan was violating the agreement by dumping in third markets and refusing to expand the foreign share of the Japanese market. Upon hearing this, members of Congress demanded that Reagan retaliate with trade sanctions. Reagan agreed to do so, and on April 17 steep tariffs were levied on certain types of Japanese computers and on electropneumatic hammers.

In response to the American penalties, MITI began watching dumping more closely. But little was done to improve the foreign share of the Japanese market, which remained at 10 percent. Even when the agreement was extended in 1991 and the 20 percent target was reaffirmed, foreign sales in Japan stagnated at 15 percent. As was the case with other trade deals with Japan, the semiconductor agreement delivered less than was promised.

The Structural Impediments Initiative

In April 1987, the United States announced that a Japanese firm, the Toshiba Machine Company, and a Norwegian company, Kongsberg Vaapenfabrik, had sold technology to the Soviet Union that could enhance the capabilities of submarines. The sale violated CoCom export rules and complicated American efforts to track the Soviet fleet. The United States also reported that the Japanese government had been informed of possible Toshiba violations, had conducted cursory investigations, and had denied that any wrongdoing had occurred.[40]

As the details of the story unfolded, members of Congress became increasingly incensed, especially with the Japanese. In fact, the Toshiba affair came at a particularly sensitive moment in 1987; Congress was considering a new trade bill, intended to give the president more power to pry open foreign markets and to eliminate unfair trade. Rep. Richard Gephardt and his allies had proposed an amendment to the bill requiring other nations to lower their trade surpluses with the United States, and Sen. Howard Metzenbaum, D-Ohio, suggested the addition of a provision requiring companies to give their workforces sixty days' notice before closing factories. The bill also contained a provision that extended the president's fast-track authority to conduct GATT negotiations.

With the Toshiba-Kongsberg controversy grabbing headlines across the country, Congress moved to include penalties for these companies in the bill. By a 92–5 vote, the Senate passed an amendment to the trade bill that banned all Toshiba and Kongsberg products from the American market for a two- to five-year period. This move, however, set off a wave of lobbying by American firms with ties to Toshiba; they wanted the penalties against the company reduced or eliminated. The White House also sought to limit the proposed sanctions. Because Congress was unable to finish the bill in 1987, it took the matter up in 1988, when tempers were cooler, and ended up toning down the penalties to forbid U.S. government purchases of products from the two companies for three years.[41]

In addition to moderating the sanctions for Toshiba and Kongsberg, the final version of the **Omnibus Trade and Competitiveness Act of 1988** eliminated Gephardt's proposal for reducing trade surpluses. Instead, Section 301 of the 1974 Trade Act was rewritten to include two new provisions, known as **Super 301** and **Special 301,** which were intended to beef up the attack on unfair trade. Super 301 required the U.S. trade representative to establish market-opening priorities for 1989 and 1990 and to identify countries and practices that posed problems for fair trade. The bill also called for negotiations to eliminate the problems within three years. Special 301 obligated the USTR to identify those countries failing to respect the intellectual property rights of American exporters and to conduct talks to guarantee such respect in the future. Both Super 301 and Special 301 gave the president the power to retaliate if the negotiations proved fruitless.[42]

The omnibus trade bill also extended fast-track; tightened the timetables for conducting escape clause, dumping, and subsidy investigations; extended the time limit for escape clause relief from five to eight years; and required American companies to give sixty days' notice when closing factories. This last provision drew the ire of President Reagan, who vetoed the bill and demanded that Congress send him legislation without the plant closing provision. A version without the offending passage was passed and signed into law in August.[43]

For most members of Congress, the centerpieces of the omnibus trade law were the Super 301 and Special 301 provisions. Although Japan was not explicitly mentioned in the law, it was clear to everyone, including the Japanese, that the law took dead aim at Japan. The Office of the U.S. Trade Representative was required to announce its Super 301 list of priority countries by the end of May 1989, and leading figures in Congress made it known they expected the list to include Japan. As Republican senator John Danforth put it, although Super 301 "was designed to be aimed at more than Japan, it was not aimed at anything less than Japan."[44]

In 1988, Reagan's vice president, George Bush, succeeded in his bid for the presidency. The new administration found itself boxed in as it considered its moves on trade. Most members of the Bush team were free traders who disliked the coercive approach of Super 301. Yet they also recognized that the White House trade agenda, which included a new GATT round and negotiations to create a free trade area throughout North America, could be derailed if the administration refused Congress's bidding. As a result, the Bush White House cited Japan for its government procurement problems for satellites and super computers and for its technical barriers to imported forest products. Brazil and India were cited as well.

At the same time, Bush decided to push a new negotiating initiative meant to eliminate some basic Japanese obstacles to trade. The trade discussions Bush was proposing represented an entirely new approach to dealing with Japan. In the past, the United States had attempted to reduce Japanese barriers to specific American products, as in the MOSS talks, and had tried to specify the share of the Japanese market that should be reserved for foreign goods, like in the semiconductor agreement. Yet neither of these approaches had produced as much as the United States had hoped for. By 1989, many American trade specialists had concluded that the reason for the continuing trade problems between the United

States and Japan was the basic structure of the Japanese economy. Japan had too many interlocking domestic companies (or *keiretsu*) that did business with one another but not with foreigners, and it had a host of distribution problems and business practices that made it nearly impossible for foreigners to operate in Japan. The new trade talks, dubbed the **Structural Impediments Initiative (SII),** were designed to change the way at least part of the Japanese economy was set up.[45]

The United States called on Japan to include five areas in the SII negotiations: (1) the Japanese distribution system, (2) public works spending, (3) land reform, (4) exclusionary keiretsu business practices, and (5) antimonopoly enforcement. For their part, many Japanese resented the U.S. presumption that it had the right to intrude into domestic Japanese affairs and its insinuation that American-Japanese trade problems were entirely Japan's fault. Japanese negotiators insisted that if the SII agenda was to include alleged Japanese deficiencies, then American problems such as its poor educational system and a huge federal budget deficit also must be on the bargaining table.

The SII talks were highly publicized and operated with a clear deadline, May 1990—the date Congress was due to receive a new Super 301 report. When the talks opened, the U.S. negotiating team found it had some allies in Japan, because the U.S. call for changes in the Japanese distribution system, in public works, and in land use policies would benefit Japanese consumers. Changes in the Japanese distribution system were constrained by the Large Store Law of 1974, which made it difficult to open the kind of super-sized discount stores found in the United States. American negotiators reasoned that larger discount stores would be more likely than smaller stores to sell imported goods. On public works, the Americans were seeking a better Japanese highway system, better airports, better sewers, and such; they expected public works spending to increase the demand for imported construction equipment and other products. The American land reform goals were similar to those for public works: to encourage housing and apartment construction that would require imported building materials and equipment. In these areas, the Japanese agreed to meet most of the American demands.

When it came to keiretsu business practices and to antimonopoly laws, the going was much tougher. The U.S. negotiators argued that the cozy working relationships found within keiretsu business groups made it almost impossible for foreign companies to sell in the Japanese market. Moreover, lax enforcement of Japanese antimonopoly laws was seen as leading to price fixing, manufacturer-controlled distribution networks that excluded foreigners, rigged bids for many construction projects, and a slow patent approval process. Rather than accede to American demands in these areas, the Japanese argued that the practices in question were essential features of Japanese culture that could not be changed.[46]

In the end, the SII talks did manage to achieve progress on some fronts—public works, land reform, and rules relating to retail sales in Japan. The talks also led to a government-sponsored publicity campaign to encourage people to buy foreign goods. As a result, Japan was not on the Super 301 citation list when it was released in 1990. Over time, however, new complaints emerged about U.S. access to Japanese markets, leaving Americans wondering how tough negotiations and an ingenious new approach to bargaining could have yielded so much less than the United States had anticipated. The puzzle of how to do business in Japan remained.

THE URUGUAY ROUND OF THE GATT

Japan was not the only source of frustration for American trade specialists in the 1980s. They fielded complaints about foreign violations of the intellectual property rights of American firms, international restrictions on trade in such services as banking and insurance, continuing frictions over agricultural trade, and the need to better protect trade-related foreign investments. The special interests joined Congress in exerting growing pressure on the executive branch to do something about each of these issues, several of which appeared to be costing American producers billions of dollars a year in business.

Economic conditions in the United States, where unemployment stood at 11 percent in 1982, provided another reason for action; many in the White House feared that Congress would pass protectionist laws to safeguard American workers from foreign competition unless the trade complaints were solved.[47] Moreover, the Reagan team believed that opening foreign markets would be an effective way to handle America's economic problems. As the U.S. trade representative, Bill Brock, said in November 1982, "There is just no chance of recovery without an expansion of trade."[48]

Trade also was seen as the best medicine for American agriculture, which by the early 1980s was depending heavily on foreign markets. In 1980, 40 percent of American acreage was devoted to producing exports, and 60 percent of the wheat, 50 percent of the soybeans, and 33 percent of the corn grown by American farmers went to other countries. But in spite of these impressive figures, by 1982 American farmers were under assault. High American interest rates and the high value of the dollar hurt farm exports by pushing up the prices of American agricultural goods. In addition, by 1982 the European Community was aggressively subsidizing its agricultural exports.[49]

These changes in international agricultural markets were bad news for American farmers. They saw their net farm income fall from $35 billion in 1979 to $19 billion in 1982, when farm debt reached $127 billion. To administration observers, increasing exports was the best way out of the mounting agricultural mess, which meant initiating new GATT negotiations.[50]

Getting Started

U.S. Trade Representative Brock first made the case for a new GATT round at a Geneva meeting in November 1982. He pointed out that "at stake . . . is $3 trillion worth of world trade, economic recovery and real growth for all nations."[51] Europeans, and especially the French, were cool to the GATT idea, fearing that it would put the EC's Common Agricultural Policy on the bargaining table. For their part, developing countries were ambivalent; they favored negotiations to open agricultural markets and water down the Multi-Fiber Arrangement, but feared allowing foreign competition in their service sectors.[52]

As time passed, the situation in the agriculture arena became even bleaker. By the end of 1984, American farmers owed a total of $215 billion in debt, and 30 percent of all government-backed loans were delinquent, requiring additional spending just as the Reagan administration was under pressure to reduce the federal budget deficit. In Europe, the Common Agricultural Policy also was getting unbearably expensive, accounting in 1983 for over 60 percent of the EC budget at a time when many European analysts called for channeling more money to the high-technology and aerospace sectors.[53]

With these problems in mind, President Reagan issued a formal call for a new GATT round in his State of the Union address on February 6, 1985, and he persisted in his quest at the annual Group of Seven meeting in Bonn in May 1985.[54] The French resisted, but when it became clear they were alone in their opposition, they insisted on a more complete agenda that would not focus exclusively on farm goods. The next month, the European Community announced its support for a multifaceted GATT round.[55] Finally, in November 1985 a GATT committee decided to open the new round in Punta del Este, Uruguay, in September 1986.

The Punta del Este meeting set the agenda for the new GATT negotiations, known as the **Uruguay Round.** The primary issues of interest to the United States were trade in services, **trade-related intellectual property rights (TRIPs), trade-related investment measures (TRIMs),** and agricultural trade. In pushing for agriculture, the United States found itself cooperating with developing countries and the so-called **Cairns Group**—fourteen food-exporting countries that agreed with the need to reduce agricultural trade barriers.[56] Working with the Cairns countries, the United States was able to convince the EC to negotiate over farm subsidies. At the same time, American delegates made it clear they did not wish to eliminate the CAP, but simply to phase out trade-distorting policies.

The United States pushed for a discussion of services because it wanted to open markets to American banks, insurance companies, brokerage firms, and other such industries. The service sector was one of the strongest and fastest-growing sectors of the American economy, and lower foreign trade barriers promised to bring substantial new business to American companies. The U.S. desire to secure protection for intellectual property was motivated by the illegitimate manufacturing operations in some countries that copied and sold American products without paying American firms any royalties. Because many European and Japanese companies faced similar problems, they cooperated with the United States on the services and TRIPs issues.

Europe, Japan, and the United States also worked together on the foreign investment (TRIMs) issue; after all, many European and Japanese firms also maintained subsidiaries in other countries. The major goal here was assurances that corporations operating abroad would receive the same legal treatment and rights as local corporations. Known as **national treatment,** such guarantees would eliminate the advantages governments often conferred on domestic companies that made it difficult for foreigners to compete.

By the time the Punta del Este meeting ended in late September, the United States could point to an agenda containing virtually all it wanted. In fact, the agenda was the most ambitious negotiating program the GATT had ever set out to tackle. In addition to agriculture, services, intellectual property, and foreign investments, it included tariffs, nontariff barriers, tropical goods, textiles, subsidies and countervailing duties, dispute settlement procedures, and the organization and operation of the GATT system.[57]

The Negotiations

After the Punta del Este meeting, the Uruguay Round negotiations bogged down as the United States and the EC fought over agriculture. In January 1986, an issue unrelated to the GATT fanned the flames of this dispute when the United States demanded compensation for the estimated $500 million in farm exports it expected to lose when Portugal and Spain entered the EC. As President Reagan said in late March, "We cannot allow the American farmer . . . to pay the price for the European Community's enlargement."[58] The EC disagreed with the American claims, and for nearly a year acrimony clouded U.S.-EC trade relations. Finally, a compromise ended the conflict in January 1987.[59]

The EC enlargement conflict left Americans more convinced than ever that the members of the EC, particularly the French, were so tied to the CAP that they would never engage in meaningful negotiations. For the EC, it became apparent that the United States was determined to dismantle many key parts of the CAP, a move that would lead to the demise of agriculture in Europe given the more efficient nature of American agricultural production.

European fears about agriculture were confirmed in June 1987 when the United States announced a new negotiating position known as the "double zero" proposal. It called for eliminating all agricultural support programs and export subsidies by 2000. This proposal was a clear change from the previous American position which had focused only on export subsidies, and it represented just the challenge to the CAP that the EC feared. An EC Uruguay Round delegate voiced Europe's concerns when he reacted by saying that "it's unrealistic to [expect] that in the future there will be no support for agriculture."[60] Many Americans knew the double zero approach was controversial, but they also feared that anything less than a dramatic move would doom Uruguay Round negotiations to the same futility experienced during the Kennedy and Tokyo Rounds when almost no progress was made on agriculture.

This, then, was the climate when a GATT meeting convened in Montreal in November 1988 to assess the state of the negotiations. Several negotiating teams reported progress, including those working on the GATT system, dispute settlement procedures, trade in tropical products, and trade in services. The ongoing U.S.-Europe argument over agriculture, however, became so contentious that it nearly wrecked the meeting. The essence of the agricultural conflict was Europe's refusal to accept the American double zero proposal. In an effort to bridge the differences between the two trading giants, members of the Cairns Group suggested a compromise 20 percent reduction in farm support payments and in trade subsidies over the short run; the parties would lay the groundwork for more substantial cuts over a longer period of time. But neither the United States nor the Europeans accepted the proposal. The meeting therefore ended with the agricultural talks at an impasse.[61]

Over the course of the next several months, dramatic international events slowed Uruguay Round progress by diverting the attention of world leaders to other issues. The first, in 1989, was the collapse of the Soviet empire in Eastern Europe, which led eventually to the unification of Germany and to the integration of East Germany into the EC in 1990 (several other Eastern European nations also expressed an interest in joining the EC). Second, the Iraqi invasion of Kuwait in August 1990 created a crisis that left global oil markets jittery and threatened for a time the stability of the world economy.

Another surprise was Canada's call in April 1990 for the creation of a World Trade Organization to replace the GATT. In making the proposal, Canadians pointed out that the GATT was a nonorganization (see Chapter 4) that was not meant to be permanent and that the complex new rules emerging from the Uruguay Round would require a true international organization to administer them properly. Because such an organization was not on the original Uruguay Round agenda, it added an unexpected complication to negotiations. Further complicating matters was the counterproposal from several developing countries that, instead of a WTO, an international trade organization be created within the United Nations framework.

From the American point of view, bargaining over the WTO was something that could detract from the discussion of the substantive issues such as agriculture, services, and TRIPs. Moreover, there was always the possibility that Congress would refuse to allow the United States to join a new trade organization. The U.S. delegates to GATT therefore urged that the matter be set aside until other issues were cleared up.[62]

Thus when another GATT meeting assembled in Brussels on December 3, 1990, to assess progress on the Uruguay Round, the delegates faced a crowded agenda. One issue—whether or not to liberalize trade in textiles—was resolved quickly. In mid-1989, the textile working group had recommended elimination of the Multi-Fiber Arrangement over ten years. After at first resisting the idea, President Bush had agreed to the proposal in October 1990. Developing countries were delighted, and most now expressed a willingness to cooperate on other issues.[63]

Even so, problems again emerged over agriculture. As thirty thousand European farmers protested, the United States offered a new position that included a 75 percent reduction in domestic farm support programs and a 90 percent cut in export subsidies over ten years. The Europeans countered by offering a 30 percent cut in support programs and no reduction in export subsidies.[64] When it became apparent that the gulf between the Americans and Europeans could not be closed, the talks collapsed.

The Final Negotiations

The fiasco in Brussels left many wondering whether any Uruguay Round agreement was possible. Adding to the bleak atmosphere was the fact that the Bush administration's fast-track negotiating authority was set to expire at the end of May 1991. Bush made it known that he was not prepared to request an extension from Congress unless there was progress on agriculture. The collapse of the round thus seemed possible. In late February, however, the EC finally agreed to discuss reductions in export subsidies for agriculture. In response, Carla Hills, Bush's new trade representative, approached Congress about extending fast-track.

Yet fast-track renewal was far from automatic because it would apply not only to the Uruguay Round, but also to the controversial North American Free Trade Agreement negotiations under way in early 1991 (and described later in this chapter). Organized labor and several environmental groups opposed NAFTA and therefore the extension of fast-track. But when an administration report asserted that NAFTA would benefit the American economy and allow the United States to work with Mexico to improve the environment, Congress responded favorably. The House renewed fast-track on May 23 by a 231–192 vote, and the Senate did the same the next day by a 59–36 vote.[65]

Fast -track renewal kept the Uruguay Round alive, but there was little progress in 1991. The French continued to oppose reductions in export subsidies, and protests by 200,000 French farmers in September illustrated the depth of the political problems facing the French government.[66] Protests or no, GATT director-general Arthur Dunkel announced that it was time for all parties to compromise. German economic minister Jürgen Möllemann agreed, stating that "there has to be a change in the EC's position on agriculture, including export subsidies."[67]

Despite these demands for progress, the agricultural negotiations continued to go nowhere. A compromise American offer in November 1991 to accept a 30–35 percent cut in export subsidies for farm goods, instead of the much higher cuts originally demanded, brought only a tepid European response. And things only got worse. During a Group of Seven summit in Munich in the spring of 1992, French foreign minister Roland Dumas told American secretary of state James Baker that the French had no interest in compromising on agriculture.[68]

The U.S. presidential election of November 3, 1992, spelled the end of the Republican Bush administration and brought Democrat Bill Clinton to office. Among his last acts as president, Bush decided to try to pressure the EC to negotiate by imposing stiff penalties on agricultural goods from Europe.[69] The move nearly worked. Several EC members angrily accused the French of precipitating the American move, and EC negotiators agreed to meet with U.S. Trade Representative Carla Hills November 18–20 at the Blair House in Washington. During the meeting, the parties agreed to a 21 percent reduction in EC agricultural export subsidies over six years. This deal seemed to pull a Uruguay Round victory from the jaws of defeat—that is, almost. When other EC representatives examined the agreement, things fell apart.[70]

After Clinton assumed the presidency, one of his first goals was to finish the Uruguay Round. Clinton chose Mickey Kantor, a Los Angeles attorney who had helped manage Clinton's presidential campaign, as the new U.S. trade representative. In December 1993, Kantor accompanied Secretary of State Warren Christopher and Secretary of Agriculture Mike Espy to Brussels to negotiate with the newly formed European Union (EU). (The EU, made up of the members of the former European Community, was created on November 1, 1993, when the Maastricht Treaty went into effect.[71]) The American team proposed altering the Blair House deal to meet several French objections. The 21 percent export subsidy cut was retained, but technical calculations about how the reductions would be made were reworked to the advantage of the French. The EU, including the French, agreed to the deal.[72]

The final issue on the Uruguay Round table was the Canadian proposal for a WTO. When the United States agreed to go along with the creation of the new organization, the last item on the GATT agenda was laid to rest.

With the Uruguay Round agreement in hand and with the proper fast-track notification having been given in December 1993, the Clinton administration sent a trade bill to Congress. During the congressional debate, environmental and labor groups questioned whether the Uruguay agreement would promote pollution and hurt workers. Political activists such as Ross Perot, Ralph Nader, and Pat Buchanan voiced their opposition to the agreement. But the most telling issue to emerge had to do with a possible loss of sovereignty if the United States joined the WTO. Despite President Clinton's explanation that the WTO could not force the United States to change its laws if a WTO panel ruled against an American trade practice, many members of Congress remained unconvinced. Clinton noted that instead of changing a law, the United States could either accept foreign retaliation in the form of trade barriers against American exports or offer compensation to the offended WTO party.[73]

To head off trouble over this problem, Clinton accepted a suggestion from Sen. Bob Dole that a board of judges be established to evaluate adverse WTO panel rulings. If over a period of five years the judges found that three WTO panels ruled incorrectly against the United States, then Congress could initiate proceedings to withdraw the United States from the WTO.[74] Satisfied with this proposal, Congress approved the Uruguay Round results—the House by 288–146 on November 29 and the Senate by 76–24 on December 1. The way was cleared for the United States to join the WTO (see box for the provisions of the Uruguay Round).[75]

THE NORTH AMERICAN FREE TRADE AGREEMENT

In addition to the Uruguay Round of the GATT, the United States pursued free trade talks with both Israel and its North American neighbors in the 1980s and early 1990s. When the free trade negotiations were first initiated, they were regarded by most American trade analysts as an interesting sideshow to the discussions within the GATT. As time passed and frustrations over the GATT talks increased, however, many trade specialists began to consider the possibility of using a series of free trade agreements either to pressure other governments to give ground within the GATT or to serve as an imperfect alternative to the stalled GATT framework.[76]

Provisions of the Uruguay Round Agreement

The parties agreed to:

- Cut tariffs by one-third.
- Tighten the nontariff barrier codes negotiated during the Tokyo Round.
- Phase out over a ten-year period the quotas for textiles established under the Multi-Fiber Arrangement.
- Cut agricultural tariffs by 36 percent, agricultural export subsidies by 21 percent, and trade-distorting farm support programs by 20 percent.
- Standardize antidumping and subsidy investigation procedures according to specific international regulations.
- Standardize procedures relating to the escape clause according to specific international guidelines.
- Establish a general agreement on trade in services (GATS) to require "national treatment" for most trade in services and eliminate other restrictions on trade in this area.
- Establish rules for protecting intellectual property rights such as patents, copyrights, and trademarks.
- Protect foreign investors from local rules designed to impede their ability to compete fairly in the local market.
- Establish rules related to the use of sanitary and phytosanitary measures as a means for restricting trade.
- Establish the World Trade Organization (WTO) to handle the Uruguay Round agreements.
- Establish new dispute settlement procedures to moderate a country's ability to evade adverse WTO panel findings.

Sources: See Stephen D. Cohen, Joel R. Paul, and Robert A. Blecker, *Fundamentals of U.S. Foreign Trade Policy: Economics, Politics, Laws, and Issues* (Boulder: Westview Press, 1996), 267–272; Edward S. Kaplan, *American Trade Policy, 1923–1995* (Westport, Conn.: Greenwood Press, 1996), 128–129; and Ernest H. Preeg, *Traders in a Brave New World: The Uruguay Round and the Future of the International Trading System* (Chicago: University of Chicago Press, 1995), 53–54, 190–201.

Note: In setting up the WTO, the parties agreed that all previous GATT agreements and all new Uruguay Round accords would fall within the authority of the WTO, which was scheduled to commence operations on January 1, 1995.

The U.S.-Canada Negotiations

The impetus for the negotiations that led to the creation of the North American Free Trade Agreement came first from Canada and later from Mexico. As a result, the negotiations to set up NAFTA were a two-step process. Step one consisted of the talks that led to an accord with Canada, and step two was the three-way bargaining process with Canada and Mexico that produced the final NAFTA agreement. The fact that Canada and Mexico approached the United States about free trade talks is somewhat remarkable because both countries had long been concerned about domination by the United States.

The first moves toward NAFTA came in the early 1980s amid a deep recession in Canada and the United States. As often happens during hard times, American industries sought protection from imports to reduce the competitive pressures they confronted. Among the imports some American industries wished to restrict were several from Canada, most notably lumber and other building materials and various agricultural goods. Even though most of these protectionist moves failed, many Canadians became worried about possibly losing access to an American market that absorbed two-thirds of Canada's exports and bought approximately one-fifth of the total output of the Canadian economy.[77]

To secure access to the United States, the Canadian government approached the Reagan administration with a proposal for limited talks to improve trade relations between the two countries. Reagan's trade representative, Bill Brock, gave an immediate affirmative answer to the idea, stating, "I'd like to expand trade in any areas the Canadians would like to expand trade." For Brock, talks with Canada not only provided the chance to gain better entry to the Canadian market, but also held the possibility of pushing along the new GATT negotiations Brock was attempting to start.[78]

When the negotiations with Canada began in 1984, they ran into trouble right out of the starting gate. Each side attempted to deal only with the issues it regarded as important and avoid trade-offs between issues. As a result, the talks soon collapsed, and the possibility of a special trade deal between the United States and Canada appeared dead.

The Canadian elections in September 1984, however, brought Brian Mulroney and the Progresssive Conservatives to office. Although Mulroney had spoken out against a U.S.-Canada trade agreement during the campaign, he soon changed his mind. Key factors in his decision were the fear of losing the American market and the arguments of many larger Canadian businesses that they needed to operate from an expanded North American base if they were to remain internationally competitive. Thus when Mulroney met Reagan in March 1985 for the "Shamrock Summit," he proposed negotiating a free trade agreement between the United States and Canada. Reagan immediately agreed, and the two leaders released a communiqué stating that "we have today agreed to give the highest priority to finding acceptable means to reduce and eliminate existing barriers to trade in order to secure and facilitate trade and investment flows."[79]

When the talks finally started in February 1986, the Canadian team was led by Simon Reisman, the Canadian deputy minister of finance, and the U.S. delegation was headed by Peter Murphy, a relatively junior official in the USTR office. As some Canadians saw it, this disparity in the ranks of the negotiators reflected the differing priorities of the two sides.[80] The Canadians also were sensitive to the lack of U.S. news coverage of the talks—an indicator, they thought, that most Americans did not care much about trade with Canada—and to the relatively slow pace at which the United States seemed to be negotiating.

The major issues in the negotiations were the elimination of tariffs and non-tariff barriers, the rights investors would have in each country, trade in services, the rules that would determine what qualified as a Canadian or an American good and would therefore be covered by the agreement (known as rules of origin), U.S. antidumping and antisubsidy laws, and dispute resolution. These last two issues became the primary sticking points in the bargaining and nearly brought about the collapse of negotiations in September 1987.

To save the negotiations, Treasury Secretary James Baker intervened to work out a compromise. The dispute resolution question was resolved by agreeing to establish a joint U.S.-Canada panel that would evaluate problems as they arose. As for dumping and subsidies, the Canadians demanded that the United States promise not to change its current laws so that Canadians could be sure they would not face new rules at some point in the future. Baker could not make such a promise, but he did manage to finesse the point by agreeing that future changes in these laws only would apply to Canada if Congress stated they applied. Because Congress rarely specified which countries laws would cover, this proviso settled the matter.[81] Once these issues were out of the way, negotiations moved quickly to completion in December 1987 (see box).

The agreement produced little public or congressional debate in the United States. The House agreed to the deal on August 10, 1988, by a 366–40 vote; the Senate on September 19 by 83–9. In Canada, where the agreement was more controversial, Mulroney called an election for November 21, 1988, to give the Canadian people an opportunity to conduct what was in effect a national referendum on the accord. The Progressive Conservatives won the election, and the Canadian Parliament endorsed the agreement on December 24, 1988.[82]

The Three-Way Talks

The second set of negotiations leading to the NAFTA accord began in June 1990 when Mexican president Carlos Salinas de Gortari asked President Bush to agree to discussions aimed at eliminating trade barriers between the United States and Mexico. Salinas decided to move in this direction because of the poor state of the

Provisions of the 1988 U.S.-Canada Free Trade Agreement

- All tariffs shall be eliminated over a ten-year period.
- Carefully worded rules of origin set out in the agreement shall determine which products qualify under the agreement.
- Government procurement contracts over $171,000 shall be open to companies from either country.
- U.S. firms shall have the right to invest in Canadian energy projects on a nondiscriminatory basis.
- U.S. financial firms may operate in Canada on a nondiscriminatory basis.
- U.S. companies may sell used autos and aircraft in Canada.
- U.S. broadcasters shall be compensated for their television programs picked up in Canada.
- Subsidized Canadian agricultural exports to the United States shall be eliminated.
- Both countries shall extend "national treatment" to service companies from the other country.
- A panel established by the agreement shall handle disputes.

Source: Edward S. Kaplan, *American Trade Policy, 1923–1995* (Westport, Conn.: Greenwood Press, 1996), 138.

Mexican economy. Too many state-run businesses were losing money, economic growth was slow but inflation was high, government budget deficits were absorbing too much of the investment capital needed for modernization, and many of those who had money to invest were sending their funds out of the country in search of better opportunities abroad. As Salinas saw it, Mexico desperately needed to reverse decades of economic isolation and inefficiency, and the best way to do so was to guarantee Mexico's access to foreign markets and to encourage foreign corporations to invest in Mexico.

Salinas also was aware that several East Asian countries had achieved rapid growth by focusing their development strategies on promoting exports, many of which went to the United States. To Salinas, these Asian countries represented both a model for development and a threat, because a large portion of Mexico's exports went to the United States and thus had to compete with the exports of the Asian dynamos. A free trade agreement with the United States was one way to ensure that Mexico would not be driven from its most important foreign market.[83]

Bush responded to Salinas's proposal with enthusiasm. As a former oil company executive, Bush recognized that a free trade agreement could pave the way

Provisions of the North American Free Trade Agreement

- All tariffs and nontariff barriers shall be eliminated over a fifteen-year period.
- All agricultural quotas and nontariff barriers shall be converted to tariffs, which then shall be eliminated over a fifteen-year period.
- Rules of origin are carefully specified in the agreement to establish which products it covers.
- Corporations in any of the three member countries may invest in any of the three countries on a nondiscriminatory basis.
- Restrictions on travel by business people within any of the member countries shall be eliminated.
- Companies engaged in the provision of services may operate in any member country on a nondiscriminatory basis.
- Barriers to trade in autos and auto parts shall be dismantled over a fifteen-year period.
- Barriers to trade in textiles shall be eliminated over a fifteen-year period.
- Government procurement contracts are open to bids by companies in the member countries on a nondiscriminatory basis.
- The intellectual property rights of businesses in the member countries shall be given appropriate protection.

Sources: Stephen D. Cohen, Joel R. Paul, and Robert A. Blecker, *Fundamentals of U.S. Foreign Trade Policy: Economics, Politics, Laws, and Issues* (Boulder: Westview Press, 1996), 241; and Edward S. Kaplan, *American Trade Policy, 1923–1995* (Westport, Conn.: Greenwood Press, 1996), 152–154.

toward greater opportunities for American companies to invest in Mexican natural resource projects, an area in which investments had been sharply curtailed. Bush also saw the chance to offer services such as telecommunications, banking, and insurance to the Mexican market and to lower substantially the formidable tariff wall that affected Americans' ability to sell goods in a country that bought over 70 percent of its imports from the United States. In addition, Bush feared that if the United States did not react favorably to Mexico's invitation, then it would turn to Japan or the European Community, and the United States would face a serious new economic challenge in the Western Hemisphere.[84]

In view of the preexisting free trade agreement between the United States and Canada, it was only natural that Canada be invited to join the negotiations between the United States and Mexico. The Canadians agreed to do so in June

1991. From that point, and in marked contrast to the Uruguay Round under way at the same time, the talks moved ahead quickly with a minimum of conflict among the negotiating teams. A final agreement was reached on August 12, 1992 (see box), just as the American presidential election season was moving toward a climax.

The negotiations leading to the establishment of the NAFTA accord were relatively straightforward, but congressional approval of the agreement was anything but that. As it turned out, NAFTA was one of the most hotly debated and controversial trade deals in American history.

Congressional Approval

One indication of the controversy that would eventually engulf NAFTA came in 1991 when the Bush administration requested fast-track renewal from Congress. As noted earlier in this chapter, labor and environmental groups were against the extension because of their opposition to free trade with Mexico. When fast-track was renewed in spite of their strong objections, these groups prepared even more carefully for their next chance to block the deal. That chance came when the finished NAFTA agreement arrived on Congress's doorstep for approval.

NAFTA also was a major issue in the 1992 presidential election.[85] The primary issues associated with NAFTA were Mexico's lax enforcement of laws to curb pollution; the effects of the agreement on American workers, who feared that the lower cost of labor in Mexico would entice American companies to set up shop south of the border, thereby pulling jobs out of the United States; and whether the agreement would tie the American economy to a relatively unstable developing country that could be a source of trouble in the future.

On the campaign trail, the incumbent president, Republican George Bush, strongly favored NAFTA, arguing that it would greatly benefit the United States. Reform Party candidate Ross Perot opposed the accord and warned that NAFTA would lead to a substantial loss of jobs. Democrat Bill Clinton, mindful of labor's position on the issue, offered a qualified endorsement, insisting that trade adjustment assistance be provided for any workers and farmers hurt by the agreement, that foreign workers not be allowed to enter the United States as strike breakers, and that the concerns of environmental groups be addressed by providing funds for cleaning up any pollution and other problems resulting from the accord.

When Clinton won the 1992 election, he made it clear he wanted to negotiate side agreements to NAFTA to safeguard American workers and to protect against environmental degradation. At a January 8, 1993, meeting between Clinton and Salinas, the Mexican leader agreed to proceed with the additional talks

Clinton had in mind. When completed, the side agreements set up two commissions, one to monitor environmental matters and the other to keep an eye on labor standards.[86]

Despite Clinton's side agreements, objections to NAFTA continued to increase in the spring and summer of 1993. The AFL-CIO put enormous pressure on Democrats to vote against the agreement, and several prominent public figures announced their opposition, including Pat Buchanan, Jesse Jackson, and Ralph Nader. And, of course, Ross Perot continued his campaign, warning time and again that if NAFTA was approved by Congress there would be a "giant sucking sound" of manufacturing jobs leaving the United States.

Environmental groups also were seeking to obstruct NAFTA. In June, the Sierra Club secured a decision from a federal court requiring that an environmental impact study be conducted before Congress could consider NAFTA. This ruling threatened to hold up consideration of the agreement for months, perhaps even years. The Clinton administration immediately appealed the decision, and in late September a federal appeals court overruled the lower court.[87]

Meanwhile, the Democratic majority leader in the House of Representatives, Richard Gephardt, announced in August that he would not support NAFTA. Gephardt was joined in his opposition by several other House Democrats, making the fate of the agreement uncertain. It was generally understood in Washington that the vote in the Senate probably would be pro-NAFTA. The House, however, was much less certain, and Gephardt's defection, even though expected by the White House, seemed an ominous sign.

In late summer, realizing just how much sentiment in the House was running against NAFTA, Clinton organized a strong campaign in behalf of the agreement. He began by appointing William Daley, the brother of Chicago mayor Richard Daley, to orchestrate the campaign for passage of NAFTA. Another move came in mid-September when Clinton asked the five living former presidents to visit Washington to express their support for the agreement. Ford, Carter, and Bush made the trip; Nixon and Reagan sent messages of support. In early November, Clinton held a similar White House meeting with Carter and former Republican secretaries of state Henry Kissinger and James Baker. In addition, Clinton made numerous personal appeals to undecided members of Congress. Finally, in November the administration challenged diehard NAFTA opponent Perot to debate Vice President Al Gore on the popular CNN show "Larry King Live." Gore's calm and deliberate style contrasted sharply with Perot's exaggerations and led most people to conclude that Gore was the victor.

By the time the House voted on November 17, the White House had the votes it needed. The final tally was 234–200 in favor of NAFTA. Three days later, the Senate also voted yes by 61–38. The Canadian Parliament had already granted its approval in May, and the Mexican Senate voted for the agreement on November 23. The three-way free trade deal was set to go into effect.[88]

CHAPTER SUMMARY

During the 1980s and early 1990s, the United States confronted several trade issues that challenged America's commitment to more open international markets. Foremost among these problems were the difficulties some U.S. industries had competing on an international level. For many Americans, the most visible and troubling source of competition was Japan, a country that until the late 1960s seemed to pose no threat to America's international economic supremacy.

Beginning in the 1970s, several Japanese industries moved into the American market, offering increasing volumes of goods that were equal in quality to anything produced in the United States. Indeed, in many cases Japanese goods actually outperformed American-made ones. As Japanese imports flooded into the United States, industries producing such things as autos, steel, electronic devices, machine tools, tires, sporting goods, and computers approached Congress through their lobbyists for assistance in competing with what some referred to as the Japanese "invasion." In addition, their attorneys filed dumping complaints and escape clause cases with the proper federal agencies.

The problems stemming from Japanese imports were only part of the story, however; complaints also surfaced about the difficulties American producers faced when they tried to enter the Japanese market. Early on, the Reagan administration tended to attribute industry comments about a closed Japanese market to America's inability to produce goods the Japanese wanted or to Americans' unwillingness to work hard enough to operate successfully in Japan. Over time, however, as they heard more and more stories of market closure, the president and Congress realized they needed to take action.

The first efforts to handle the closure of the Japanese market took the form of negotiations over specific products. But as time passed and the Japanese market remained difficult to penetrate, the parties resorted to more all-encompassing negotiations such as the MOSS talks, the semiconductor negotiations, and the bargaining associated with the SII. In each case, the United States found that progress was slow and that improvements in American access to the Japanese market often were illusory.

One of the most interesting features of these American efforts is that they were designed to open Japanese markets and not to close U.S. markets to Japanese goods. The same can be said of much of the legislation produced by Congress during the same period of time. Bills designed to close the American market were introduced in Congress, but few of them passed, and those that did were shot down by presidential vetoes. Instead, with the exception of the auto bills discussed in Chapter 7, most "protectionist" legislation from Congress generally was designed to promote the opening of foreign markets. For example, the Omnibus Trade and Competitiveness Act of 1988 and its Super 301 provision may have been labeled protectionist, and the act certainly was heavy-handed, but Super 301 was in fact supposed to pry open foreign markets. In fact, by the mid- to late 1980s American trade policy makers, including many on Capitol Hill, were so intrinsically committed to liberal trade that their natural response to illiberal policies in other countries was not to close the American market, but instead to open foreign markets.

These moves by U.S. policy makers to open foreign markets included not only trade legislation, but also attempts to initiate a new GATT round and to negotiate free trade agreements with Canada and Mexico. The Uruguay Round of GATT was intended to secure international trade rules for a variety of new problems confronting American exporters. These problems included tightly restricted foreign agricultural markets, barriers to trade in services, inadequate protection for intellectual property, and discrimination against foreign investors.

As much as anything that happened since World War II, the Uruguay Round illustrates how deeply American decision makers value a liberal trading system governed by internationally accepted rules. The Uruguay Round was agonizingly long and frustrating: it took the United States nearly four years to convince other countries of the need for negotiations, which, once begun, dragged on for seven years. Not only was the bargaining lengthy, but it also was contentious, especially in the agricultural arena where one American compromise after another was turned down by the Europeans. The fact that American negotiators persisted in the face of such slow progress was a clear sign both of their commitment to liberal trade and of the need to trim agricultural support budgets.

Perhaps the severest test of America's interest in liberal trade was the NAFTA negotiations. The initial deal with Canada elicited little controversy, but the accord with Mexico was another story altogether. Open trade with Mexico worried several American special interests, particularly organized labor and environmentalists. These groups made the strongest possible effort to defeat NAFTA, and yet a determined president was able to obtain congressional approval. Once again, the promise of opening a foreign market outweighed the fear of competition from imports. As the United States moved toward a new millenium, then, the American people and their government seemed more comfortable with a world of trade than at any time in American history.

NOTES

1. The quote is found in Michael Mastanduno, *Economic Containment: CoCom and the Politics of East-West Trade* (Ithaca: Cornell University Press, 1992), 220.

2. Jimmy Carter, *Keeping Faith* (New York: Bantam Books, 1982), 472.

3. Zbigniew Brzezinski, *Power and Principle* (New York: Farrar, Straus, Giroux, 1983), 430.

4. David A. Baldwin, *Economic Statecraft* (Princeton: Princeton University Press, 1985), 261–262; Brzezinski, *Power and Principle*, 432; Philip J. Funigiello, *American-Soviet Trade in the Cold War* (Chapel Hill: University of North Carolina Press, 1988), 192; and Mastanduno, *Economic Containment*, 223. Carter's trade-related moves were made under the authority granted to him by Congress in the Export Administration Act of 1979, which was originally passed in 1969.

5. Carter, *Keeping Faith*, 478; and Baldwin, *Economic Statecraft*, 271.

6. Robert L. Paarlburg, "Lessons of the Grain Embargo," *Foreign Affairs* 59 (fall 1980): 144–162.

7. Ronald Reagan, *An American Life* (New York: Simon and Schuster, 1990), 270.

8. Mastanduno, *Economic Containment*, 228–232.

9. Quoted in Bruce W. Jentleson, *Pipeline Politics: The Complex Political Economy of East-West Energy Trade* (Ithaca: Cornell University Press, 1986), 178.

10. Jentleson, *Pipeline*, 176.

11. George Shultz, *Turmoil and Triumph: My Years as Secretary of State* (New York: Scribner's, 1993), 135; and Margaret Thatcher, *The Downing Street Years* (New York: HarperCollins, 1993), 253.

12. Thatcher, *Downing Street Years*, 256.

13. Shultz, *Turmoil and Triumph*, 140.

14. Jentleson, *Pipeline*, 197; and Shultz, *Turmoil and Triumph*, 142.

15. These figures are from United Nations, *Yearbook of National Accounts Statistics*, 1981, 7–9, 242–243, 294–295.

16. United Nations, *Yearbook of National Accounts Statistics*, 1981, 242–243, 294–295.

17. Bureau of the Census, Department of Commerce.

18. Edward J. Lincoln, *Japan's Unequal Trade* (Washington, D.C.: Brookings Institution, 1990), 14.

19. The European Economic Community (EEC) that was created by the Treaty of Rome in 1957 gave way in 1967 to the European Community (EC), which was formed by the merger of the European Coal and Steel Community and Euraton. Nevertheless, the acronym EEC was used frequently until the Single European Act went into effect in 1987.

20. Bela Balassa and Marcus Noland, *Japan in the World Economy* (Washington, D.C.: Institute for International Economics, 1988), 50.

21. Steve Dryden, *Trade Warriors: USTR and the American Crusade for Free Trade* (New York: Oxford University Press, 1995), 229.

22. Bureau of the Census, Department of Commerce.

23. Lincoln, *Japan's Unequal Trade*, 18.

24. For a more complete presentation of these views, see James Fallows, *Looking at the Sun: The Rise of the New East Asian Economic and Political System* (New York: Vintage Books, 1995); and Clyde V. Prestowitz Jr., *Trading Places: How We Are Giving to Japan and How to Reclaim It* (New York: Basic Books, 1988).

25. An exception to this attitude was the negotiation of a VER to limit Japanese auto sales in the United States after 1981.

26. Dryden, *Trade Warriors*, 280.

27. Ibid., 281.

28. Prestowitz, *Trading Places*, 399.

29. Dryden, *Trade Warriors*, 271, 298.

30. Bureau of the Census, Department of Commerce.

31. See I. M. Destler, *American Trade Politics* (Washington, D.C.: Institute for International Economics, 1995), 85–87.

32. Destler, *American Trade*, 84.

33. Leonard Schoppa, *Bargaining with Japan: What American Pressure Can and Cannot Do* (New York: Columbia University Press, 1997), 66.

34. The following discussion draws on Lincoln, *Japan's Unequal Trade*, 148–151; Schoppa, *Bargaining with Japan*, 65–66; and Laura D'Andrea Tyson, *Who's Bashing Whom? Trade Conflict in High-Technology Industries* (Washington, D.C.: Institute for International Economics, 1992), 58–65. Many of those who discuss these talks call them the Market-Oriented *Sector*-Specific talks, but official USTR and Department of Commerce publications use the title found in the text.

35. Tyson, *Who's Bashing Whom?* 67–71.

36. Both quotes are from Dryden, *Trade Warriors*, 305–306.

37. Quoted in Dryden, *Trade Warriors*, 311.

38. Yoichi Funabashi, *Managing the Dollar: From the Plaza to the Louvre* (Washington, D.C.: Institute for International Economics, 1989), 16; and Schoppa, *Bargaining with Japan*, 67.

39. Much of the discussion of the semiconductor negotiations relies on Dryden, *Trade Warriors*, 312–320; Prestowitz, *Trading Places*, chap. 2; and Tyson, *Who's Bashing Whom?* chap. 4.

40. For a complete discussion of the Toshiba affair, see Raymond Vernon, Debora L. Spar, and Glenn Tobin, *Iron Triangles and Revolving Doors: Cases in U.S. Foreign Economic Policymaking* (New York: Praeger, 1991), chap. 5.

41. Dryden, *Trade Warriors*, 336–337; and Vernon, Spar, and Tobin, *Iron Triangles*, 120–125.

42. Patrick Low, *Trading Free: The GATT and U.S. Trade Policy* (New York: Twentieth Century Fund Press, 1993), 64–66.

43. John H. Jackson, *The World Trading System: Law and Policy of International Economic Relations* (Cambridge: MIT Press, 1997), 192; and Edward S. Kaplan, *American Trade Policy, 1923–1995* (Westport, Conn.: Greenwood Press, 1996), 116–118.

44. Dryden, *Trade Warriors,* 357.
45. For a detailed discussion of the SII talks, see Schoppa, *Bargaining with Japan,* chaps. 3–8.
46. Ibid., 92–93.
47. Dryden, *Trade Warriors,* 284.
48. Jarod Wiener, *Making Rules in the Uruguay Round of the GATT* (Aldershot, U.K.: Dartmouth Publishing, 1995), 96.
49. Ibid., 85–86.
50. Ibid., 86–87.
51. Dryden, *Trade Warriors,* 284.
52. Low, *Trading Free,* 195–203; and Wiener, *Making Rules,* 92.
53. Wiener, *Making Rules,* 103, 106.
54. The Group of Seven consists of Canada, France, Germany, Great Britain, Italy, Japan, and the United States. In the early 1970s, these nations began holding annual summit meetings to coordinate their economic policies.
55. Wiener, *Making Rules,* 114–116; and Ernest H. Preeg, *Traders in a Brave New World: The Uruguay Round and the Future of the International Trading System* (Chicago: University of Chicago Press, 1995), 53–54.
56. The Cairns Group was made up of Argentina, Australia, Brazil, Canada, Chile, Colombia, Fiji, Hungary, Indonesia, Malaysia, New Zealand, the Philippines, Thailand, and Uruguay. The group is named for the Australian city where it held its first meeting.
57. Preeg, *Traders,* 60–62.
58. Dryden, *Trade Warriors,* 321, 326; and Kaplan, *American Trade Policy,* 121. The quote is from Wiener, *Making Rules,* 138.
59. Wiener, *Making Rules,* 151.
60. Ibid., 156–157.
61. Low, *Trading Free,* 215–218; and Preeg, *Traders,* 84–88.
62. Preeg, *Traders,* 113–114.
63. Ibid., 101, 117.
64. Dryden, *Trade Warriors,* 367; Low, *Trading Free,* 219–225; and Preeg, *Traders,* 118–119.
65. Preeg, *Traders,* 129–131.
66. Ibid., 135–136.
67. Ibid.
68. Ibid., 138, 141.
69. Kaplan, *American Trade Policy,* 126.
70. Dryden, *Trade Warriors,* 378–379; and Preeg, *Traders,* 146.
71. The European Union is intended to put the members of the European Community on the path to total economic and monetary integration and to begin the process of moving toward a common foreign policy.
72. Kaplan, *American Trade Policy,* 127–128; and Preeg, *Traders,* 167–172.

73. Susan A. Aaronson, *Trade and the American Dream: A Social History of Postwar Trade Policy* (Lexington: University Press of Kentucky, 1996), 146.

74. Ibid., 156.

75. See Stephen D. Cohen, Joel R. Paul, and Robert A. Blecker, *Fundamentals of U.S. Foreign Trade Policy: Economics, Politics, Laws, and Issues* (Boulder: Westview Press, 1996), 267–172; Kaplan, *American Trade Policy,* 128–129; and Preeg, *Traders,* 190–201.

76. Anne O. Krueger, *American Trade Policy: A Tragedy in the Making* (Washington, D.C.: AEI Press, 1995), 6.

77. Cohen, Paul, and Blecker, *Fundamentals,* 239; and Vernon, Spar, and Tobin, *Iron Triangles,* 22.

78. Vernon, Spar, and Tobin, *Iron Triangles,* 26–28. The quote is on p. 28.

79. Cohen, Paul, and Blecker, *Fundamentals,* 239; and Vernon, Spar, and Tobin, *Iron Triangles,* 27–28.

80. Dryden, *Trade Warriors,* 341–342.

81. Ibid., 342; and Vernon, Spar, and Tobin, *Iron Triangles,* 46–47.

82. Vernon, Spar, and Tobin, *Iron Triangles,* 50.

83. Cohen, Paul, and Blecker, *Fundamentals,* 240.

84. Ibid., 242; and Kaplan, *American Trade Policy,* 140.

85. Excellent accounts of the battle surrounding congressional approval of NAFTA are found in Cohen, Paul, and Blecker, *Fundamentals,* chap. 12; Kaplan, *American Trade Policy,* 143–152; and Robert A. Pastor, *Integration with Mexico: Options for U.S. Policy* (New York: Twentieth Century Fund Press, 1993), chap. 2.

86. Kaplan, *American Trade Policy,* 145.

87. Ibid., 146, 148.

88. Ibid., 146, 151–152.

9 Approaching a New Century of Trade

Throughout most of the post–World War II period, America's trading relationships with the rest of the world took a backseat to the strategic and security issues that crowded the U.S. foreign policy agenda. From the late 1940s until the 1980s, Americans focused on containing the Soviet Union and communism. Although trade was always a priority for the special interests affected by trade agreements, the American public as a whole paid little attention to the subject, and trade issues were rarely featured prominently in the media. Few people seemed to know much about trade, even fewer appeared to care, and for some of those who did care, trade issues often seemed arcane.

In the late 1970s and 1980s, the public's attention shifted as the oil crisis and Japanese imports began to cause problems for the economy as a whole and for a variety of specific industries. Not only did the companies and workers affected by imports respond vigorously to trade-related problems, but so did the media, which began to ask whether America was losing its international leadership. In addition, the end of the Cold War, dramatically symbolized by the destruction of the Berlin Wall in 1989 and the collapse of the Soviet Union in 1991, freed Americans from their preoccupation with communism and allowed them to concentrate on issues related to their economic well-being, including trade.

Thus by the 1992 election more people than ever were concerned with the economy and their pocketbooks. Many also had a strong sense that something should be done about America's competitive position in international commerce. Commentators across the country remarked on the growing importance of economic performance to national security and on the role played by trade in the health of the economy. Among those concerned with the question, a lively debate ensued over whether the United States was properly positioned for the post–Cold War era and how American trade policy could be better shaped to contribute to American welfare and security.[1]

The debate itself was more than academic. As the discussion of the North American Free Trade Agreement in Chapter 8 indicates, it evolved into a hotly contested and well-publicized discussion of whether the United States had gone far enough, or perhaps too far, in integrating its economy with that of the rest of the world through trade and foreign investments. Labor leaders and environmentalists were especially vocal in questioning the costs associated with the post–World War II pattern of increasing America's economic linkages to other countries by lowering American trade barriers and pushing for others to do the same. Lost jobs and a more polluted environment were alleged to be just two of the many penalties associated with the expansion of trade. Other suspected costs included at least partial loss of national sovereignty that went with allowing the World Trade Organization to monitor trade practices across the globe and the possibility that economic problems in another part of the world might have deleterious effects on the U.S. economy. For the critics of America's involvement in what people increasingly referred to as the "global village," the prices of participation were too high.

As it happened, the 1992 Democratic presidential candidate, Bill Clinton, positioned himself nicely to take advantage of these new questions and doubts about the United States and global ties. Running against an incumbent known for his experience in handling the Cold War, Clinton steered his campaign toward economic and trade issues and promised to end the recession of the early 1990s by focusing on managing the American economy. A sign in Clinton's campaign headquarters in Little Rock, Arkansas, said it all—"It's the economy, stupid." In other words, the number one issue concerning most Americans at the time was the recession and how the United States could best cope with international competition.

As he campaigned, Clinton offered a qualified endorsement of trade and globalization, stating that he did not oppose trade deals as long as they were part of a strategy for strengthening the United States. He repeatedly stressed that the primary difference between his approach to trade and that of Republican Presidents Ronald Reagan and George Bush was that he did not see freer trade as an end in itself, as had many of the ideologues in previous administrations. For Clinton, freer trade was a tool to be used for improving the economy by opening foreign markets to American exports and for supplying the American consumer with more goods and services. In addition, trade pushed American companies to sharpen their competitive skills and to become more efficient.

Clinton also argued that the United States should place a higher priority on its economic relationships with other nations and should not treat trade issues as a poor cousin to supposedly more important national security questions. One way to do this was to establish an economic equivalent to the National Security Council that advised the president on political and strategic affairs. Such an economic council could serve as an advocate of the importance of trade and could devise a strategy to guarantee that trade would benefit the common American citizen. Furthermore, the economic council could push for fairer trade and for the elimination of the trade barriers American products confronted in other countries. The American people were assured that during a Clinton presidency the United States would no longer accept foreign trade barriers as the price they had to pay for world leadership. Instead, the United States would insist on eliminating obstacles to trade and on achieving results, not making promises.

When he assumed office in January 1993, Clinton faced many of the issues described in earlier chapters. He had to finish the NAFTA deal by securing congressional approval; he confronted a seemingly endless Uruguay Round; and he had bilateral problems with several countries and regions, most notably China, Japan, and the European Union. This chapter examines how Clinton and Congress handled these and other problems. In particular, it focuses on the strategies that were used to continue to open markets in Europe, the Americas, Asia, and Africa for U.S. exports. The push to open markets was built on two foundations. First, the government sought to expand current free trade and WTO agreements and to negotiate new accords. Second, it continued to try to eliminate the unfair trade practices that were robbing the United States of foreign sales opportunities.

JAPAN

In dealing with the continuing problem of unfair trade and closed markets in Japan, Clinton drew on previous American approaches and used a "results-oriented" strategy modeled on the semiconductor negotiations of 1985–1986—that is, the United States would obtain an agreement on the specific numbers of imports to expect from an expansion of trade. The Clinton team concluded that merely seeking the elimination of import barriers or encouraging changes in Japanese policy and business practices—the goals of the Market-Oriented Sector-Selective and Structural Impediments Initiative talks—simply allowed the Japanese to find new ways to prevent Americans from selling in Japan. Commerce Secretary Ron Brown mapped out the new American goals during a 1993 visit to Tokyo when he said that the ultimate measure of success would not be the removal of barriers but sales and open markets—that is, "when we see that American products, successful all over the world, have equal success in Japan."[2]

The Framework Talks

The new negotiations, known as the **Framework Talks,** began in the fall of 1993. Included in the talks were some of the same issues tackled in the MOSS and SII bargaining: government procurement, regulatory reform, and imports of autos and auto parts, medical technology, insurance services, and telecommunications equipment and services. The bargaining was contentious from the start because the Japanese refused to conclude any agreement containing the numerical indicators the United States wanted for measuring progress in market opening. Even a meeting between President Clinton and Japanese prime minister Morihiro Hosokawa in Washington in February 1994 did not resolve these differences. The two leaders admitted during a joint press conference that the trade problems between their countries could not be solved at that time. U.S. Trade Representative Mickey Kantor underscored the depth of the dispute when he told the press that "there's no more business as usual" with Japan.[3]

In response to the lack of progress in the negotiations, Clinton decided in March to reinstate the Super 301 provision of the Omnibus Trade and Competitiveness Act of 1988. As originally passed, Super 301 expired after two years unless the president extended its provisions. The Bush administration had allowed Super 301 to die in 1990, but Clinton regarded it as a useful tool in the struggle to open markets. After renewing Super 301, Clinton set October 1 as the date for determining which countries to cite.

Meanwhile, the Framework negotiations went nowhere until September 30, when, under the pressure of the October 1 Super 301 deadline, a deal was reached on medical technology, insurance, and telecommunications sales. The language of the deal fell short, however, of what the United States wanted. Instead of specifying numbers, the Japanese committed themselves to "a significant increase in access and sales of competitive foreign products and services" and agreed that "recent trends in the value, rate of growth and share" of the Japanese market would be used as indicators of progress. This language allowed the Japanese to define "significant increase" and left the door open to continuing disputes over whether the Japanese were keeping their word.[4]

A deal on autos and auto parts, however, was elusive even under the pressure of a possible Super 301 citation. The United States therefore began a Section 301 investigation to determine if Japan's market was unfairly closed to foreign goods. One consequence of this investigation was the possibility that the president would impose penalties on Japanese goods if it was found that Japan was unfair and if the Japanese refused to make the necessary market opening moves. Even the added pressure of the Section 301 investigation did not budge the Japanese on autos and auto parts. To introduce still more pressure, Clinton announced in May 1995 that if the negotiations were not successful by June 28, he would place 100 percent tariffs on the $5.9 billion in luxury cars Japan was selling in the American market. The United States also threatened to file a World Trade Organization case against Japan for discriminating against American autos and auto parts.

Once again, an agreement was hammered out just before the June 28 deadline. And again, the agreement was not what the administration had hoped for. Numerical targets for increased imports were not set, but the Japanese did agree to encourage car dealers in Japan to carry foreign as well as domestic autos. The Office of the U.S. Trade Representative estimated that this would lead to two hundred new dealership outlets for American-made cars by 1996 and a thousand new outlets by 2000. The Japanese also decided to relax their rules for inspecting autos and for determining what auto parts could be used to repair cars that failed an inspection. The United States expected this move to increase the sale of American auto parts in Japan.[5]

The Enhanced Initiative

As so often had been the case in the past, the Framework agreements did not end trade frictions between the United States and Japan. By 1997, the U.S. trade deficit with Japan had hit $56.1 billion, and many American trade analysts were concluding that several of the structural and regulatory problems that had been discussed as part of the Structural Impediments Initiative were still causing problems. Seeking a solution, Clinton approached Japanese prime minister Ryutaro Hashimoto during the Group of Eight summit in Denver in June 1997 about new negotiations to address the structural sources of the trade problems between the United States and Japan.[6]

Labeled the **Enhanced Initiative on Deregulation and Competition Policy,** the new discussions examined Japanese regulatory policy in four areas: (1) telecommunications, (2) housing and construction, (3) financial services, and (4) medical devices and pharmaceuticals. Some of these issues were carryovers from previous negotiations. The Enhanced Initiative was envisioned as an ongoing process that would address trade conflicts between the United States and Japan as they arose. In addition to this initiative, the United States continued to press Japan to further open its market to foreign autos and auto parts.

The United States has secured agreement in several areas under the Enhanced Initiative. In telecommunications, the Japanese have promised to facilitate long-distance competition by changing the fees foreign companies are charged for access to the Japanese telephone system, to increase the number of programming channels available for use by foreign satellite broadcasters, and to ensure that Japanese fiber optic cables are available for use by foreigners on an equitable basis. For medical devices, the Japanese have consented to speed up the approval process for foreign products and to revise the Japanese pricing system to ease the entry of foreign goods into the Japanese market. The Japanese also have pledged to accept international housing and building materials codes and to sponsor seminars to encourage Japanese builders to use foreign products. And in the financial arena, the Japanese have agreed to expand the services foreign banks and brokerage firms may offer to Japanese customers. In addition, the Japanese repealed the Large Store Law in 1998 and will be including the Japanese energy industry in future Enhanced Initiative discussions.[7]

For autos and auto parts, progress has been minimal. This stalemate can be attributed in part to a recession that struck Japan in the early 1990s and continued unabated through the end of the century. As a USTR press release in 1998 put it, "Japan's recession is compounding the trade and regulatory barriers that have long impeded U.S. auto and auto parts sales to Japan."[8] But the recession tells only part of the story. A joint report by the Department of Commerce and the Office of the U.S. Trade Representative notes that "Japanese government policies serve to hold back needed changes and preserve the status quo." The same report also points out that "we are disappointed with the overall Japanese government actions to open and deregulate its automotive market."[9] Evidence of the continuing problems U.S. producers confront in Japan is found in the 1998 sales figures: that year sales of American auto parts to Japan declined by 7.4 percent and auto sales by 35 percent.[10] In addition, the Framework Talks were expected to result in 200 new dealership outlets by 1996 and a thousand new outlets by 2000, but in fact only 187 additional dealerships were selling American cars by 1998.[11]

Progress in opening the Japanese market thus has been slow, with misunderstandings and disputes between the United States and Japan a constant source of controversy. One reason for these problems is the differences between the two countries in the social and economic relationships found among commercial actors. The more arm's-length relationships characterizing U.S. businesses make it easier for foreigners to establish ties with those businesses and to penetrate the American market. In Japan, the close-knit ties between firms often lead to the exclusion of outsiders. Even if it is possible to change these Japanese practices, it will take a long time.

Another source of trouble is the differing attitudes the countries have toward trade. The United States, a large society with an abundance of resources, feels able to cope with foreign commerce. A resource-poor country, Japan feels compelled to maintain a trade surplus in order to pay for the natural resources it needs. The Japanese therefore are wary of opening their market too wide for fear it might bring trade deficits that would leave them unable to pay their international bills. Given these distinctions between the two countries, it is likely that trade disputes will continue into the next century.

Finally, trade is much more complex than it has been in the past. Lowering tariffs and eliminating quotas used to be the keys to opening foreign markets, but today policy makers must take into account such things as the types of auto parts a government-certified repair shop is permitted to use and the rules regulating access time to satellite transmissions. These and thousands of other technical standards can serve as formidable barriers to trade. Opening markets thus becomes a tedious task, accomplished by identifying the problems a few at a time and negotiating a solution. In short, there are no quick fixes, and extensive trade discussions between the United States and Japan are likely to be an ongoing feature of American trade policy.

THE EUROPEAN UNION

Maintaining a smooth trading relationship is among the most important items on the respective agendas of the United States and the European Union as the two economic giants move into the new century. The United States and the EU absorb approximately one-fifth of each other's merchandise exports and nearly one-third of each other's trade in services. More broadly, the EU provides 59 percent of the foreign investment in the United States, and the United States provides 51 percent of the foreign investment in the EU.[12] As these figures illustrate, commerce between Europe and the United States is essential to the performance of the economies on both sides of the Atlantic.

Several initiatives were implemented in the 1990s to guarantee that commercial contacts across the Atlantic function smoothly. The **Transatlantic Business Dialogue (TABD)** gives American and European businesses an opportunity to work with their respective governments to eliminate trade frictions before they become serious.[13] The **Transatlantic Economic Partnership (TEP)** was launched in May 1998 in London to promote ongoing government negotiations to reduce trade barriers and to exchange information. In recent months, TEP has sponsored talks to reduce barriers to trade in services and to encourage more cooperation on trade in biotechnology products.[14]

Despite these attempts to facilitate relations between the United States and the EU, trade conflicts continue. Among the most serious of these disputes have been continuing clashes over agriculture, most related to the CAP and to export subsidies. Additional problems have arisen recently over EU food import policies that, according to the United States, discriminate against American producers. Among the most visible of these issues are Europe's decisions to ban the import of hormone-fed beef and to discriminate against bananas produced by U.S. companies in Central America.

Beef Hormones

The beef hormone dispute illustrates the complexity of agricultural trade in the contemporary world. These days, the United States and other countries employ biotechnology to enhance the yields of food from different types of crops and animals. Biotechnology involves everything from feeding animals special diets to using designer fertilizers and engaging in genetic engineering. This scientific manipulation of the food supply can spark anxiety in consumers and demands that the government protect their food supply. In the United States, political action of this sort has been poorly organized, but in Europe the protestors are better organized, and the press delights in writing about what has been labeled "frankenfood." Thus European politicians have been pressed to do something to limit the production and import of such goods, even when those actions fly in the face of scientific evidence.

The beef hormone dispute began in October and December 1985 when the European Community decided to ban the import of animals, and the meat from animals, fed growth hormones. The EC claimed it was protecting the health of EC citizens from the possible adverse effects of eating the meat from hormone-fed animals. Because hormones were, and still are, used widely in the United States to promote the growth of animals, particularly cattle, the EC ban closed the European market to American meat.

The United States immediately protested the EC prohibition, which was to take effect January 1, 1988, saying it had no scientific foundation. Indeed, the U.S. Department of Agriculture and the Office of the U.S. Trade Representative noted that scientific studies in the United States and Europe had demonstrated that hormone meat was safe for human consumption. They also reminded Europeans that foods such as eggs, milk, wheat germ, and soybeans had far higher levels of the hormones in question than the beef that was banned.[15] Europeans rejected the American protests and insisted that the ban be implemented.

In response to the EC action, the United States attempted in 1986 and 1987 to invoke a GATT dispute settlement procedure that called for technical experts to evaluate the EC policy. The EC refused to accept this move, which only could proceed with the concurrence of both parties to the conflict. In November 1987, however, the EC did, under pressure from the United States, agree to postpone the implementation of the import ban for one year, until January 1, 1989. A month later, President Reagan announced and suspended 100 percent retaliatory tariffs on $100 million in European exports to the United States.[16]

Over the course of the next year, U.S.-EC negotiations went nowhere. In fact, two months before the ban was to take effect, the EC broadened its action to include meats, such as pork, that are not fed growth hormones, claiming that the United States was not supplying data to prove that these meats were not tainted.[17] On January 1, 1989, the EC prohibition went into effect. Within a few days, the United States imposed retaliatory tariffs on selected European agricultural exports. At the same time, the U.S. trade representative and the Department of Agriculture worked with the Food and Agriculture Organization (FAO), the

World Health Organization (WHO), and European scientific officials to establish acceptable human consumption levels for the hormones involved in the dispute.[18] Despite a joint FAO/WHO report in 1993 indicating that the banned meat was safe, the European Union (the former European Community), refused to budge. It also refused to reconsider its restrictions when an EU scientific conference held in November 1995 concluded that meat with hormones posed no risk to humans.[19]

At this point, the United States requested that a WTO dispute settlement panel be formed. The EU blocked the request, but the United States persisted and a panel was set up in July 1996. In October, Canada also asked for a panel. In May 1997, interim reports from the panels found in favor of the United States and Canada. On May 29, 1998, the WTO directed the EU to drop its import ban by May 13, 1999. When the EU refused to comply, a panel of arbitrators decided on July 12, 1999, that the United States was entitled to retaliate against $116.8 million in EU exports.[20] This retaliation was implemented and continues.

The beef hormone dispute illustrates the degree to which the campaign against trade barriers is moving into uncharted territory where obstacles to trade are a product of the way people respond to new technologies. Trade barriers based on an emotional and fearful reaction to biotechnology may be among the most difficult for negotiators to tear down. And because biotechnology is here to stay, trade frictions of this sort no doubt will increase in the future.

Bananas

The banana conflict between the United States and the EU is a product of the increasingly global economy. The controversy has little to do with protecting domestic producers and consumers from imports; after all, the United States and Europe produce almost no bananas. Instead, the dispute centers on the reaction by U.S. companies who grow bananas in Latin America to Europe's attempt to provide banana producers in Africa with preferential access to the EU market. In other words, the EU has decided to assist selected developing countries by opening its market to their bananas, and the United States has protested that this arrangement works to the disadvantage of developing countries in another part of the world and harms American companies.

The banana dispute originated in a program established by the European Community in the 1970s and 1980s to aid the economic development of former European colonies in Africa, the Caribbean, and the Pacific. Known as the Lome Accords, the program gave the countries special access to EC markets. In the late 1980s and early 1990s, the EC/EU negotiated new understandings with the Lome countries, also called the ACP states, that gave them special privileges in European markets for a variety of products, including bananas. The new rules for bananas, which went into effect in July 1993, provided ACP states with duty-free access to Europe for 900,000 metric tons of bananas and established new quotas and tariffs that limited the ability of Latin American banana producers to sell in Europe. The Office of the U.S. Trade Representative estimated that U.S. banana companies operating in Latin America lost nearly one-half of their share of the European market because of the Lome Accords.[21]

In 1993, several Latin American countries lodged a complaint with the General Agreement on Tariffs and Trade, alleging that the EU banana policy was discriminatory because it subjected ACP bananas to one set of rules and other bananas to different regulations. A GATT panel ruled in early 1994 that the European banana system violated GATT rules. The EU responded by negotiating an agreement with Colombia, Costa Rica, Nicaragua, and Venezuela that did little to change the overall thrust of the EU program.[22] Thus even though these countries received a better deal, other countries and companies involved in the dispute still suffered from discrimination.

In October 1994, Chiquita Brands International and the Hawaii Banana Industry Association filed a formal complaint with the Office of the U.S. Trade Representative under Section 301 of the 1974 Trade Act. The complainants asserted they were denied market access because of unfair European practices. A USTR investigation and negotiations with the EU yielded no change in the European position. The U.S. trade representative also initiated Section 301 investigations of two (Colombia and Costa Rica) of the four Latin American countries that had made special deals with the EU earlier in the year.[23]

While the Section 301 investigations were under way, the United States also filed cases with the World Trade Organization in October 1995 and February 1996. Guatemala, Honduras, and Mexico joined the October case, and Ecuador added its voice in February. After first trying to block the formation of a WTO dispute panel, the EU agreed in March to cooperate.

After the WTO panel found against the EU in early 1997, the EU appealed, and in September a WTO appellate panel ruled that the EU had violated over a dozen GATT and GATS (General Agreement on Trade in Services) rules when forming its banana import policy. The WTO gave the EU until January 1, 1999, to comply with the panel rulings.

When it came in January 1999, the European Union response proved inadequate. It rearranged the calculations of tariffs and quotas, but it maintained the practice of varying standards for setting import rules by country. U.S. Trade Representative Charlene Barshefsky immediately noted the inconsistencies between the EU response and the rulings of the WTO panels.[24] But in spite of the protests, the EU announced in June that it would move ahead with its reformulated banana rules.[25]

In the face of the EU's refusal to change policy, the United States announced plans to retaliate by imposing penalties on selected EU goods sold in America. It then asked a WTO dispute settlement panel for authority to retaliate with 100 percent tariffs against $520 million in European goods. After three months of deliberation, the panel ruled in the spring of 1999 that the United States had actually suffered $191.4 million in damages and could retaliate in that amount. The tariff increases were imposed soon thereafter.[26] Although the United States and the EU continue to discuss the banana issue, no mutually satisfactory solution appears on the horizon.

The beef hormone controversy and the banana dispute together illustrate the lengthy WTO dispute settlement process and how the losing party can ignore a WTO finding. In the hormone case, three years passed between the creation of a WTO panel in 1996 to hear the American complaint and the final decision to authorize retaliation. For bananas, the process took even longer. The first ruling against the EU was in early 1994 when EU banana regulations were declared violations of GATT. Even after the EU response was termed insufficient, two more years passed before another WTO panel was set up in 1996 and three additional years before American retaliation was authorized. Thus in the bananas case more than five years passed between creation of the first panel and the decision to allow the United States to take action. This, then, was hardly the hasty decision-making process that so worried American critics of the WTO when Congress debated the Uruguay Round agreement in 1994. Moreover, such a time lag could cripple parties that rely heavily on trade and need a quick resolution to a problem.

As for the retaliation of the United States against the EU in the beef and bananas cases, in both instances American tariffs were levied against many types of EU exports from a variety of countries. This strategy was undertaken in the hope that European producers who were losing sales in the American market would pressure the EU to change its beef and banana policies. To date, though, it has been ineffective.

CHINA

America's trade relations with the People's Republic of China have been unlike those maintained with any other country. Prior to the communist revolution in 1949, most Americans saw China as a country with vast economic potential that had been wasted by weak governments and excessive foreign influence. But after the communists seized power in 1949 and the Chinese intervened in the Korean War in late 1950, the American public began to view China as one of the most virulent threats to peace in the international arena.

Indeed, that was the impression most Americans had of China when Richard Nixon became president in 1969. Nixon believed that a Sino-Soviet political split and border clashes between the military forces of the two countries had created a chance for the United States to alter its relationship with China. In February 1972, Nixon launched the new American stance toward China by flying to Beijing to meet Chinese leaders. Almost overnight, the American public's image of China became more positive, and American companies started contemplating the potentially vast Chinese market. A transformation in U.S.-China trade relations seemed just around the corner.

The Chinese market, however, was slow to develop. For one thing, the Chinese people were poor and unable to buy many American goods. For another, the Chinese government carefully controlled imports and exports. In addition, the United States had no formal diplomatic ties with China until President Jimmy Carter extended formal recognition in December 1978. Without such ties, American corporations found it difficult to function in China. And finally, the United States only restored China's most-favored-nation status, which had been rescinded during the Korean War, in 1980. With the termination of MFN status, Chinese goods sold in the United States were burdened by the high tariff rates established under the Smoot-Hawley Tariff of 1930.

Reinstatement of China's MFN status was handled according to procedures established under Title IV of the Trade Act of 1974. Under this law, to restore MFN status to a communist country the president must negotiate a trade agreement in which the United States and the communist country extend MFN to each other and must certify that the communist country permits freedom of emigration. Congress will then approve both the trade agreement and the certification of free emigration. The Carter administration completed the negotiations for the required trade agreement in July 1979 and sent the agreement and the emigration certification to Congress, where they were approved in January 1980. Until recently, China's MFN treatment remained in force only if the 1980 trade agreement was renewed every three years, if the president certified yearly that China allowed freedom of emigration, and if Congress gave its approval of the annual certification.[27]

U.S.-China trade grew quickly during the 1980s, facilitated by the policies of Chinese leader Deng Xiaoping that opened the Chinese economy to foreigners and allowed for some capitalist activity. By 1989, China was selling $12 billion in goods to the United States; American exports to China totaled $5.8 billion. As these figures indicate, China consistently has run a trade surplus with the United States. By 1990, this surplus was beginning to alarm members of Congress, who also were increasingly upset by China's human rights record, trade barriers, violations of American intellectual property rights, and attempts to acquire strategic goods.

Human Rights

Human rights has remained at the forefront of U.S.-China relations. Although the China of the last two decades is a far cry from the totalitarian society of the 1950s, the Chinese government remains repressive. In fact, many Americans believe trade should be used as a lever to push China toward respect of civil liberties.

One of the most public examples of the Chinese government's disregard for human rights occurred in June 1989 when the government ordered the Chinese armed forces to disperse pro-democracy demonstrators in Tiananmen Square in the heart of Beijing. The resulting violence led to hundreds of deaths and thousands of arrests.[28] The United States reacted immediately to these events; President Bush suspended the sale of military goods to China, cut off high-level political contacts, postponed the Chinese foreign minister's visit to Washington, and asked the International Monetary Fund and the World Bank to defer any new lending to China. Bush did not, however, withdraw the request he had already sent to Congress for renewal of China's MFN privileges, feeling that, as Secretary of State James Baker later put it, such a move "would have been detrimental to the United States economically, hurt the forces of reform in China, and isolated the Chinese to a dangerous degree."[29]

Although Congress allowed China to retain its MFN status, in June and July the House and Senate voted by veto-proof margins to institute limited economic sanctions against China. The congressional restrictions affected the sale of satellites and satellite equipment, loans from the International Development Association, and Export-Import Bank funds. In addition, in February 1990 Congress passed a law restricting export licenses for the sale of sensitive goods to China.[30]

The legislation mandating economic sanctions gave the president discretionary power to suspend sanctions if it was in the national interest. Within a few weeks of the crackdown in Tiananmen Square, the administration did just this. On July 7, it modified the suspension of arms shipments to permit China to buy four Boeing 757-200 commercial planes that had navigation systems that could be used for military purposes. In November and December 1989, Bush also waived sanctions prohibiting the sale of satellites.[31]

Although these actions enraged critics of Bush's China policy, they illustrated how reluctant the majority in Congress was by 1989 to tie the president's hands when it came to managing American trade with a country the size of China. Congress was ready to pass legislation restricting trade with China, but it was not prepared to strip China of its MFN status. Moreover, the trade-limiting legislation was set up to allow the president to make exceptions when it was advisable to do so. The initiative for action was therefore left in the president's hands.

Another issue connecting human rights and trade is that of goods made by forced labor. American law forbids the importation of such goods,[32] but in China prison laborers often work in factories producing for export. As one of its last acts, the Bush administration finalized an accord in August 1992 under which China agreed to refrain from selling prison-made goods in the United States.[33]

When he assumed office in 1993, Bill Clinton was confronted with reports that China was ignoring the prison labor agreement. As a result, his administration negotiated a new accord in 1994 that clarified the earlier agreement and gave American inspectors the right to examine facilities suspected of using prison labor. However, even with the new accord, the dispute over forced labor has continued. In 1998 and 1999, the State Department labeled Chinese cooperation in investigating forced labor production as "inadequate" and stated that Chinese officials were unresponsive to requests from U.S. Customs inspectors who wanted to exercise their right to investigate.[34]

The Chinese government has been equally unreceptive to American inquiries about the use of child labor, the sentencing of political dissidents to long terms in prison, and the suppression of religious groups.[35] Although such activities anger many Americans and have spurred lively debates in Congress during renewal time for China's MFN status, they have never been sufficient to move Congress to block continuation of MFN. Indeed, after declaring in 1993 that human rights would serve as a key consideration in his decisions about MFN renewal, President Clinton changed course in 1994 and explicitly delinked the issues, preferring instead to promote human rights in China through a policy of "engagement." Engagement is predicated on the belief that trade fosters contacts with China that will lead to the acceptance of Western values, including respect for human rights.[36] Thus it is probably safe to say that human rights have had at best a marginal effect on America's trade policy toward China.

Chinese Trade Barriers

A second problem clouding trade with China has been the trade barriers that prevent American producers from fully participating in the Chinese economy.[37] Once the United States granted MFN status to China in 1980, the American market was opened to Chinese goods. The Chinese, however, have been far slower in lowering their trade barriers to American goods, and the result has been a growing American trade deficit with China. In 1989, the United States bought $6.2 billion more goods from China than it was able to sell to that country. Five years later, in 1994, the trade deficit with China was nearly five times higher, $29.5 billion. This figure in turn almost doubled by 1998, reaching a staggering $56.9 billion. Indeed, the trade deficit with China has grown so quickly that by the late 1990s it ranked second only to that with Japan.

As might be expected, these trade figures concern analysts in the executive branch and members of Congress, who point to Chinese trade practices that they consider unfair. Among the trade barriers that have drawn the most attention are Chinese tariff levels, nontariff barriers, rules relating to trade, the restricted distribution of foreign goods, and limitations on foreign investments.

Chinese tariffs are among the highest in the world. In 1996, the average Chinese import duty was 42 percent, a figure rivaling the infamous Smoot-Hawley tariffs of the 1930s. By 2000, negotiations had succeeded in pushing this level down to an average of 17 percent, but that level is still higher than the tariffs of any other major American trading partner. Moreover, Chinese tariffs on some goods, such as automobiles, are as high as 100 percent, which effectively excludes such products from the Chinese market.

Nontariff barriers and excessive rules on imports also impede trade. The Chinese government maintains a complex and secretive maze of licensing, certification, and technical procedures for imports. In addition, the right to sell directly to consumers is severely restricted in China, which means that foreigners must work through local distributors, a process most international businesses find cumbersome and time-consuming. Beyond this, importers often find local laws vague, enforcement uneven, and government restrictions on imports arbitrary.

Foreign investors also have found China a tough country to do business in. Foreign ownership rights are tightly controlled and non-Chinese businesses frequently are subjected to discrimination. Moreover, foreign exchange is carefully regulated, making it difficult to buy and sell abroad, and foreign businesses often are required to transfer technological secrets to China as the price for operating in the Chinese market.[38]

The Chinese handling of technological secrets touches on another sensitive area in U.S.-China trade—intellectual property. One of the most persistent problems confronting American firms in China has been that country's refusal to protect the patents, copyrights, trademarks, and production secrets of foreign companies. Time and again, American corporations have complained that the Chinese government has allowed Chinese producers to replicate American products and market them in China and other parts of Asia.

In view of these trade practices, the United States, largely beginning with the Bush administration, has tried several times to convince the Chinese government to reform the way it handles foreign trade. In April 1991, the U.S. trade representative cited China under the Special 301 provision of the Omnibus Trade and Competitiveness Act of 1988 as one of three countries (India and Thailand were the others) that did not provide adequate protection for the intellectual property of American businesses. An investigation and negotiations followed. When the negotiations produced insufficient progress, the U.S. trade representative announced in November that it would impose penalties against $1.5 billion in

Chinese exports to the United States unless a resolution was reached by January 1992. Under the threat of sanctions, Beijing agreed on January 16 to strengthen China's laws related to patents, copyrights, and trade secrets. In addition, the Chinese promised to protect American computer software, sound recordings, and pharmaceuticals from illegal copying.

In October 1991, the Bush administration tried again to secure greater cooperation from China. The U.S. trade representative filed a Section 301 complaint against China for maintaining unfair trade barriers in the form of licensing procedures, discriminatory technical practices, and the uneven enforcement of local laws. As was the case for the Special 301 citation, however, the Chinese were unwilling to negotiate meaningful changes until the U.S. trade representative threatened in August 1992 to levy increased duties against $3.9 billion in Chinese sales to the United States. Finally, in October the Chinese agreed to eliminate or modify several of the procedures that American businesses said most hampered their activities.

Regrettably, some of the Chinese pledges yielded less than was expected. In June 1994, the U.S. trade representative again cited China under Special 301 for its unwillingness to protect intellectual property. The United States was particularly concerned about China's failure to prevent the pirating of foreign compact and laser disks. Eight months of desultory negotiations followed, until in February 1995 the trade representative again threatened to impose punitive tariffs on $1.1 billion in Chinese goods. As had happened on the two occasions discussed earlier, the Chinese agreed almost immediately, in March, to prevent piracy and to provide greater access for American goods in the expectation that the temptation to buy pirated goods would be reduced if the genuine products were available for purchase.

Within a little over a year after the March agreement, however, China was once again hit with a Special 301 citation for not meeting its earlier enforcement promises. In particular, the U.S. trade representative noted that although China was limiting the retail sale of pirated goods, it was not doing enough to stop the production of those items. The USTR report pointed to thirty factories, some owned by the Chinese army, that were suspected of making pirated products. Following the now-familiar pattern, the trade representative announced that $2 billion in Chinese exports would be subject to penalties unless the Chinese stepped up their efforts against piracy. And again, on the eve of the June 17 date when the sanctions were scheduled to go into effect, the two countries reached an agreement calling for the Chinese to close the factories in question and to better monitor the problem in the future.

Even with the resolution of this most recent dispute, officials in the Office of the U.S. Trade Representative and in the Commerce Department continue to regard the protection of intellectual property and the elimination of piracy in China as issues that require the constant attention of the United States. In addition to the piracy of computer software and sound recordings, USTR Barshefsky has noted that the United States currently is monitoring the production of pharmaceuticals in China that may violate the rights of American firms.[39]

U.S.-China WTO Negotiations

Another prominent trade issue in the U.S.-China relationship has been Beijing's interest in joining the World Trade Organization. The Chinese first expressed an interest in joining the world trading community when they applied to become a GATT contracting party in 1986. In the late 1980s and early 1990s, GATT took no action on the Chinese application. When the WTO was created in 1995, the Chinese updated their previous application by indicating they wished to join that organization.

To attain WTO membership, China had to negotiate on two levels. The first was bilateral talks with individual WTO members to set the conditions under which each member would agree to extend the privileges of membership to China. The second was with the WTO Working Party that would establish the nature of China's obligations to the WTO.[40]

As one of the most influential members of the WTO, the United States was crucial to Chinese membership. U.S.-China negotiations, which began in 1994 but moved very slowly until 1997, became a lightning rod in the United States both for the many economic, security, and political issues dividing the two countries and for the frustrations felt by those opposing the expansion of American trade. Thus, instead of concentrating solely on trade, Sino-American talks about the WTO became the occasion for digressions about human rights, Chinese weapons transfers to third countries, the role played by China in American political campaigns, and questions about Chinese espionage in the United States.

In conducting its negotiations with China, the key issues for the United States were the conditions under which the United States would support China's entry into the WTO and grant most-favored-nation status to China on a permanent basis (recall that a basic feature of the WTO is members' willingness to extend most-favored-nation status to all other members—see Chapters 4 and 8). If the United States agreed to Chinese WTO membership, Congress would have to pass a law replacing the annual MFN review procedure with a grant of permanent MFN status.[41]

In many ways, the question of permanently granting MFN to China became the heart of the Sino-American WTO negotiations. Indeed, by 1998 the issue had become so hot politically that Congress felt compelled to pass legislation specifying that in the future the United States would employ the term **normal trade relations (NTR)** in place of the term *most-favored-nation* because too many people in the public and the media misunderstood the meaning of the latter term.[42]

Among the problems that arose during the U.S.-China WTO talks, one was whether China would be treated under WTO rules as a developing country and another was the types of market access concessions China would make in return for a grant of permanent NTR status. The Chinese insisted that the low average incomes of the Chinese people qualified their country as developing, thereby entitling China to preferential WTO rules. For its part, the United States pointed out that the size of the Chinese economy and the sophistication of many Chinese industries disqualified China from special WTO treatment. As for market access, the United States pushed China to eliminate many of its discriminatory and trade-distorting rules. Chinese officials countered these American demands by arguing that too much market opening would bankrupt Chinese businesses and could lead to instability.[43]

Just as the trade talks began heating up in late 1996 and early 1997, problems arose that nearly derailed the negotiations. The first problem was questionable campaign contributions to the Democratic National Committee. In February 1997, news reports suggested that the Chinese government, in seeking to curry favor with the Clinton administration, channeled money to the Democratic Party during the 1996 election.[44] In addition, a Clinton appointee to an advisory panel on Pacific and Asian trade, Charles Yah Lin Trie, was accused of playing a role in collecting the Chinese campaign donations.[45]

Americans who opposed a China trade deal quickly claimed that the Clinton administration could not be trusted to negotiate with China. In response to these concerns, Clinton's nominee for the USTR job, Charlene Barshefsky, stated during her 1997 congressional confirmation hearings that the United States would block Chinese entry into the WTO unless Beijing agreed to open its market to American products.[46]

Also clouding the trade talks were intelligence findings indicating that Chinese companies had sold Iran equipment that could be used to make chemical weapons. These reports came on the heels of evidence that China had assisted Pakistan with its nuclear weapons program. Although Secretary of State Madeline Albright asserted there was no evidence linking the Chinese government to the Iranian sales, these transactions reinforced the perception held by many in the United States that China could not be trusted.[47] Especially troubling for some members of Congress was the fact that China had pledged in 1992 to accept the Nuclear Non-Proliferation Treaty and in 1993 to abide by the terms of the Chemical Weapons Convention, both of which required adherents to refrain from transferring certain types of equipment and knowledge to other countries.[48] Some people asked whether a China that was lax in keeping these promises would be prepared to honor a trade agreement.

In response to these controversies, the Chinese government slowed the pace of negotiations over WTO membership. Reports circulated that the political troubles confronting the Clinton administration made it unlikely that a deal could be reached before Clinton left office. By August 1997, American trade negotiators were telling media representatives that the WTO/NTR talks were going nowhere, that China was offering few of the market access concessions the United States wanted, and that the Chinese appeared to be reassessing their interest in the WTO.

The fall of 1997 brought more gloom for those seeking a China trade deal; the Clinton administration was unable to convince the House of Representatives to renew its fast-track authority. Fast-track fell prey to a beefed-up version of the coalition that opposed NAFTA. In addition to labor unions and environmentalists, those attempting to kill fast-track included human rights activists, religious leaders, and conservatives who distrusted the Chinese government. The ultimate goal for many wishing to block fast-track was to prevent the United States from negotiating any additional trade deals resembling the NAFTA and Uruguay Round accords. Although Clinton attempted throughout September and October to cobble together the votes needed to extend fast-track, by November it appeared doomed and the authorizing legislation was withdrawn. A second attempt at renewal in September 1998 also was defeated.

Further complicating the U.S.-China WTO/NTR talks was a financial crisis in the Far East in the summer of 1997. Thailand's baht currency was hit by a sudden wave of speculative selling that cut its value in half almost overnight. In the coming months, one Asian currency after another was affected by surges of selling that reduced their values dramatically. As time passed, the crisis began spreading to other parts of the developing world and to some of the countries once part of the Soviet Union.

The ongoing crisis affected the negotiations in two ways. First, it reduced the ability of Asian countries to import goods, which in turn affected China's economy. Second, the Chinese became more hesitant than ever to make the market opening concessions the United States was demanding. As a result, the Chinese began debating among themselves the wisdom of moving ahead on WTO/NTR, and they became less willing to bargain with the United States.

The climate for an agreement improved in the spring of 1999. The worst of the Asian crisis was over, and the furor in Washington over campaign contributions and weapons sales no longer clouded the horizon. American and Chinese negotiators targeted the April visit of Prime Minister Zhu Rongji to the United States for completing the talks. By the end of the first week of April, a deal appeared to be imminent. Although it did not contain everything the United States wanted, it was far better than anything most analysts had thought possible. All that remained was for American and Chinese leaders to bestow their blessings on the agreement.

At the eleventh hour, however, Clinton pronounced the deal inadequate. For one thing, American banks, securities firms, and audiovisual services still lacked adequate access to China. The Chinese also were reluctant to accept U.S. dumping regulations and textile quotas.[49] At any rate, the Chinese responded with fury to Clinton's decision. The American businesses that expected to benefit from the deal also were angry. Observers in Washington and Beijing speculated that Clinton's political problems—campaign donations and a sex scandal—had forced him to take an unnecessarily tough stand on the China deal.[50]

But worse was yet to come. Just as the United States and China reopened negotiations, NATO warplanes accidentally bombed the Chinese embassy in Belgrade, Serbia, during a May military operation in Kosovo. Amid anti-American outbursts in several cities, the Chinese government suspended the talks. Moreover, the bombing incident appeared to strengthen the standing of Chinese leaders who questioned the wisdom of joining the WTO and moving forward with economic reforms.

The Final Agreement

After a four-month hiatus, U.S.-China WTO/NTR talks resumed in September 1999. For two months, United States and Chinese negotiators sparred with one another amid rumors that U.S. rejection of the April accord would make it impossible to reach an understanding while Clinton remained in office. Finally, after lengthy discussions in November in Beijing, American and Chinese officials announced they had reached a mutually acceptable agreement.

Under the accord, the United States agreed to confer permanent normal trade relations status upon China and to back Chinese membership in the WTO in exchange for Chinese concessions on tariffs and quotas, expanded rights for American businesses in China, the opening of Chinese service sectors to U.S. firms, and agricultural trade. The Chinese continued to refuse, however, to allow majority foreign ownership of businesses operating in certain parts of the Chinese economy. Otherwise, the deal gave the United States almost everything the Clinton administration had requested (see box).

The reaction to the Chinese trade deal was intense. Businesses that stood to benefit strongly supported the accord. These included aerospace, auto, auto parts, and office machine companies; farmers; industrial machinery and appliance manufacturers; and a variety of service companies. Vehement opposition sprang from

Highlights of the 2000 U.S.-China Trade Agreement

Under the agreement, China pledged to take the following steps:

Tariffs, Quotas, and Subsidies

- Reduce tariffs on agricultural products from an average of 31.5 percent to 14.5 percent by 2004 and allow private trade in agricultural products.
- Reduce tariffs on industrial products from an average rate of 24.6 percent to 9.4 percent by 2005.
- Reduce tariffs on information technology from an average of 13.3 percent to zero by 2005.
- Reduce tariffs on autos from an average of 80–100 percent to 25 percent and on auto parts to an average rate of 10 percent by 2006; eliminate auto quotas by 2005.
- Expand quotas for most products by 15 percent a year until quotas are eliminated altogether.
- Eliminate export subsidies.
- Accept special U.S. rules for dumping, subsidy, and import surge investigations.

Rules Governing Foreign Firms

- Allow American firms full trading and distribution rights in China.
- Open Chinese service sectors to foreign trade and investment.
- Permit American financial firms to make loans for auto sales in China.
- Drop government rules requiring foreign firms in China to transfer technology, to use locally made products, and to export a proportion of their production.
- Allow American firms to compete for sales to government-owned Chinese firms on a nondiscriminatory basis.

Sources: Wayne N. Morrison, *China-U.S. Trade Issues,* Congressional Research Service, Washington, D.C., April 25, 2000, 10; and House Ways and Means Committee, "Testimony of Ambassador Charlene Barshefsky on China's WTO Accession," February 16, 2000, 5–11.

labor unions, environmentalists, industries that competed directly with Chinese imports (for example, pottery, textile, and shoe manufacturers), human rights activists, and citizens suspicious of Chinese security policy. One indication of the intensity of the opposition to the agreement were the demonstrations in Seattle in November against the WTO meeting in particular and globalization and expanded trade in general (see Chapter 1). Protesters also hit the streets four months later in Washington during the annual meetings of the International Monetary Fund and the World Bank.

In January 2000, President Clinton began an all-out effort to secure congressional approval of the China agreement. Businesses around the country let members of Congress know how greatly they valued the deal. Opponents also bombarded Congress, and organized labor made it known that those voting for the deal would be held accountable in the 2000 election. Presidential candidates George W. Bush and Al Gore announced their support for the trade pact, but with qualifications related to human rights and protections for American workers.

As the debate intensified, it became clear that the House of Representatives was the key battleground; passage in the Senate appeared certain. Thus both supporters and detractors focused on securing 218 votes, either for or against. Because the agreement was negotiated without the benefit of fast-track, crippling amendments were a source of concern until the Republican-controlled Rules Committee voted not to permit changes in the accord.

In the end, two legislative developments helped to swing votes toward the trade deal: the creation of a commission to monitor human rights in China and the passage of a trade bill granting sub-Saharan African nations special trading privileges with the United States. The human rights commission helped to convince several legislators who wished to prod China on civil liberties to support the trade agreement. The African bill, which had been under consideration for more than two years, helped persuade several African American legislators to vote aye.

Even though the outcome had appeared doubtful just two weeks earlier, on May 24 the House voted 237–197 in favor of the China trade pact. Four months later, on September 19, the Senate also gave its approval, 83–15.

THE UNITED STATES AND THE WTO

In the years since the United States joined the WTO, two of the most important issues to arise have been the WTO's role in settling disputes and America's desire for a new round of WTO negotiations.

Dispute Settlement

Since it joined the WTO on January 1, 1995, the United States has made frequent use of the WTO Dispute Settlement Understanding (DSU) to resolve conflicts with other countries.[51] Of the fifty-three DSU complaints it has filed, twenty-five currently are under WTO consideration, twelve were settled to the satisfaction of the United States through bilateral negotiations before a WTO panel issued a ruling, and thirteen resulted in a favorable ruling from the WTO. The United States has lost only three of the cases it initiated, but in each of these cases it was able to obtain a reasonably acceptable solution even with the unfavorable ruling.

Of the twenty-five cases the United States brought to a favorable solution either through negotiations or by way of a WTO panel decision, twelve dealt with food and agricultural trade, six with the protection of intellectual property rights, and three with trade in services. The most frequent targets of American complaints have been the EU and Japan (three cases apiece) and Australia, Canada, India, and Korea (two cases each).

The three cases the United States initiated and lost involved the EU classification of computer equipment for calculating tariffs, Japanese regulations for photographic film and paper, and Korean procurement for the construction of an airport. In the EU case, the United States later negotiated the complete elimination of the tariffs in question, and in the Korean case Korea promised to liberalize procurement procedures in the future. The United States continues to monitor Japanese photographic import rules.

In addition to the cases it has filed, the United States has been the target of thirty-nine WTO panel complaints. Of these, ten were resolved through negotiations, eleven are currently inactive, and ten are still under WTO consideration. Of the eight cases that were resolved by WTO panels, the United States lost seven. The sole American victory pertained to an EU complaint that Section 301 of the 1974 Trade Act violated WTO rules. The American losses were related to, among other things, the pollution standards applied to imported gasoline (brought by Brazil and Venezuela), restrictions on importing shrimp caught in nets harmful to endangered sea turtles (brought by India, Malaysia, the Philippines, and Thailand), limitations on textile imports from Costa Rica and India and on computer chips from Korea, American tax exemptions for exporters (brought by the EU), and the Commerce Department's calculations of countervailing duties on lead imports from the EU.

In most of the cases the United States has lost, remedy has been found in changes in bureaucratic procedure. For example, in the gasoline and shrimp cases the WTO ruled that the United States may retain its laws to protect the environment. The application of those laws was the problem; foreign and domestically produced gasoline were held to different pollution standards, and shrimp from Asia was held to a different standard than shrimp from Latin America. The standards were ruled acceptable as long as they were applied consistently. In the two textile cases, the law in question for Costa Rica expired one month after the ruling was handed down, and the U.S. agency regulating textile imports voluntarily altered the way it was applying the law in question in the Indian case. The computer chip case and the lead countervailing duty case were resolved through minor changes in the way the Commerce Department regulates dumping and subsidy investigations. Only the EU complaint about American tax breaks for exporters remains unresolved. Even though the United States lost this case, negotiations between the parties continue on the action the United States will take to resolve the complaint.

On the whole, the American experience with the WTO dispute settlement system has been positive. There have been no threats to American sovereignty, and the United States has not been forced to change any laws because of a WTO ruling. Indeed, the WTO served the valuable role of validating American complaints against the EU in the beef hormone and bananas cases described earlier in this chapter. One valid concern about WTO dispute settlement procedures is the secrecy that governs the deliberations. WTO panels do, however, publish a full discussion of their decisions and the reasons behind them. For the most part, the United States has had little reason to complain.

A New Round of Negotiations

From the moment the House and Senate approved the Uruguay Round, American trade negotiators began planning for new discussions to handle the problems left unresolved when the WTO was formed in 1995. Three trade areas of special concern to the United States in such talks are information technology, telecommunications, and financial services.[52] American companies are among the world leaders in each of these areas and would benefit from any expansion of trade.

During a WTO conference in Singapore in December 1996, the United States worked with its WTO partners to create the Information Technology Agreement, which entered into force on July 1, 1997. This agreement committed its participants to eliminating by January 1, 2000, tariffs on $600 billion in products such as computers, semiconductors, software, and telecommunications equipment. A WTO committee was created to monitor progress in this area.

The WTO Basic Telecommunications Agreement negotiated in 1997 was designed to end the monopolies many countries maintain in their telecommunications sectors. The agreement, which became effective in February 1998, allows American firms to enter once-closed markets in Europe, Asia, the Pacific, Africa, and Latin America. Before the agreement, only 17 percent of the global market was open to American companies. Since the agreement took effect, 95 percent of the world market has become open to foreign competition.

The WTO Financial Services Agreement completed in December 1997 took effect in March 1999. The accord has begun to open global markets in banking, insurance, and financial services to foreign competition. Globally, bank lending is a $38 trillion market, and the financial services and insurance markets are valued at $19.5 trillion and $2.1 trillion, respectively. Given the dominant position of American firms in these areas, the Financial Services Agreement represents a major opportunity for these businesses.

The information technology, telecommunications, and financial services agreements are only part of the American agenda for the WTO. As described in Chapter 8, at the conclusion of the Uruguay Round American negotiators felt that trade in agriculture and in several other areas had not been handled adequately. In addition, the recent furor over workers' rights and the environment raised new issues to address in a multilateral setting. Beyond this, new forms of trade, such as electronic commerce, were demanding attention. Thus the Clinton administration decided to push for a new round of WTO talks. A ministerial meeting scheduled for Seattle from November 30 to December 4, 1999, was targeted for launching the negotiations.

When preparing for the talks, the United States placed agricultural trade "at the heart of [the] agenda."[53] It was particularly concerned about four issues: (1) terminating or reducing export subsidies; (2) eliminating barriers to agricultural trade; (3) abolishing domestic farm support programs; and (4) formulating better international regulations for the use of biotechnology in farming. The first three issues were carryovers from the Uruguay Round, and the fourth pertained to the problems arising during the beef hormone dispute.[54]

Another matter for a WTO round was enlarging the General Agreement on Trade in Services. Although GATS and the information technology, telecommunications, and financial services agreements were valuable starting points for more open trade in services, American trade analysts also wanted to reduce trade barriers in law, finance, health care, electronic commerce, satellite entertainment broadcasts, and education. Many American corporations expected to reap huge benefits from agreements in these areas.[55]

Other items of interest to the United States included setting rules for admitting former communist countries to the WTO, providing more assistance to developing countries, setting standards to guarantee workers' rights, and regulating the effects of trade on the environment. Bringing former communist countries into the WTO and helping developing countries were steps designed to promote peace and to eliminate misery. The workers' rights and environmental issues were the focal points for special-interest group demands in the United States and Europe.[56]

The attempt to launch the new WTO round in Seattle did not go as the Clinton administration planned. Several weeks before the meeting, special interests announced they would use the occasion to protest against the WTO in general and the American trade agenda in particular. Most of the demonstrations were meant to be peaceful and to express concerns about the absence of labor and environmental standards in trade agreements and about the secrecy surrounding the operation of the WTO. However, groups with more violent intentions also converged on Seattle. Many of these protestors were anarchists or were members of groups that feared the WTO was the forerunner to a world government. When the protests began, the anarchists and their allies quickly initiated a chaotic free-for-all that made it virtually impossible for the meeting to go ahead as scheduled. As a result, much of what the United States hoped to achieve was set aside for the moment.

The disruption of the Seattle meeting probably will not prevent a new WTO round. In fact, in testimony in February 2000 before the Subcommittee on Trade of the House Ways and Means Committee, U.S. Trade Representative Barshefsky made it clear that the American interest in a new WTO round was unchanged and that the agenda, which contained several issues of interest to the peaceful protestors, would remain the same.[57] It is almost certain, however, that no one will refer to the new negotiations as the Seattle Round.

REGIONAL TRADE

Although America's trade ties with Japan, the European Union, China, and members of the World Trade Organization tend to attract the spotlight, the United States has in recent years also confronted issues related to several other countries and regions throughout the world. This section briefly examines these issues.

Asia

The United States conducts more trade with Asia than with any other region in the world. Over 30 percent of total American exports go to Asia and 40 percent of American agricultural products are sold in the Far East. In its relations with Asia, the United States has been guided by the same goals it has followed with other countries and regions—opening markets to American goods and services and eliminating unfair trade practices.

America pursues these goals by participating in the Asia-Pacific Economic Cooperation (APEC) forum, an association of twenty-one countries that border the Pacific. Established in 1989, APEC first met in 1993 in Seattle. At a meeting the following year in Bogor, Indonesia, member countries agreed to move in phases toward a Pacific free trade area, by 2010 for the advanced country participants and by 2020 for APEC's less-developed members.[58]

The Osaka Action Agenda of 1995 called for the creation of the APEC free trade area through the individual and collective efforts of APEC participants to lower trade barriers. In moving toward this goal, a majority of APEC nations set up in 1997 a program for voluntarily liberalizing trade in fifteen sectors, including environmental goods and services, energy, fish products, forest products, medical equipment and pharmaceuticals, and chemicals. The idea was that some APEC participants would move immediately toward reducing trade barriers in the specified sectors and that other participants would do so later. Some of the countries currently participating in this program are Australia, Canada, Hong Kong, New Zealand, Singapore, and the United States. So far, China, Japan, and Korea have been reluctant to take part; Chile and Mexico favor an even broader effort at liberalization.[59]

In another move toward opening markets, APEC requested in 1999 new WTO negotiations. APEC asked that the new talks focus on eliminating barriers to agricultural trade, reducing impediments to industrial trade, and promoting trade in the sectors APEC selected for carrying out the Osaka agenda.[60] These APEC goals for a future WTO round conform closely with those of the United States. APEC therefore has been useful in America's attempt to boost trade not only in the Pacific but also throughout the world.

U.S. relations with Asia have not been worry-free, however. In 1997 and 1998, a currency crisis in Asia threatened for a time to both upset the march toward more open markets and disrupt the American economy. As noted earlier, this crisis began in 1997 in Thailand, where a speculative assault on the baht forced the government to devalue its currency. Rather than dampen the speculation, the Thai devaluation appeared to indicate that economic conditions in Asia were shaky, and speculators began selling their holdings in Philippine pesos and Malaysian ringgits, causing those currencies to fall in value. By August, the Indonesian rupiah and the Hong Kong dollar were in trouble. October brought an assault against Taiwan's dollar, and November saw the Korean won weaken. As currency values fell, stock markets throughout the Far East plunged. In the fall of 1997, other developing regions also had problems, and Brazilian, Argentinian, Mexican, and Venezuelan stock prices tumbled.

These developments wreaked havoc on several Far Eastern and Latin American economies. Declining values for local currencies made it impossible for Asian and Latin American corporations to pay their debts to foreign firms, and many companies in the developing world were forced into bankruptcy. Falling currency values also increased the price of developing country imports and made it difficult for those countries to buy a range of items from consumer goods to medicine and construction equipment.

With the falling Asian currencies, a part of the world that normally bought nearly a third of American exports was no longer able to do so. At the same time, exports from that region to the United States became cheaper and thus more attractive to U.S. buyers. The result of the greater volume of goods flowing into the United States and the smaller amount flowing out was larger trade deficits. In fact, the trade deficit mushroomed from $104.7 billion in 1997 to $164.3 billion in 1998 and $271.3 billion in 1999.[61]

The falloff in exports to Asia affected some parts of the American economy more than others and some states, such as California and Washington, more than others. Some industries—such as those producing chemicals, transportation equipment, scientific instruments, industrial machinery, wood products, and agricultural goods—also suffered substantially because they were the leading American exporters to the Far East. In those industries, profit margins were squeezed, and workers faced smaller wage increases or even layoffs.[62] In addition, the cheaper exports produced by declining Asian currency values meant more competition for some American industries such as autos and auto parts, textiles, semiconductors, steel, and electronics. Moreover, many in Congress wondered about the wisdom of negotiating additional trade deals, because they might render the United States even more susceptible to the sort of instability that was afflicting Asia and other parts of the developing world.[63]

All this being said, the Asian crisis did have a few positive effects on the American economy. In particular, with falling Asian currency values many Asian goods were available at bargain basement prices. As a result, American consumers were able to buy more goods, which helped to control inflation in the United States— a subject of growing concern in late 1997 as the American economy continued to expand rapidly.

In part, the United States responded to the crisis by agreeing to buy more Asian exports and by encouraging the EU and Japan to do the same. The hope was that an increased flow of exports would allow the afflicted Asian countries to right their economies by producing goods for export. In addition, the United States worked with the International Monetary Fund and the World Bank to provide economic advice and loans. This advice was often controversial, however, because it usually included calls for local austerity measures, and the poor frequently suffered the most.

As American imports from Asia grew, complaints from affected American industries mounted. In particular, American companies alleged that Asian firms were dumping. In response, President Clinton warned in November 1998 that the United States would prevent unfair trade. Dumping investigations were conducted, and several negotiated arrangements, including one in mid-1999 on steel imports, were set up to guarantee against the practice.

Most analysts agreed that the Asian crisis offered lessons about interdependence and the need for mechanisms to prevent rampant speculation. As for interdependence, the crisis revealed that the ties from increased trade enable the ripples from unsettling events to spread quickly from one part of the globe to another and that these forces may be difficult to control once they are in motion. Such situations call for international institutions that can handle problems such as currency speculation before they get out of hand. These institutions are especially useful when the crisis affects relatively small countries, as was the case in Asia.

Expanding NAFTA

Almost from the moment Congress approved NAFTA in November 1993, the Clinton administration began working to expand the agreement to include other Latin American participants as part of its goal of opening new markets for American exports. After all, some 470 million people live in Latin America and the Caribbean. From 1992 to 1999, approximately 40 percent of the region's imports came from the United States, and the sale of American products in the region increased by 57 percent. During the same period, the number of U.S. jobs tied to Latin American exports grew by 43 percent. Given the fact that the average Latin American tariff is four times higher than the average U.S. tariff, one can only imagine how much American exports would grow if trade barriers in Latin America were reduced.[64]

To this end, the United States played a leading role in organizing a Summit of the Americas in Miami in December 1994. At the summit, the leaders of thirty-four nations in North and South America agreed to create a **Free Trade Area of the Americas (FTAA)** by 2005. Further discussion at another Summit of the Americas in Santiago, Chile, in April 1998 brought a consensus to set up nine negotiating groups to address market access, competition, dumping and subsidies, intellectual property rights, government procurement, investments, agriculture, services, and dispute settlement. Most of the thirty-four nations also agreed to eliminate excessive import regulations by the end of 2000.[65]

Mindful of the controversy that surrounded NAFTA, the Clinton administration attempted to address some of the issues that might arise over a FTAA. Among other things, the White House called for an assessment of the environmental effects of such a free trade area and an analysis of how workers' rights and consumers interests might be affected. In addition, the United States pushed for the creation of a special negotiating committee to seek comments about the talks from special interests in the countries attempting to set up the FTAA.[66]

Despite these moves to calm potential critics, the efforts to create an FTAA drew heavy opposition from special interests in the United States. In February 1997, the AFL-CIO issued a statement opposing an enlarged NAFTA. The United Steel Workers and the Made in the USA Foundation also condemned the idea. In addition, the desire to block American participation in FTAA talks was a key consideration in Congress's refusals to extend the president's fast-track negotiating authority in November 1997 and September 1998.[67]

Although the United States has continued to participate in FTAA discussions even without fast-track, the absence of such authority has affected the calculations of other American nations. Some of the thirty-four countries involved in the FTAA bargaining have concluded that they should move to establish trading deals among themselves even if the United States cannot be a party to the agreements. Others have attempted to set up new trading arrangements with the EU and Japan. An example of the former is a Chilean agreement in June 1996 to join the Mercosur common market with Argentina, Bolivia, Brazil, Paraguay, and Uruguay. Another example are the discussions between the Andean Free Trade Group (Bolivia, Colombia, Ecuador, Peru, and Venezuela) and Mercosur about the possibility of a merger. Finally, Canada and Chile signed their own free trade agreement in November 1996 that called for the elimination of all trade barriers between the two countries by 2001.

Several countries also have attempted to deal with the EU. In July 1999, the leaders of thirty-three Latin American and Caribbean nations met with their EU counterparts in Rio de Janeiro in the first Latin America-European Union summit. The topic was free trade. Even though no agreement was reached, participants set a date of July 2001 to begin formal negotiations. Beyond this, in November 1999 Mexico and the EU completed a free trade deal covering 95 percent of their commercial exchanges, including agricultural and industrial goods and services such as banking and insurance.

In the end, then, the Clinton administration made only slow progress toward its goal of expanding American trade in the Western Hemisphere in large part because U.S. special interests believed they had a lot to lose from such an arrangement. This inability of the United States to move ahead quickly has opened opportunities for others in markets that are expanding and that historically have imported heavily from the United States.

Sub-Saharan Africa

Sub-Saharan Africa comprises the forty-eight countries that lie south of the Sahara Desert in Africa. With a total population of approximately 640 million, these countries represent a vast potential market for American goods and services. The trade potential of the region, however, has been limited for decades by poverty and political instability. In 1996, the average annual income in this part of the world was only $451, compared with nearly $30,000 in the United States. In large measure, the poverty in sub-Saharan Africa accounts for the low U.S. exports to the region of only $6 billion in 1996. By contrast, the United States exported approximately $140 billion in goods and services that same year to Canada, a country with only one twenty-fifth the population of sub-Saharan Africa.[68]

Over the years, the United States has provided substantial foreign aid to the countries in the sub-Saharan African region, but factors ranging from poor transportation and communications systems to inadequate education and corrupt governments have undermined the efficacy of that aid. In the 1990s, Congress and the Clinton administration decided to pursue another approach for helping Africa. In Section 134 of the Uruguay Round Agreements Act passed in 1994, Congress directed the president to formulate a comprehensive trade and development policy for the countries of Africa and to submit annual reports to Congress through 2000.[69]

In response to this congressional mandate, the Clinton administration unveiled in June 1997 its Partnership for Growth and Opportunity in Africa. The Partnership called for providing increased duty-free access to the American market and technical and other assistance to African countries that committed themselves to market-oriented reforms and the promotion of democracy. Democratic African countries with free market economies would be invited to negotiate free trade agreements with the United States. Other African nations would be offered technical assistance, opportunities to work with American specialists to set up better policy management structures, and encouragement to work more closely with the WTO. The White House also drew up the **African Growth and Opportunity Act** to give the president the legal authority to implement the Partnership (see box).[70] Finally, in March 1998 President Clinton made the first presidential visit in two decades to Africa as a sign of America's commitment to the continent.

No action was taken on the African trade bill in 1996 and 1997, but it did pass the House of Representatives just days before the president departed for Africa. Unfortunately, the Senate took no action, and the bill died. The legislation was reintroduced in 1999, and the House again passed it in July by a 234–163 vote. The bill was harder to sell in the Senate, where Ernest Hollings, D-S.C., organized a filibuster to protest provisions allowing duty-free and quota-free access to the American market for African textiles. Hollings feared that textile mills in South Carolina would be harmed by imports from Africa. On November 2, the Senate voted 74–23 to break the filibuster, and the next day the bill passed, 76–19. After work by a conference committee, Congress passed the bill and President Clinton signed it in May 2000.

The United States also has pursued other initiatives with Africa. For example, in February 1999 Trade and Investment Framework Agreements were signed with South Africa and Ghana and in February 2000 with Nigeria. These agreements opened talks to pave the way for trade understandings covering agricultural and industrial products, services, intellectual property rights, market access, labor rights, and environmental standards. The United States has worked as well to

Provisions of the 2000 African Growth and Opportunity Act

- African nations may participate in the program only if the president certifies that they have established a market-based economy or are doing so.
- The United States grants eligible African countries duty-free and quota-free access to the U.S. market for ten years.
- The president is directed to assist sub-Saharan African countries in setting up a free trade area among themselves.
- The president is directed to work out a debt relief plan for sub-Saharan countries.
- The president is directed to initiate negotiations with African countries to promote trade.
- The act amends previous foreign assistance laws to allow foreign aid to be used to promote democratization and conflict resolution.
- The act establishes an African section within the Office of the U.S. Trade Representative.

Sources: New York Times, July 17, 1999, A1; and International Trade Commission, The Year in Trade, 1997, 83.

expand the products covered by the WTO's generalized system of preferences, which helps sub-Saharan African countries.

But even with these American moves, Africa's poverty and political problems remain formidable obstacles to economic progress, and trade can do only so much to help overcome these problems. As long as prosperity and stability continue to elude Africa, the continent's tremendous promise as a market for American goods and services will remain out of reach.

CHAPTER SUMMARY

As the world moves into the twenty-first century, American trade policy has become more committed than ever to the opening of foreign markets to goods and services from the United States. This pursuit of new foreign markets is taking place at several levels. Globally, the United States is pushing for a new round of WTO negotiations. In its view, these talks should address old issues left unresolved in earlier negotiations, such as eliminating policies that distort agricultural trade, and new problems that have arisen from the rapid technological change found in the contemporary world, such as electronic commerce and biotechnology.

At the regional and bilateral levels, the United States has opened discussions to create free trade areas in the Pacific, throughout the Americas, and between the United States and some countries in sub-Saharan Africa. In addition, a process has been established that may result in a free trade arrangement between the United States and the European Union. The regional approach to freer trade began in the Reagan administration with the talks that led to U.S.-Canada free trade. The Clinton administration then pushed the idea to new levels as it pursued hub-and-spoke arrangements in which the United States would be at the center of a collection of free trade deals with various countries. Whether these free trade agreements eventually will be tied to the World Trade Organization remains to be seen.

Another aspect of the American market-opening strategy of the past decade has been the use of American trade law to push other countries to allow better access to their markets and to eliminate what many Americans regard as unsavory trade practices. In particular, Section 301 of the 1974 Trade Act and Super 301 and Special 301 of the 1988 Omnibus Trade and Competitiveness Act have been employed to prod various countries to terminate violations of intellectual property rights and to modify domestic rules that inhibit trade.

Even as the executive branch has attempted to extend American access to foreign markets, trade has become increasingly controversial on the domestic scene. In part, questions about the value of trade come from those, such as labor unions, who stand to lose political and economic influence as trade between the United States and the rest of the world increases. Also unhappy are those who are concerned about the plight of workers in the less-developed countries and those who want to safeguard the environment from industries that might strip away irreplaceable resources and engage in wanton acts of pollution as they make goods for the world market. Because many of these labor and environmental groups are closely associated with the Democratic Party, it should be no surprise that the last three decades have witnessed an increasingly rapid shift among Democrats from support for freer trade, which inspired early party leaders such as Cordell Hull, to the more protectionist stance that motivates some current leaders such as Richard Gephardt.

Despite the widely heard talk throughout the United States about the problems associated with trade, America as a society has reached the point where it simply does not have the option of turning its back on trade. For one thing, too many people and businesses owe their livelihoods to trade. Any action threatening to turn back the clock on trade could bring with it an unparalleled economic disaster. Beyond this, there are good reasons to believe that trade has delivered exactly what Cordell Hull promised: peace and prosperity. It is probably no coincidence that the world's leading trading countries have the highest national incomes in their histories and that those same countries have not fought against one another for over half a century.[71] Attempting to halt or reverse the tide of trade could prompt very unfortunate changes in the patterns of peace found in the contemporary world.

This being said, it should be recognized that trade does not eliminate conflict between countries. Indeed, the evidence presented in this book illustrates that increased trade produces more conflict. But it is not the type of conflict fought with guns and bombs; trade conflicts are verbal clashes—over beef growth hormones, bananas, market access in Japan, and Chinese violations of intellectual property rights. And the means chosen for battle in a trade conflict is a retaliatory tariff on French wine, not a retaliatory attack by nuclear or other weapons. The expansion of trade does not mean the world will become a utopian community. It does mean, however, that many of the world's most urgent problems—past, present, and future—can be resolved in a more satisfactory way.

NOTES

1. The following books examine aspects of the debate discussed here: Norman J. Glickman and Douglas Woodward, *The New Competitors: How Foreign Investors Are Changing the U.S. Economy* (New York: Basic Books, 1989); Tim Jackson, *The Next Battleground: Japan, America, and the New European Market* (Boston: Houghton Mifflin, 1993); Edward N. Luttwak, *The Endangered American Dream: How to Stop the United States from Becoming a Third World Country and How to Win the Geo-Economic Struggle for Industrial Supremacy* (New York: Simon and Schuster, 1993); Henry R. Nau, *The Myth of America's Decline: Leading the World Economy into the 1990s* (New York: Oxford University Press, 1990); and Wayne Sandholtz et al., *The Highest Stakes: The Economic Foundations of the Next Security System* (New York: Oxford University Press, 1992).

2. Leonard J. Schoppa, *Bargaining with Japan: What American Pressure Can and Cannot Do* (New York: Columbia University Press, 1997), 258.

3. Steve Dryden, *Trade Warriors: USTR and the American Crusade for Free Trade* (New York: Oxford University Press, 1995), 392; and Schoppa, *Bargaining with Japan*, 266.

4. Schoppa, *Bargaining with Japan*, 266.

5. Ibid., 269, 273.

6. By 1997, the Group of Seven (Canada, France, Germany, Italy, Japan, the United Kingdom, and the United States) had expanded to include Russia and was renamed the Group of Eight.

7. Office of the U.S. Trade Representative, "Second Annual Joint Status Report from the United States and Japan regarding the Enhanced Initiative," May 3, 1999; and White House, "The United States-Japan Enhanced Initiative on Deregulation," press release, May 15, 1998.

8. Office of the U.S. Trade Representative, "Japanese Progress under the Auto Agreement," press release, August 12, 1998.

9. U.S. Department of Commerce and Office of the U.S. Trade Representative, *Report to President William Jefferson Clinton of the Interagency Enforcement Team regarding the United States-Japan Agreement on Autos and Auto Parts,* Washington, D.C., June 3, 1999.

10. Ibid.

11. Office of the U.S. Trade Representative, "Japanese Progress."

12. United States Mission to the European Union, "The Transatlantic Economic Partnership," May 18, 1998.

13. U.S. Department of State, *Country Commercial Guides, FY 1999: The European Union,* Washington, D.C., 1999, chaps. 1 and 2.

14. Office of the U.S. Trade Representative, "Progress in Transatlantic Trade," press release, June 21, 1999.

15. Foreign Agricultural Service, *A Primer on Beef Hormones,* U.S. Department of Agriculture, Washington, D.C., February 24, 1999, 2.

16. Foreign Agricultural Service, *Chronology of the EU Hormone Ban,* U.S. Department of Agriculture, Washington, D.C., March 1, 1999, 1.

17. Ibid.

18. Office of the U.S. Trade Representative, "WTO Finds U.S. Trade Damaged by EU Beef Import Ban," press release, July 12, 1999, 2.

19. Foreign Agricultural Service, *Chronology,* 2.

20. World Trade Organization, "European Communities—Measures concerning Meat and Meat Products (Hormones), Original Complaint by the United States, Decision by the Arbitrators," July 12, 1999, 17.

21. Office of the U.S. Trade Representative, *2000 National Trade Estimate Report on Foreign Trade Barriers,* Washington, D.C., 2000, 90.

22. Office of the U.S. Trade Representative, *1995 National Trade Estimate Report on Foreign Trade Barriers,* Washington, D.C., 1995, 5.

23. Office of the U.S. Trade Representative, *1996 National Trade Estimate Report on Foreign Trade Barriers,* Washington, D.C., 1996; "Costa Rica," 3, and "Colombia," 4.

24. Barshefsky became acting U.S. trade representative in April 1996 when President Clinton appointed Mickey Kantor to fill out the late Ron Brown's term as secretary of commerce. Barshefsky was appointed for a full term as USTR in December 1996 and was confirmed by Congress the following January.

25. U.S. International Trade Commission (USITC), *The Year in Trade: Operation of the Trade Agreements Program during 1998,* USITC Publication 3192, May 1999, 53–54.

26. Office of the U.S. Trade Representative, *2000 National Trade Estimate, Report,* 90.

27. Vladimir N. Pregelj, *Most-Favored Nation Status for the People's Republic of China,* Congressional Research Service, Washington, D.C., April 13, 2000, 2.

28. James A. Baker III, *The Politics of Diplomacy* (New York: Putnam's, 1995), 101–103; and Dianne E. Rennack, *China: U. S. Economic Sanctions,* Congressional Research Service, Washington, D.C., October 1, 1997, 2.

29. Baker, *Politics of Diplomacy,* 105–107. The quote is on p. 106.

30. Rennack, *China,* 2.

31. Ibid., 17–19.

32. The Smoot-Hawley Tariff Act of 1930 states that goods made by forced labor cannot be sold in the United States.

33. Wayne M. Morrison, *China-U.S. Trade Issues,* Congressional Research Service, Washington, D.C., April 25, 2000, 8.

34. Ibid.

35. See *New York Times* articles on June 6, 1996, I1; December 31, 1996, A1; and January 26, 1997, I1.

36. Pregelj, *Most-Favored Nation Status,* 3.

37. Much of the material in this section is from Morrison, *China-U.S. Trade Issues,* 3, 6–8; and Senate Finance Committee, "Testimony of Ambassador Charlene Barshefsky on Renewal of Normal Trade Relations with China," July 9, 1998, 4–5.

38. *New York Times,* March 4, 1997, A1.

39. Senate Finance Committee, "Testimony of Ambassador Charlene Barshefsky," 5–6.

40. Morrison, *China-U.S. Trade Issues,* 9; and Pregelj, *Most-Favored Nation Status,* 5.

41. Actually, the United States could invoke Article XIII of the GATT (the rules of which are a subsection of the WTO), indicating that it did not consent to MFN for China. See Pregelj, *Most-Favored Nation Status,* 5.

42. Ibid., 2.

43. Morrison, *China-U.S. Trade Issues,* 9. Also see *New York Times,* January 2, 1997, C12; and March 2, 1997, I1.

44. See *New York Times,* February 25, 1997, A27; and February 28, 1997, A24.

45. *New York Times,* December 18, 1996, B10.

46. *New York Times,* January 30, 1997, D7.

47. *New York Times,* February 21, 1996, A9; and May 23, 1997, A1.

48. Kerry Dumbaugh, *China-U.S. Relations,* Congressional Research Service, Washington, D.C., April 14, 2000, 4.

49. Morrison, *China-U.S. Trade Issues,* 10; and Senate Finance Committee, "Testimony of Ambassador Charlene Barshefsky on U.S. Trade Policy in China," April 13, 1999, 3–8.

50. *New York Times* April 9, 1999, A1; April 10, 1999, A1, A35; and April 13, 1999, A1.

51. The material in this section draws on the Subcommittee on Trade, Senate Finance Committee, "Testimony of Ambassador Charlene Barshefsky on the WTO Dispute Settlement System," June 20, 2000.

52. The discussion in this section is based on Office of the U.S. Trade Representative, "The Clinton Administration 2000 Trade Policy Agenda and 1999 Annual Report," press release, March 2, 2000; and Office of the U.S. Trade Representative, *2000 Trade Policy Agenda and 1999 Annual Report of the President of the United States on the Trade Agreements Program*, Washington, D.C., 2000, 74, 110–113.

53. Charlene Barshefsky, "The Road from Seattle," speech to the National Press Club, November 23, 1999, 4.

54. Ibid.; "Communication from the United States to the World Trade Organization, Preparations for the 1999 Ministerial Conference," May 20, 1999, 1; and Subcommittee on Trade, House Ways and Means Committee, "Testimony of Ambassador Charlene Barshefsky on the Next Steps at the WTO," February 8, 2000, 8.

55. Barshefsky, "Road from Seattle," 5; and U.S. Department of State, *Fact Sheet: Clinton Agenda for WTO Ministerial Meeting*, Washington, D.C., November 24, 1999, 3.

56. Barshefsky, "Road from Seattle," 5–9; U.S. Department of State, *Fact Sheet*, 4; and Subcommittee on Trade, "Testimony of Charlene Barshefsky on the Next Steps at the WTO," 6–7.

57. Subcommittee on Trade, "Testimony of Charlene Barshefsky on the Next Steps at the WTO."

58. Office of the U.S. Trade Representative, *1997 Trade Policy Agenda and 1996 Annual Report of the President of the United States on the Trade Agreements Program*, Washington, D.C., 1997, 171–172.

59. U.S. International Trade Commission, *Year in Trade, 1998*, 1999, 46–47; and Office of the U.S. Trade Representative, *1999 Trade Policy Agenda and 1998 Annual Report of the President of the United States on the Trade Agreements Program*, Washington, D.C., 1999, 167–168.

60. Office of the U.S. Trade Representative, *2000 Trade Policy Agenda*, 179.

61. U.S. Department of Commerce, Bureau of Economic Analysis, February 18, 2000. The currency crisis in Asia was not the only reason for the climbing American trade deficit. Other factors, such as the booming American economy, also played a role.

62. *New York Times*, December 20, 1997, D1; and U.S. Department of the Treasury, *Impact of the Asian Crisis on the States*, Washington, D.C., March 24, 1998.

63. *New York Times*, December 20, 1997, D1.

64. Office of the U.S. Trade Representative, *2000 Trade Policy Agenda*, 171.

65. U.S. International Trade Commission, *Year in Trade, 1998*, 48–49; Office of the U.S. Trade Representative, *2000 Trade Policy Agenda*, 168; and Charlene Barshefsky, "Toward a Free Trade Area of the Americas," speech to the Council of the Americas, May 2, 2000.

66. Office of the U.S. Trade Representative, *2000 Trade Policy Agenda*, 168.

67. *New York Times*, May 15, 1997, D4.

68. Office of the U.S. Trade Representative, *Future Free Trade Area Negotiations,* Washington, D.C., May 1, 1997, 28; and Office of the U.S. Trade Representative, *2000 Trade Policy Agenda,* 12.

69. U.S. International Trade Commission, *The Year in Trade: Operation of the Trade Agreements Program during 1997,* USITC Publication 3103, May 1998, 78.

70. Ibid., 79.

71. For a more complete elaboration of this argument, see John M. Rothgeb Jr., *Defining Power: Influence and Force in the Contemporary International System* (New York: St. Martin's Press, 1993), 67–84.

Glossary

ad valorem Procedure for calculating tariffs that is based on the value of the goods entering a country. *Chap. 3*

African Growth and Opportunity Act Law passed in 2000 during the Clinton administration to provide special trade privileges and assistance to sub-Saharan African countries. *Chap. 9*

American Selling Price (ASP) Procedure established in 1922 that allowed the president to base the calculation of some tariffs on the amount it would cost American producers to make a similar good. *Chap. 3*

Anti-Dumping Act A 1921 law that established procedures to protect American businesses from the sale of goods in the United States at prices below normal value. *Chap. 5*

balance of trade Difference between the value of a country's exports and imports. *Chap. 2*

barrel The 52-gallon unit of measure for crude oil. *Chap. 7*

barter trade Arrangement in which countries agree to exchange specific quantities of goods instead of selling goods for cash. *Chap. 3*

Battle Act Formally known as the Mutual Defense Assistance Control Act of 1951, a law that allowed the president to prohibit exports of strategic goods to communist countries and to terminate aid to countries that did not go along with American trade restrictions. The law applied in both war and peace. *Chap. 5*

Bretton Woods System International organizations created at a conference in Bretton Woods, New Hampshire, in the closing months of World War II to facilitate postwar international commercial activity. *See* International Monetary Fund and World Bank (International Bank for Reconstruction and Development). *Chap. 4*

Cairns Group Fourteen food-exporting countries that cooperated with one another during the Uruguay Round of the GATT talks in an attempt to lower agricultural trade barriers. *Chap. 8*

Cannon Amendment A 1950 addition to the Foreign Assistance Act of 1948 that applied whenever American forces fought under United Nations command and gave the president the authority to halt trade with any country that traded with the Soviet Union. *Chap. 5*

capitalism Economic system in which commercial activity is based on competition between and among those who produce and purchase goods and services. *Chap. 2*

cash and carry Neutrality legislation first passed in 1937 that permitted American companies to sell goods to belligerent countries on the condition that the purchasing country paid for the goods immediately and transported the goods in its own ships. *Chap. 4*

Common Agricultural Policy (CAP) Plan established for European farmers in the early 1960s by the European Economic Community. It provides protection from imports, income guarantees, and assistance to help make European farm exports competitive. *Chap. 6*

competitive tariff Tax designed to ensure that imports do not sell for less than what American producers charge for similar products. *Chap. 3*

Coordinating Committee for Multilateral Export Controls (CoCom) Secretive organization set up by the United States and its Cold War allies to regulate restrictions on trade with communist countries. *Chap. 5*

countervailing duties Fees collected by the customs officials of an importing country to offset subsidies that the government of an exporting country may pay to its exporters. *Chap. 5*

dumping Term applied to a situation in which foreign producers offer products for sale in the United States at prices that are below normal value in an attempt to take markets away from American businesses. *Chap. 5*

economic warfare Term applied to situation in which all trade with a country is terminated because of the fear that commercial contacts of any kind will enhance the military capabilities of the other society. *Chap. 5*

Enhanced Initiative on Deregulation and Competition Policy Negotiations with Japan conducted by the Clinton administration to eliminate Japanese administrative and other regulations that inhibit trade. *Chap. 9*

escape clause Provision in American trade law and under Article XIX of the General Agreements on Tariffs and Trade that allows any party to a trade agreement to temporarily withdraw from the agreement in order to give domestic producers a chance to adjust to international competition. *Chap. 5*

Export Control Act of 1949 Law giving the president the authority to restrict exports in peacetime. The act was designed to limit exports to communist countries. *Chap. 5*

fast-track Procedure under which Congress pledges to vote on trade deals, without amendments, within sixty days after they are sent to Congress. *Chap. 6*

favorable balance of trade Term applied to the situation in which the value of a country's exports exceeds the value of its imports. *Chap. 2*

Framework Talks Negotiations conducted with Japan by the Clinton administration to open the Japanese market to American autos and auto parts, medical technology, services, and telecommunications equipment. *Chap. 9*

free trade Term applied to a situation in which governments refrain from creating political barriers to international commerce. *Chap. 2*

Free Trade Area of the Americas (FTAA) Project launched by the Clinton administration in 1994 to expand the North American Free Trade Agreement to include other countries in the Western Hemisphere. *Chap. 9*

GATT codes Provisions in the Tokyo Round of the General Agreement on Tariffs and Trade that set rules for regulating nontariff barriers to trade. *Chap. 6*

General Agreement on Tariffs and Trade (GATT) Set of rules and procedures set up in 1947-1948 to regulate both negotiations to lower trade barriers and international commercial exchanges. *Chap. 4*

generalized system of preferences (GSP) Rules of the General Agreement on Tariffs and Trade under which lower-than-normal tariff rates are applied by advanced countries to goods coming from developing countries. *Chap. 6*

graduation Procedure under the General Agreement on Tariffs and Trade rules that determines when a developing country is no longer eligible for special low tariff rates. *Chap. 6*

Imperial Preference System Agreement established in 1932 that created privileged trading relationships within the British Empire and Commonwealth. *Chap. 3*

import substitution Policy that uses trade barriers to encourage the local production of goods formerly bought abroad. *Chap. 2*

intellectual property rights The privileges producers receive from the patents, copyrights, and trademarks they hold. *Chap. 8*

interdependence Situation in which differing societies become reliant on one another for the production and distribution of goods and services. *Chap. 7*

International Energy Agency (IEA) International organization created in 1974 to help countries cooperate in handling international energy emergencies. *Chap. 7*

International Monetary Fund (IMF) International organization created at the Bretton Woods conference in the closing months of World War II to maintain a fixed exchange rate system between the world's major currencies and to finance balance-of-payments problems. *Chap. 4*

International Trade Commission (ITC) New name given to the Tariff Commission in the Trade Act of 1974. The ITC, a U.S. government agency, conducts trade investigations and holds hearings to determine when protection should be granted to American producers. *Chap. 6*

International Trade Organization (ITO) Proposed international organization that would have created and maintained rules for regulating world commerce. Negotiated in the late 1940s, the ITO died when the U.S. Congress refused to permit American membership. *Chap. 4*

internationalism Political tradition built on the belief that the United States is best served by policies that emphasize a high degree of involvement with the rest of the world. *Chap. 1*

isolationism Political tradition built on the belief that the United States is best served by policies that minimize American involvement with the rest of the world. *Chap. 1*

Jackson-Vanik Amendment Provision in the Trade Act of 1974 that required communist countries to grant their citizens the freedom to emigrate before the country could receive most-favored-nation status from the United States. *Chap. 6*

Lend-Lease Legislation passed by Congress in 1941 that permitted the president to transfer any defense article to any country when it was in the security interests of the United States to do so. *Chap. 4*

liberalism Political tradition that values free markets, open trade, individual liberty, and limited government. *Chap. 6*

Long-Term Arrangement (LTA) Program negotiated by the United States to restrict cotton textile imports from 1962 until 1967. *Chap. 6*

Market-Oriented Sector-Selective (MOSS) Trade talks between the United States and Japan in the mid-1980s that were designed to reduce Japanese barriers to such American exports as medical equipment and pharmaceuticals, telecommunications equipment, forest products, and electronics items. *Chap. 8*

mercantilism View of commercial activity as subordinate both to the government's accumulation of power and to the overall needs of society as defined by the government. *Chap. 2*

Ministry of International Trade and Industry (MITI) Japanese government agency that regulates that country's participation in international commerce. *Chap. 7*

most-favored-nation (MFN) Agreement to conduct trade on a nondiscriminatory basis. All trading partners covered by a MFN agreement are extended the same trading privileges offered to a nation's best trading partner. *Chap. 3*

Multi-Fiber Arrangement (MFA) Orderly marketing arrangement created in 1974 that set quotas on almost all types of textile exports to nearly every market in the world. *Chap. 6*

National Defense Act of 1940 Legislation that permitted the president to restrict American exports whenever it was in the security interests of the United States to do so. *Chap. 4*

national treatment Guarantee that foreign products and business subsidiaries will not be subject to legal discrimination. *Chap. 8*

neutrality laws Series of laws passed by Congress between 1935 and 1939 that attempted to prevent U.S. participation in foreign wars by limiting American trade with belligerent countries. *Chap. 4*

New Economic Policy (NEP) Policy announced by President Richard Nixon in August 1971 that included a wage and price freeze, a suspension of the convertibility of the dollar into gold, and a 10 percent surcharge on imports. *Chap. 6*

nontariff barriers (NTBs) Administrative, safety, health, and other regulations that are used to obstruct trade in the absence of tariffs. *Chap. 6*

normal trade relations (NTR) Term created by Congress in 1998 to replace the term *most-favored nation*. *Chap. 9*

normal value Term applied in a situation in which a foreign good is sold in the United States for the same price that is charged in its home market or other export markets or for a price that adequately reflects the cost of production and distribution. *Chap. 5*

North American Free Trade Agreement (NAFTA) Agreement concluded in 1993 among the United States, Canada, and Mexico to eliminate trade barriers among the three countries. *Chap. 8*

Omnibus Trade and Competitiveness Act of 1988 Law designed to provide the president with enhanced power to fight unfair trade; noted for its Super 301 and Special

301 provisions. Among other things, this act extended fast-track and tightened rules for escape clause, dumping, and subsidies investigations. *Chap. 8*

orderly marketing arrangement (OMA) Agreement that importers and exporters of a product will allocate shares of importers' markets to each exporter. *Chap. 6*

Organization of Petroleum Exporting Countries (OPEC) International cartel created in 1960 by oil-producing states to regulate the price and production of the oil sold on world markets. *Chap. 7*

peril point Provision in American trade law during the late 1940s and 1950s that called for the Tariff Commission to establish the minimum tariff level below which American producers would be harmed by imports. *Chap. 5*

protectionism Policy that calls for shielding local American businesses from foreign competition by restricting imports. *Chap. 1*

protective tariff Tax designed to raise the price of imports to such high levels that consumers are induced to buy locally made goods. *Chap. 2*

quota Specific numerical limit set by a country on the quantity of a particular item it will import over a specific period of time. *Chap. 3*

Randall Commission Commission established in September 1953 to study all aspects of American trade policy and to recommend policy changes. Formally known as the Commission on Foreign Economic Policy. *Chap. 5*

Reciprocal Trade Agreements Act (RTAA) Law first passed in 1934 that allowed the president to negotiate the reduction of trade barriers with other countries on a product-by-product basis. Congress renewed this legislation several times until 1962. RTAA served as the legal basis for American participation in the General Agreement on Tariffs and Trade. *Chap. 3*

reciprocity Arrangement in which countries reduce trade barriers by equal amounts. *Chap. 3*

scientific tariff Tax on imports designed to ensure that foreigners are not able to undercut the prices American producers charge for similar goods. *Chap. 3*

Section 201 Section of the Trade Act of 1974 that sets the rules under which the escape clause is applied. *Chap. 6*

Section 301 Section of the Trade Act of 1974 that outlines foreign unfair trade practices from which American producers can seek relief. *Chap. 6*

Section 337 Section of the Tariff Act of 1930 (Smoot-Hawley Tariff) that sets up procedures to restrict imports that violate the intellectual property rights of American businesses. *Chap. 5*

Short-Term Arrangement (STA) Program negotiated by the United States to restrict cotton textile imports. Remained in effect from October 1961 until September 1962. *Chap. 6*

Smithsonian Agreement Agreement reached in December 1971 during a conference of advanced industrialized countries in Washington, D.C., that devalued the dollar by 10 percent. *Chap. 6*

Special 301 Provision of the Omnibus Trade and Competitiveness Act of 1988 that requires the U.S. trade representative to identify countries that fail to respect the intellectual property rights of American firms and mandates negotiations to end such abuses. *Chap. 8*

special trade representative (STR) Presidential appointee in the executive branch who is charged with conducting trade negotiations and advising the president on trade matters. Now known as the U.S. trade representative (USTR). *Chap. 6*

strategic embargo Prohibition of trade that has direct military implications. The commercial exchange of nonmilitary goods is usually allowed. *Chap. 5*

Structural Impediments Initiative (SII) Negotiations between the United States and Japan in 1989 and 1990 that aimed to open Japanese markets to American products by changing public policies and business practices that were regarded as stunting trade. *Chap. 8*

subsidies Payments provided by a foreign government to its exporters, allowing them to sell their goods in foreign markets at abnormally low prices. *Chap. 5*

Super 301 Provision of the Omnibus Trade and Competitiveness Act of 1988 that requires the U.S. trade representative to identify countries and practices that abuse fair trade and mandates negotiations to end those abuses. *Chap. 8*

tariff Tax collected on goods entering a country from abroad. *Chap. 2*

Tariff Commission U.S. government agency created in 1882 to investigate the trade practices of other countries and to provide advice to the president and Congress. Name changed to the International Trade Commission in 1974. *Chap. 3*

Trade Act of 1974 Major trade law that established the fast-track procedure for trade agreements, eased escape clause requirements, allowed for the generalized system of preferences for developing countries, conferred cabinet rank on the special trade representative, and renamed the Tariff Commission as the International Trade Commission. *Chap. 6*

trade adjustment assistance Funding provided by the U.S. government to assist American workers, companies, and communities adversely affected by imports. *Chap. 6*

Trade Agreements Act of 1979 Act that wrote into law the results of the Tokyo Round of the General Agreement on Tariffs and Trade. First trade law passed by Congress under fast-track procedures. *Chap. 6*

Trade Agreements Extension Act of 1951 Law that reauthorized the president's authority to negotiate under the Reciprocal Trade Agreements Act program and stripped communist countries of their most-favored-nation status. *Chap. 5*

Trade and Tariff Act of 1984 Law that reauthorized American participation in the generalized system of preferences of the General Agreement on Tariffs and Trade and gave the president the power to negotiate a free trade agreement with Israel. *Chap. 8*

Trade Expansion Act of 1962 Law that authorized the president to participate in the Kennedy Round of the General Agreement on Tariffs and Trade negotiations, established trade adjustment assistance, and directed the president to create the post of special trade representative by executive order. *Chap. 6*

trade policy Rules and procedures that governments use to regulate commerce between their own society and other countries. *Chap. 1*

trade-related intellectual property rights (TRIPs) Guarantee that the patents, copyrights, and trademarks of companies that engage in international trade will be respected. This was one of the primary issues that motivated the United States to call for the Uruguay Round of the General Agreement on Tariffs and Trade talks. *Chap. 8*

trade-related investment measures (TRIMs) Issue negotiated during the Uruguay Round of the General Agreement on Tariffs and Trade talks that involves attempts to guarantee that businesses setting up operations in other countries will not be subject to discrimination. *Chap. 8*

Transatlantic Business Dialogue (TABD) Forum set up by the Clinton administration to allow European and American businesses to work with each other and their governments to promote trade. *Chap. 9*

Transatlantic Economic Partnership (TEP) Ongoing negotiations launched during the Clinton administration to promote U.S.-European cooperation in identifying and reducing trade barriers. *Chap. 9*

transparency Principle that requires countries to publicize their trade rules and the procedures for complying with those rules. *Chap. 4*

unfair trade Defined by Congress as a situation in which a foreign producer or its government manipulates market conditions to its advantage and to the detriment of an American business. *Chap. 5*

Uruguay Round General Agreement on Tariffs and Trade negotiations conducted between 1986 and 1994. Established the World Trade Organization, reduced barriers to agricultural trade, set rules for trade in services, and established guidelines to protect intellectual property and foreign investments. *Chap. 8*

variable levy Tax on agricultural imports established in the 1960s to protect farmers in the European Economic Community. *Chap. 6*

voluntary export restraint (VER) agreements Arrangement in which a country limits its exports to a specific foreign market in response to political pressure from a foreign government. *Chap. 3*

windfall profits tax President Jimmy Carter's proposal to tax the profits oil companies would receive from deregulated oil prices. Proceeds from the tax were meant to assist the poor with energy bills and to promote mass transit and energy research. Congress never approved the idea. *Chap. 7*

World Bank (International Bank for Reconstruction and Development) International organization set up in the closing months of World War II to finance recovery from wars and natural disasters and to assist countries with economic development. *Chap. 4*

World Trade Organization (WTO) International organization established in 1995 that regulates trade among its members through the creation and maintenance of rules and procedures that facilitate commercial activity. *Chap. 1*

Suggestions for Further Reading

CHAPTER 2

Classic discussions of nineteenth- and early twentieth-century American trade policy are found in F. W. Taussig, *The Tariff History of the United States* (New York: Augustus M. Kelley Publishers, 1967); and E. E. Schattschneider, *Politics, Pressures, and the Tariff* (New York: Prentice-Hall, 1935). More recent treatments of the same period are found in Judith Goldstein, *Ideas, Interests, and American Trade Policy* (Ithaca: Cornell University Press, 1993); and Carolyn Rhodes, *Reciprocity, U.S. Trade Policy, and the GATT Regime* (Ithaca: Cornell University Press, 1993). An excellent presentation on free trade is provided by Douglas A. Irwin, *Against the Tide: An Intellectual History of Free Trade* (Princeton: Princeton University Press, 1996); and the theoretical role special-interest groups play in the trade policy-making process is described in J. A. Frieden, "Invested Interests: The Politics of National Economic Policies in a World of Global Finance," *International Organization* 45 (autumn 1991): 425–451; and Ronald Rogowski, *Commerce and Coalitions: How Trade Affects Domestic Political Alignments* (Princeton: Princeton University Press, 1989).

CHAPTER 3

Post–World War I trade is discussed in Edward Kaplan and Thomas Ryley, *Prelude to Trade Wars: American Tariff Policy, 1890–1922* (Westport, Conn.: Greenwood Press, 1994); and F. W. Taussig, *The Tariff History of the United States* (New York: Augustus M. Kelley Publishers, 1967). The classic treatment of the Smoot-Hawley Tariff is found in E. E. Schattschneider, *Politics, Pressures, and the Tariff* (New York: Prentice-Hall, 1935). Cordell Hull's role in trade policy is described in his own book, *The Memoirs of Cordell Hull,* Vol. I (New York: Macmillan, 1948); and in Michael Butler, *Cautious Visionary: Cordell Hull and Trade Reform, 1933–1937* (Kent, Ohio: Kent State University Press, 1998). An interesting explanation of the Reciprocal Trade Agreements Act of 1934 is in Stephan Haggard, "The Institutional Foundations of Hegemony: Explaining the Reciprocal Trade Agreements Act of 1934," *International Organization* 42 (winter 1988): 91–119.

CHAPTER 4

Discussions of isolationism and neutrality are found in Wayne S. Cole, *Roosevelt and the Isolationists, 1932–1945* (Lincoln: University of Nebraska Press, 1983); and Robert Divine, *The Illusion of Neutrality* (Chicago: University of Chicago Press, 1962). America's entry into World War II is discussed by Robert Dallek, *Franklin D. Roosevelt and American Foreign Policy, 1932–1945* (New York: Oxford University Press, 1979); and Waldo Heinrichs, *Threshold of War: Franklin D. Roosevelt and American Entry into World War II* (New York: Oxford University Press, 1988). The creation of the Bretton Woods System is described in Armand Van Dormael, *Bretton Woods: Birth of a Monetary System* (London: Macmillan, 1978); and Richard N. Gardner, *Sterling-Dollar Diplomacy in Current Perspective* (New York: Columbia University Press, 1980). The controversy over the International Trade Organization is analyzed by Susan A. Aaronson, *Trade and the American Dream: A Social History of Postwar Trade Policy* (Lexington: University Press of Kentucky, 1996).

CHAPTER 5

Complete discussions of east-west trade restrictions are found in Philip J. Funigiello, *American-Soviet Trade in the Cold War* (Chapel Hill: University of North Carolina Press, 1988); and Michael Mastanduno, *Economic Containment: CoCom and the Politics of East-West Trade* (Ithaca: Cornell University Press, 1992). Eisenhower's position on trade is ably described by Burton I. Kaufman, *Trade and Aid: Eisenhower's Foreign Economic Policy, 1953–1961* (Baltimore: Johns Hopkins University Press, 1982). A careful analysis of how Congress handled trade in the 1950s is found in Raymond A. Bauer, Ithiel de Sola Pool, and Lewis Anthony Dexter, *American Business and Public Policy: The Politics of Foreign Trade* (New York: Atherton Press, 1964). Postwar protectionist measures are discussed in Judith Goldstein, *Ideas, Interests, and American Trade Policy* (Ithaca: Cornell University Press, 1993).

CHAPTER 6

A discussion of the Kennedy Round is found in John W. Evans, *The Kennedy Round in American Trade Policy: The Twilight of the GATT?* (Cambridge: Harvard University Press, 1971); and the Tokyo Round is described in Patrick Low, *Trading Free: The GATT and U.S. Trade Policy* (New York: Twentieth Century Fund Press, 1993). The role of the special trade representative is discussed in Steve Dryden, *Trade Warriors: USTR and the American Crusade for Free Trade* (New York: Oxford University Press, 1995). Nixon's New Economic Policy is analyzed by Joanne S. Gowa, *Closing the Gold Window: Domestic Politics and the End of Bretton Woods* (Ithaca: Cornell University Press, 1983).

CHAPTER 7

Detailed discussions of the oil industry are found in Daniel Yergin, *The Prize: The Epic Quest for Oil, Money, and Power* (New York: Simon and Schuster, 1992); and Anthony Sampson, *The Seven Sisters, The Great Oil Companies and the World They Shaped* (New York: Bantam Books, 1991). American oil policy is described in Dankwart A. Rustow, *Oil and Turmoil: America Faces OPEC and the Middle East* (New York: Norton, 1982). The effect of the oil crisis on the auto industry is discussed by David Halberstam, *The Reckoning* (New York: Avon Books, 1986); and the industry's quest for protection is analyzed by Stefanie Ann Lenway, *The Politics of U.S. International Trade* (Boston: Pitman Publishing, 1985); and Carolyn Rhodes, *Reciprocity, U.S. Trade Policy, and the GATT Regime* (Ithaca: Cornell University Press, 1993).

CHAPTER 8

Discussions of Soviet-American trade relations in the 1980s are found in Philip J. Funigiello, *American-Soviet Trade in the Cold War* (Chapel Hill: University of North Carolina Press, 1988); and Michael Mastanduno, *Economic Containment: CoCom and the Politics of East-West Trade* (Ithaca: Cornell University Press, 1992). Issues relating to American-Japanese trade are analyzed in Clyde V. Prestowitz Jr., *Trading Places: How We Are Giving Our Future to Japan and How to Reclaim It* (New York: Basic Books, 1988); and Leonard J. Schoppa, *Bargaining with Japan: What American Pressure Can and Cannot Do* (New York: Columbia University Press, 1997). The Uruguay Round is described in Ernest H. Preeg, *Traders in a Brave New World: The Uruguay Round and the Future of the International Trading System* (Chicago: University of Chicago Press, 1995); and Jarod Wiener, *Making Rules in the Uruguay Round of the GATT* (Aldershot, U.K.: Dartmouth Publishing, 1995). NAFTA is discussed in Raymond Vernon, Debora L. Spar, and Glenn Tobin, *Iron Triangles and Revolving Doors: Cases in U.S. Foreign Economic Policy Making* (New York: Praeger Publishers, 1991); and Robert A. Pastor, *Integration With Mexico: Options for U.S. Policy* (New York: Twentieth Century Fund Press, 1993).

CHAPTER 9

Several U.S. government agencies provide excellent and comprehensive discussions of current American trade policy issues. Three of the best are the annual editions of: U.S. International Trade Commission, *The Year in Trade: Operation of the Trade Agreements Program;* Office of the U.S. Trade Representative, *National Trade Estimate Report on Foreign Trade Barriers;* and Office of the U.S. Trade Representative, *Trade Policy Agenda and Annual Report of the President on the Trade Agreements Program.* These publications are available from the sponsoring agencies. They also are available online at http://www.ustr.gov/ and at http://www.usitc.gov/.

Index